The Complete Films of
RITA HAYWORTH

The Complete Films of
RITA HAYWORTH

The Legend and Career
of a Love Goddess

by GENE RINGGOLD

A CITADEL PRESS BOOK
Published by Carol Publishing Group

First Carol Publishing Group Edition 1991

Copyright © 1974, 1991 by Gene Ringgold

A Citadel Press Book
Published by Carol Publishing Group
Citadel Press is a registered trademark of Carol Communications, Inc.

Editorial Offices   Sales & Distribution Offices
600 Madison Avenue   120 Enterprise Avenue
New York, NY 10022   Secaucus, NJ 07094

In Canada: Musson Book Company
A division of General Publishing Co. Limited
Don Mills, Ontario

Queries regarding rights and permissions
should be addressed to: Carol Publishing Group,
600 Madison Avenue, New York, NY 10022

Manufactured in the United States of America
10 9 8 7 6 5 4 3 2 1

Carol Publishing Group books are available at special discounts
for bulk purchases, for sales promotions, fund raising, or
educational purposes. Special editions can also be created to
specifications. For details contact: Special Sales Department,
Carol Publishing Group, 120 Enterprise Ave., Secaucus, NJ 07094

ISBN 0-8065-1260-1

Dedication

To *all* the talented still photographers (of Local 659 of IATS & MPMO), whose individual craftsmanship and genius has been an integral but unsung contribution to motion picture history and whose collective work has made possible the creation of pictorials such as this.

Individually, I would like to cite each of them by name, but since this is impossible, I would like to mention a few of them responsible for the still scenes and gallery portraits of Miss Rita Hayworth which appear on subsequent pages:

Clarence Sinclair Bull, Don Christie, Bob Coburn, R. S. Crandall, Eddie Cronenweth, Charles Goldie, Ray Jones, Alex Kahale, Madison S. Lacy, Irving Lippman, Bertram ("Bud") Longworth, Frank Powolny, A. E. ("Whitey") Schafer, Ned Scott, Homer Van Pelt, Joseph Walter and Scott ("Scotty") Welbourne.

I would also like the still photographers of Miss Hayworth's European-made films *(Circus World, The Happy Thieves, Road to Salina, The Rover,* and *Sons of Satan),* whose names I have not been able to verify, to know that this dedication is indeed intended to include them too.

If "one picture *is* worth a thousand words," then this book is rightly their creation and their tribute to Rita Hayworth as much as it is mine. And last, but hardly least, a special thanks to Bob Landry, the *Life* magazine photographer who took Miss Hayworth's famous World War II pinup picture, thereby uniquely contributing to the legend that is Rita Hayworth.

And, on behalf of Miss Rita Hayworth, special mention to the late Miss Louella O. Parsons, who truly loved Hollywood and its stars and who always remained a faithful Hayworth partisan—and friend. It is our misfortune that we shall not see her like again.

G. R.

Contents

Acknowledgments

For their help in locating photographs, research material and other invaluable aids, without which this book could not have been compiled, I wish to thank the following:

FIRMS:

COLLECTOR'S BOOK STORE (Leonard Brown and Malcolm Willets); LARRY EDMUNDS CINEMA BOOKSHOP (Git and Milton Luboviski); KENNETH G. LAWRENCE'S MOVIE MEMORABILIA SHOP OF HOLLYWOOD (Arthur C. Peterson); MOVIE POSTER SERVICE (Bob Smith); and, SATURDAY MATINEE (Eddie Brandt).

INDIVIDUALS:

Philip Castanza, Texas Jim Cooper, Richard Cresswell, Critt Davis, Diane Goodrich, Jerry Kropkiewicz, Madison S. Lacy, Dion McGregor, Nick Nicholls, Frank Rodriguez, Charles Smith, Lucy Smith, Lou Valentino, Jerry Vermilye, Ernest Voht and Bill Wallace. And for their unstinting cooperation, a special thanks to Rouben Mamoulian, George Marshall, George Cukor, and Stephen Oliver.

ORGANIZATIONS:

THE ACADEMY OF MOTION PICTURE ARTS AND SCIENCES LIBRARY (Mildred Simpson and her staff); THE AMERICAN FILM INSTITUTE (Ann Schlosser and her staff); and THE LOS ANGELES PUBLIC LIBRARY (and the wonderful staff that operates its Newspaper Department).

STUDIOS:

AVCO-EMBASSY; COLUMBIA PICTURES CORPORATION; COMET FILMS; FILM WORLD ENTERPRISES; METRO-GOLDWYN-MAYER PICTURES, INC.; PARAMOUNT PICTURES CORPORATION; 20th CENTURY-FOX FILM CORPORATION; UNITED ARTISTS, INC.; and, WARNER BROS.-SEVEN ARTS.

Rita, as she appeared in a 1935 Fox short subject which promoted promising starlets who were to appear in French and
Spanish language versions of Fox features. The short never had
a U.S. theatrical showing, and Rita never made a Spanish language feature film.

RITA HAYWORTH
Superstar

The Legend of a Love Goddess

Of all the beautiful women of Hollywood's world of make-believe who can be regarded as examples of that commodity called the manufactured Movie Star, Rita Hayworth is certainly among the most memorable, based solely on her accomplishments, personal and professional, against what may justly be called overwhelming odds. Now, decades after her finest hours, her name still conjures up a glorious memory of the movies' golden age of glamour.

The creation of Rita Hayworth, from the unlikely foundation of one Marguerita Carmen Cansino, surpassed the expectations of even her most impassioned mentors and attracted a legion of devotees who worshipped her as unstintingly as if her charisma had been a genuine rather than an acquired aura. Even the films of her legendary years, when she *was* the silver screen's Technicolored Love Goddess, are fairly forgettable except for her endowment of them with innate sexuality, a natural inner sensuality and an undefinable glamour that did much more than titillate audiences. Instead, her image suggested, none too subtly, that she was willing to fulfill and enjoy the promise of surrender that her face, her voice and her entire bearing proclaimed to every male she enchanted. Women found in her brash, bold-faced performances an honest and seductive sophistication that each of them secretly wished she had or could emulate.

This true Hayworth image was apparent only in isolated moments in a handful of her early films. It was actually her appearance in Rouben Mamoulian's 1941 Technicolor remake of *Blood and Sand* that led to her international stardom.

Rouben Mamoulian was actually Miss Hayworth's first director to be keenly aware of her screen potential and astute enough to take full advantage of it. And in summing up her basic appeal he said:

"Rita Hayworth was never the most beautiful woman to grace the screen. And when I first encountered her she was not even an especially resourceful actress. But all this is beside the point. Many women, much more

Marguerita Cansino, aged ten, poses outside the home in Brooklyn where she lived with her parents and two brothers, in 1928. By this time she had already danced professionally with her father, and appeared briefly in a ten-minute filmed short subject which had theatrical distribution in late 1926.

With her father, Eduardo Cansino, in 1935, as he helps Rita rehearse for her Russian dance sequence in *Paddy O'Day*.

beautiful, haven't the least idea of how to deport themselves in front of a camera or to even suggest that there is a remote possibility that they could learn to act. And some rather ordinary-looking actresses, with truly remarkable talent, are totally incapable of even suggesting they possess a quality of beauty.

"But Rita Hayworth is different. She made you believe in both her beauty and her ability whenever she was on screen. I did a test of her and instead of attempting to convey wanton lust with just her eyes or even her entire face, she used her entire body to do it—and do it with an animal grace that no actress I have ever known has come close to equaling.

"Much of her grace, I am certain, was acquired while she was a professional dancer but she conveys an inner grace that cannot be acquired and the additional lure of sending out some sort of vibrations, the lust of

which audiences immediately sensed. When I made *Blood and Sand,* classic sirens such as Doña Sol were already a bit *passé.* The many other actresses I had already tested for the part proved this. They were all ludicrous—hilariously so. But Hayworth's test was different. And, as anyone who has seen the film knows, her performance is quite brilliant.

"I don't know offhand just how many films she had made before *Blood and Sand,* quite a number of them as I recall, but it was this film and the way she played Doña Sol that made her an international star. The only credit I can honestly take for this was having the foresight to select her, against much studio opposition, I might add, and as her director, communicate to her exactly what I wanted her to do. The rest of it was entirely in her hands and she came through. . . .

"I ran into her at a party a few years ago and I

stood watching her for a few minutes before she spotted me and came over to say hello. She was then about fifty years old and among a roomful of much younger and more beautiful women. Nevertheless, she still possessed those same qualities she had when I first tested her for the Doña Sol part. I don't believe I'm exaggerating one bit by saying that every man present at that party was aware of her and all of them instinctively sensed they were in the presence of a genuine woman whose glamour has ripened but which time has not diminished."

Prior to *Blood and Sand*, Rita Hayworth had to learn to overcome inherent shyness and to acquire all the psychological traits—ambition, drive, willpower—that are so necessary for an actress to survive. Once her own ambition was established, the drive and willpower came easily, but to this day she still retains a shy quality which somehow enriches her off-screen allure. This inhibition resulted from her awe of her father, Eduardo Cansino, a successful professional dancer and teacher, who could be very lovable, but who was also demanding and domineering.

Eduardo Cansino patiently taught his only daughter to dance professionally and much more than just the basic rudiments of stage presence. More importantly, he awakened her ambition to attain better things, not just for herself but for the Cansino tradition. And so, because of her natural grace, in spite of her extreme shyness and a tendency to be overweight, she performed, seemingly for her father's approval alone, with both flash and flair.

Subsequent to appearing in *Blood and Sand,* Miss Hayworth commanded the attention of screen audiences with an ambiguous sexuality that also had flash and flair. The audience was aware that we could never be quite certain how she would use her beauty and aura of sensual desire—for good or for evil—by always keeping us guessing whether her endowments were to be a means of self-gratification or whether they were to be offered to the man whose heart she captured. In *Blood and Sand* her siren was not merely content to capture a man's heart—she wanted also to possess his soul.

But it was *Gilda* which later fully and firmly established the real standards of her on-screen image. By appearing to be a vain and mercenary creature of unlimited allure determined to drive the men with whom she was involved to their own destruction for some vaguely personal reasons, she turned out, instead, to really be a good girl at heart, simply resorting to a bizarre means of entrapment which carried only one stipulation—that mutual surrender be the condition of their love. For audiences to allow, accept, and even believe such sexual effrontery, which they had not encountered since the heyday of Mae West, who got away with the same thing by exploiting the humor in the situation of

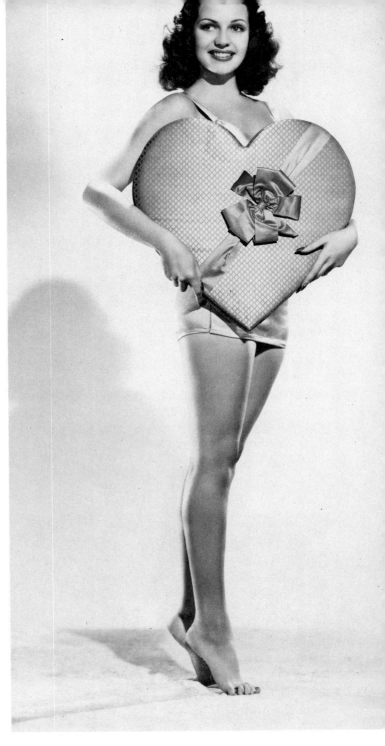

"Miss Valentine's Day" of 1939.

an aggressive female on the prowl, Miss Hayworth got away with the same thing by at all times remaining a warm and appealing creature who used femininity to prove to her man that capture meant rapture.

This appeal, merely occasionally suggested during her apprenticeship, was refined and perfected in *Gilda*. That Hayworth image became contagious to audiences during her superstardom and even now remains a potent part of her screen allure. In mediocre programmers, such as *The Money Trap,* the only memorable moments are those alloted to Miss Hayworth who, in addition to everything else, has matured into a first-rate actress. She's that rare woman who embraces each new year like an anxious and ardent lover. For her eyes, her smile and her weathered countenance still extol the verity that a woman who possesses inner beauty will be visually enchanting at any age and that facial beauty alone and a youthful facade are only fleeting externals, whereas the kind of inner beauty which Miss Hayworth possesses remains eternal. Instead of the years seemingly being kind to her, it appears as if she is the one tolerant of time.

Miss Hayworth has made no effort to fight the tides of time nor has she retreated or been relegated to the camp world of nostalgia because of a rather startling and quite amazing facet of her screen career: by design or circumstance, she has always played a woman approximately her own age! When you consider the ostensibly youthful screen assignments many of her maturing contemporaries have attempted, you can more fully appreciate just how unusual a facet of her career this really is. Allowing that, you must conclude that Rita Hayworth is both intelligent and a realist.

Another equally amazing facet of her career is that no other actress, with the exception of Myrna Loy, ever survived quite such a long apprenticeship before achieving stardom. But, unlike Miss Loy's beautifully and brilliantly conveyed image of the perfect wife, Miss Hayworth's siren's song was intriguingly different. It proclaimed: "Of all the women you will ever know or love, I am the one you will neither regret nor forget."

She was the first child of Volga Haworth and Eduardo Cansino and was born in a West Side New York hospital on October 17, 1918 and christened Marguerita Carmen Cansino. At the time of her birth her father was appearing professionally onstage at the 125th Street Theatre and living with his wife at a rather high-class theatrical hotel. Immediately after Marguerita was born, they moved to an apartment in Brooklyn but then later took residence in Jackson Heights, a section of Queens. It was during the Cansinos' tenure there that Marguerita's brothers, Vernon and Eduardo, Jr., were born and that she first attended public school.

Volga Haworth was eighteen years old when her first child was born. Partly of Irish descent, she was the daughter of an English actor whose theatrical heritage dated back a couple of centuries and included players of Shakespearean repertoire. Volga's mother Maggie

As chorus girls watch, Fred Astaire and Rita Hayworth rehearse their jive dance number for *You'll Never Get Rich* (1940).

With her husband, Ed Judson, attending the theatre in New York City to promote the opening of *You'll Never Get Rich* (1941).

O'Hara, came from an equally impressive theatrical background in Ireland. Volga's parents migrated to the United States and she was born in Washington, D.C., in the proverbial theatrical trunk. At sixteen she ran away from home to become a showgirl. Her brother, Vinton Haworth, became a screen and radio actor of some recognition who ultimately married the sister of Lela Rogers, whose own daughter, Ginger, subsequently made a name for herself.

Volga Haworth met Eduardo Cansino while working as a Ziegfeld showgirl. According to family legend, this meeting occurred during an audition for a new Follies edition when Eduardo and his sister, Elisa, had been summoned by the great showman but subsequently rejected his offer since they were then earning more on the U.S. vaudeville circuits than Ziegfeld was prepared to offer them. Eduardo's independent attitude intrigued Volga, a show business neophyte in spite of her parents' theatrical background, and her youthful, vivacious beauty impressed him.

Eduardo, one of the seven children, six sons and a daughter, of the famous Andalusian dancing master, Don Antonio Cansino, was then a vaudeville headliner in an act called "The Dancing Cansinos," which co-starred his sister Elisa. His father, Don Antonio, whose skill and renown eventually led to his performing for King Alfonso and the visiting Queen Victoria, had brought him international recognition and all his children became famous dancers although Eduardo's original ambition was to have been a bullfighter. But when he and his sister teamed up in an act and played in Madrid, they became such a sensation that they were sponsored for a U.S. appearance by Mrs. Stuyvesant

Fish, the social lioness of Newport society. They amply fulfilled all of Mrs. Stuyvesant Fish's preappearance enthusiasm and were equally sensational when performing for other social clans along the Eastern seaboard. So much so that instead of returning to Spain after their social circuit triumph, they accepted offers to appear on vaudeville bills in and around New York City.

During the next twelve years The Dancing Cansinos (several brothers had also joined their act) became headliners coast-to-coast on the Keith-Orpheum and Fanchon and Marco circuits. Appearing at the best theaters, they were often featured on programs with performers like Anna Case, Efrem Zimbalist, Mischa Elman and another very popular dance team, Fred and Adele Astaire. Later Eduardo's other brothers, his father and his uncle, Jose, also came to the United States for a concert tour which, with demands for return engagements, lasted more than four years.

Spanish dancing divides into two schools—the purely Iberian, which is classic and exempt from gypsy influence, and the flamenco, which is of gypsy origin. But it was the influence of the Andalusian natives of Southern Spain in both schools of dancing which is generally considered the most audience-pleasing, the most difficult to master and most stressed by true artists. Eduardo was master of them all and he could also perform tap, ballet and tango with equal agility. And by the time his daughter Marguerita was four years old, he was already teaching her everything he knew about dancing.

"Consequently," Miss Hayworth says, "I knew how to dance as soon as I was able to walk and by the time I was four years old I had already appeared with my father and my aunt in a Carnegie Hall recital. My par-

In 1942, the Dance Teachers Association of America presented Rita Hayworth with a scroll honoring her as "Miss Panamusicana," the highest annual award given by the organization to the female dancer of the year who, in their opinion, did the best work and had high professional standards. The award was presented at their annual convention.

ents were living in a theatrical hotel in New York when I was born which, perhaps, made me a vaudeville veteran at birth."

Marguerita's first stage experience consisted of appearing onstage near the end of the family recital, doing a few flamenco twirls, clicking a pair of miniature castanets, made especially for her by her grandfather, blushing shyly afterward and then running offstage. Her sudden appearance gave the performance, which had already thrilled the audience with its color and brilliance, a lighthearted lift and was staged to make it appear that she had just slipped on stage in a moment of enthusiasm and improvised. But Marguerita, who had a tendency toward being overweight and seldom made friends with children her own age, relished her moment in the spotlight and soon added bits of business of her own which had not been rehearsed.

Her father pointed out the error of her unprofessional upstaging and Marguerita never again made a move on stage that had not been devised, thought out and carefully rehearsed. This incident had a somewhat traumatic effect on the child. Offstage she became quite self-conscious and very shy. But Eduardo Cansino, a stern taskmaster, was also a loving and devoted father and knew exactly where to draw the line in censuring his daughter. Since neither of his sons showed any interest in continuing the dancing tradition of the family, his main concern was having Marguerita carry on the heritage. She returned his adoration, doted on his every word, followed his wishes implicitly and sought his advice and approval on everything.

In later years she transferred her acquired instinct of doing exactly as she was told to do by the men she loved, those she married and those who molded her

Outside the courtroom with her mother, who was waiting to testify in her daughter's behalf in her divorce proceedings from Ed Judson (1942).

career. Being cooperative, even on occasions when she was well in a position to be otherwise, appears to have remained an integral part of the Hayworth personality. Nevertheless, once, in a moment of rather unusual candor, she told Louella Parsons:

"Perhaps if I hadn't been so shy and unsure of myself I would not have been so malleable. I sometimes believe I have a self-destructive instinct for always picking the wrong moment to become difficult and temperamental. Later, when I'm alone, I laugh at myself for having made an issue of some trivial thing while I silently allowed myself to be talked into doing a thing I felt was wrong for me. But I don't suppose anybody who knows me gives me much credit for being a brainy dame!"

Early in 1926 The Dancing Cansinos were hired to appear in a Vitagraph short subject, filmed at the Brooklyn studio facilities, which, in slightly over ten minutes, attempted to present a cavalcade of internationally traditional dances. This short subject was intended solely as part of a stage prologue that preceded the New York premiere engagement of John Barrymore's *Don Juan,* one of the pioneer Warner films with a synchronized musical score. It was here that Rita Hayworth actually made her film debut by coming on at the conclusion of the Cansinos' appearance and doing a few flamenco twirls and clicking a pair of miniature castanets. It was indeed a most obscure film debut for an eight-year-old girl who would eventually become the screen's foremost sex symbol.

Nevertheless, it was Warner Bros., the producers of *Don Juan,* and the owners of its subsidiary company Vitagraph, who set into motion the events that indirectly led to Miss Hayworth's career. This occurred a year later when the history-making *Jazz Singer,* starring Al Jolson, revolutionized the film industry and sounded the death knell of vaudeville.

Within the next two years virtually all movies had found their voices and vaudeville was dead. Consequently, by the time of the October 1929 crash, Eduardo Cansino, no longer able to find a full season of employment on the vaudeville circuits with his expensively staged and highly paid dance act, had moved to Hollywood and opened a professional dancing school located on the busy corner of Sunset and Vine.

Cansino had shrewdly reasoned that with all the musical films being produced, and all the schools suddenly mushrooming up throughout the film capital devoted to giving vocal, diction and singing instructions, that a school dedicated to offering dancers professional training in modern, traditional, ballet, tap and interpretative instruction had a good chance of success. Can-

With Hedy Lamarr and William Randolph Hearst at a military ball banquet in 1945.

sino's Professional Dancing School was the forerunner of such institutions, which ultimately resulted in Arthur Murray's forming his cross-country chain of dance studios that were dedicated to teaching nonprofessionals the rudiments, refinements and rewarding pleasures of being a socially accomplished dancer.

Among the first of Eduardo's students were Mildred Costello, Eva Rosita, Armida, Carmelita and Carla Moretel, Luana Alcaniz and Rosita Moreno. Among the many big names to receive specialized training from Cansino personally were Lupe Velez, James Cagney, Jean Harlow, Nancy Carroll and Lilyan Tashman.

When film studios realized they could save money by training their contractees right at the studio, Cansino was deluged with offers from Samuel Goldwyn, Pathé and Fox to supervise their dance departments. But while the school still flourished, he declined such offers. Then, at the very bottom of the Depression when his school began operating at a loss, it was then too late for him to form a studio association. A proud and dedicated man whose family's well-being was always his prime concern, Cansino continued the school, assisted by his uncle, Jose, and took on the additional chores of staging the prologues at the Carthay Circle Theater and, occasionally, appearing on the program himself. (Except for Marguerita, The Dancing Cansinos also appeared in the 1936 RKO film, *The Dancing Pirate*.)

Cansino himself did not appear in the first prologue he staged at the Carthay Circle Theater when the screen attraction was Universal's first sound version of *Back Street,* but Marguerita, who had been a student at his school since its inception, was featured. At her first performance, Cansino stood at the rear of the orchestra and watched the presentation. He later said:

"All of a sudden I woke up to the fact that she was no longer a baby and although she was only fourteen years old, she already had the fully rounded figure of a mature woman. I realized then that staging prologues and attempting to operate the school was ridiculous. Here was the girl, my own daughter, with whom I could build a whole new dance act!"

Marguerita, who had been attending the Alexander Hamilton High School, transferred to the Carthay High School in order to be closer to the theater. It was also necessary that she obtain working papers from the California State Board of Education and to make up whatever school work she missed during matinee performances with long sessions of homework. Around this time Don Antonio, Marguerita's legendary grandfather, arrived in the United States to live with Eduardo and his family and help operate the school. Affectionately called "Padre" by his grandchildren, he soon spent more time operating the school than his founder-son.

This left Eduardo more time to concern himself with the prologues and to appear in them while silently contemplating his dream of a new team of The Dancing Cansinos. Ultimately, he made his dream a reality, but since Marguerita was under legal age and not permitted

Estranged from her husband, Orson Welles, Rita is seen dancing at New York's Stork Club with Stephen Crane, the estranged husband of Lana Turner, during October 1947.

by California state law to work in bistros and nightclubs where liquor was served, Eduardo accepted engagements at below the Mexican border nightclubs in Tijuana and Agua Caliente, where the Hollywood crowd spent their weekends attending the races, the bullfights, the gambling in the wide-open casinos then flourishing. And if the men were not frequenting the practically door-to-door bordellos, they passed away their nights frolicking in the boisterous, open-until-dawn nightclubs that more or less catered strictly to their weekend business. In order to avoid any problems with California school authorities, Eduardo moved his family to Mexico, a suburb near Agua Caliente since Mexico at that time had no laws governing the education or working conditions of minors.

The Dancing Cansinos were an instantaneous sensation and as big a tourist lure to the fun-seeking border spots as the other inducements which brought the wealthy and the fun-seeking Americanos from the Los Angeles area to Tijuana and Agua Caliente. The weekend exodus of Angelenos during the early 1930s to these border-town hot spots was every bit as popular as the

current weekend treks to Las Vegas, albeit on a much smaller scale.

At fifteen, Marguerita was a show-business veteran, working regularly and appearing nightly at the Foreign Club in Tijuana, then later at the Caliente Club, in the Hotel Caliente, in nearby Agua Caliente. She even was an extra in a Columbia quota quickie film, made entirely in Mexico in 1934, and released in 1935 in Spanish-speaking countries and a smattering of Los Angeles theaters which showed only Spanish-language films. This came about quite by accident when, one afternoon, while playing with a group of young Mexican girls her own age, who were intently watching the film company at work on location, she was singled out, because she could perform a street dance outside the bullfighting arena, and paid a few pesos for her contribution. Since the Columbia studios made the film, and Miss Hayworth only recalls that Fernando de Fuentes was the director and that Ramon Pereda was one of the actors working in it, it was, more than likely, *Cruz Diable (The Devil's Cross)* since all the facts concerning it that Miss Hayworth *does* recall appear to fit. She still gets a charge out of alluding to this film and the fact the director assumed she was "just another dirty-faced Mexican kid." She never let him think otherwise. (She also says she has never seen the film and knows of no one who has seen it and recognized her.)

It certainly was not unreasonable for the director to think her Mexican since she was a buxom young lady, with a tendency toward being overweight that added to her mostly acquired Latin look. Her father had insisted she dye her medium-dark brown hair to a jet black and keep it well pomaded to add a slightly swarthy effect. She also demurely followed her father's instructions about her offstage activities. So, after each performance, she retreated to her dressing room where, somewhat in frustration, she munched candy and avidly read confession-type magazine stories.

Recalls Miss Hayworth:

"I remember that at that age I always preferred the romantic-type fiction in which the men always won and the girls in the stories were always the losers in love. Years later, when Orsie (Orson Welles) started to select my reading material, he seemed appalled that I read such trash. But I think the fact that I started the day out by reading Louella Parsons' column really irked him more—although he never said anything about it."

But while she was still appearing in Mexico it was impossible for Eduardo to keep his daughter completely isolated even though he personally contended with the young men who frequented the clubs and made attempts to date her. Nevertheless, on her sixteenth birthday, he allowed her to keep a date with a young man she had met outside the nightclub world. Marguerita's euphoria, however, was short-lived. Eduardo personally attended to all the arrangements for the occasion by ordering their dinner at a swank hotel restaurant, including a bottle of the best champagne! Then, while the youngsters attempted a congenial evening, he hovered nearby at another table to make certain nothing untoward occurred.

"After that," Miss Hayworth said, "I wasn't any too anxious to accept any dates since I knew exactly how the evening would turn out. But I was also aware that rebellion would be ridiculous. After all, I was just a teenager and I still attended mass and confession regularly. I was also halfway responsible for earning the family's only income at that time and we were a very close family. The dancing school barely paid its own operating costs at that time. Looking back now, and considering all the circumstances, including the fact that Agua Calienta and Tijuana in those days weren't exactly ideal places to raise a teen-aged daughter, I think my father's strictness was well justified and certainly indicated his love and concern for my well-being."

Early in 1935, while she and her father were still performing at the Caliente Club, she came to the attention of Winfield Sheehan, who was then vice president in charge of production of the Fox Film Corporation. It seems he was one of a group of guests being entertained that particular weekend by film producer Joseph Schenck, who also happened to own the Hotel Caliente, which contained the nightclub where the Cansinos performed. Sheehan watched Marguerita perform and silently sensed some indefinable quality in her face and graceful movements which, if it was possible to capture on film, might very likely make her a good prospect for work in Fox Films. Thinking she could probably not speak English well, if at all, and deciding that other

When the enlisted men of the U.S. Navy, who had, in 1941, voted her the "Redhead They Would Most Like to Be Shipwrecked With," complained because her latest film *You'll Never Get Rich* dealt with U.S. Army personnel, Rita Hayworth invited all the sailors who could make it to a party and dance at Columbia studios where she and other starlets gave them a day to remember.

film executives must also have seen her and rejected her for one reason or another, he still wondered if there wasn't a possibility that she couldn't be worked into Fox's Spanish-language-feature program, if nothing else.

Later, after the Cansinos had performed brilliantly to an exceptionally responsive audience, Sheehan mentioned to the other guests, one of whom was columnist Louella Parsons, what he thought of Marguerita and how impressed he was with her. Schenck surprised him by saying she could speak English perfectly and was, in fact, a U.S. citizen. Without further ado, Schenck, somewhat amused because he saw Marguerita all the time and saw no possibilities in her himself, summoned a waiter and he, in turn, summoned Marguerita to join them at his table. She arrived a few minutes later, with her father.

"When she came to our table," Louella Parsons later recalled, "she turned out to be painfully shy. She could not look at strangers when she spoke to them and her voice was so low it could hardly be heard. Hardly, it seemed to me, the material of which a great star could be made.

"Yet, when we were returning to Hollywood the next day, Sheehan told me, 'I've signed her to a contract.'"

Miss Parsons, who in later years was to become one of Rita Hayworth's most faithful partisans, had very little faith in Sheehan's instincts about her. She argued that the girl was shy, overweight and not especially attractive and that while she may indeed be a very professional and expert dancer, who moved gracefully onstage, learning the rudiments of acting and facing a camera were another matter. Sheehan was not to be dismayed, however, claiming that the girl could be taught to act, taught to project her voice and that her excess pounds could be shed quite easily with a proper diet and the right kind of exercise. Just the same, he wasn't exactly truthful when he told Miss Parsons he had actually signed her to a contract. What he had offered was an expense-paid trip to Hollywood for her and her father plus a small salary while he had her make some screen tests.

When he initially had proposed the offer to Marguerita backstage later the same night that he met her, she merely looked at him, somewhat dumbfounded, but Eduardo Cansino quickly accepted, shaking Sheehan's hand happily, smiling and patting him on the back for being astute enough to realize his daughter's potential as a film personality.

Accompanied by her father, Marguerita showed up a week later at the Fox Western Avenue studio where Sheehan took them on a short tour, allowed them to watch a scene being filmed, lunched with them at the commissary and later that day turned Marguerita, whom

Clowning with Gene Kelly, director Charles Vidor and comedian Phil Silvers between scenes of *Cover Girl* (1944).

he had told at lunch to get used to being called "Rita," over to the makeup department. After working with a dialogue coach two days on her diction and some rudimentary acting suggestions on how to speak the lines assigned her for her first test, she stepped before the cameras. Ultimately she made two tests. One concentrated solely on her reading of lines and her reactions; the other a photographic exploration of her facial and figure features—good and bad.

Sheehan was exuberant when the tests turned out better than even he had anticipated. On screen she appeared to project a ripe and somewhat brazen sensuality that was slightly muted by an aura of shy, wide-eyed innocence. The effect was intriguing and Sheehan summoned her and her father to his office several weeks later and proposed a deal in which he would sign Rita to a short-term contract with options for renewal in just six months at a much higher salary if she agreed to follow to the letter a rigid program he had planned to groom her for stardom. She would attend daily acting classes with other Fox starlets, take special diction lessons to improve her voice projection and, most importantly, diet off her excess pounds. The contract conditions were agreed to, but because she was still under legal age, Eduardo's consent and approval was needed. Without a moment's hesitation, Eduardo consented.

Rita dieted strenuously, exercised vigorously in the studio gymnasium, attended classes faithfully, listening and learning. In a matter of a few weeks she had bicycled four inches off her hip measurements!

"And," Miss Hayworth added, "I developed a burning ambition—as only a too-fat seventeen-year-old can burn—to become a good actress. I got to know a few of the other girls Mr. Sheehan was also grooming and I felt each of them had advantages I did not. But this was merely an added incentive for me to work twice as hard. I paid strict attention to the acting coach and to the woman who trained me to project my voice. At home I'd lock myself in the bathroom, stand in front of a mirror over the sink, and practice for hours. I learned to correct flaws in my posture and pose for pictures in the studio gallery for hours without complaining. It didn't require my being a genius to realize Fox was spending a great deal of time and money on my behalf and I intended for them to get their money's worth!"

Within a month she worked in her first Fox film, a Spanish-language short subject used as an exploitation film in countries where that was the native language to show off new contract players and give an inkling of the Spanish-language film products planned or already in production. Footage from *Rosa de Francia,* which co-starred Antonio Moreno and Rosita Diaz, was included in this short as well as candid glimpses of Miss Diaz, herself, who had already made a name for herself in Europe and such other starlets as Frances Grant, Rosina Lawrence and Barbara Blane. But like Miss Hayworth's first short, and her unbilled extra bit in the Mexican quota quickie, this Fox film is also something of a curiosity since, ostensibly, it never had a U.S. showing—save a few theaters in Los Angeles and New York City where only Spanish-language products were screened. 20th Century-Fox still carries this short on their inventory of nonsafety films in their vaults but no print of it appears to exist in their archives!

Officially, of course, Rita Hayworth's screen debut was her dance sequence in *Dante's Inferno,* a 1935 Fox cosmic drama that starred Spencer Tracy and one of Winfield Sheehan's earlier starlet discoveries who had made good: Claire Trevor. Rita's dance contribution to this modestly budgeted potboiler was supposed to have been completed within a week since her sole contribution was a ballroom dance number, choreographed by her father, that teamed her with Gary Leon. But during the first hour of filming Leon sprained his ankle and three weeks elapsed before they were able to complete

Shopping in Wilshire district before the birth of her daughter, Rebecca Welles.

the sequence. Consequently, Rita's second Fox feature film, *Under the Pampas Moon,* in which she had a small role, a few lines of dialogue and even a dance sequence of sorts, called "The Zamba," was her first released Fox feature. Although it was booked into New York's Radio City Music Hall, "the showplace of the nation," *Under the Pampas Moon* turned out to be anything but a showcase production for Rita, French actress Ketti Gallian, whom Fox was also trying to promote, or anyone else associated with it, including the star, Warner Baxter. It was, in fact, Baxter's first sound film to be received with less than critical enthusiasm, and his slow-but-steady decline as one of the screen's ten top box-office stars of that era started with the release of this film.

Although Warner Baxter's decline was not immediately apparent at that juncture, Rita's prospects in Fox

Conveying the look and allure that was "Gilda" which made "Put the Blame On Mame" one of the most popular songs of 1946.

products appeared to be very good. She was awarded an important supporting role in *Charlie Chan in Egypt,* also released ahead of *Dante's Inferno.* The *Chan* series of that time were well scripted and produced and big money-makers. Consequently, much of the public became mildly conscious of the existence of Rita Cansino, especially since some of her footage in this *Chan* film included swimming in the pool of an underground cavern that's eerie enough to be remembered (even by producer Val Lewton, whose 1942 horror classic *Cat People,* which contains a famous and frightening swimming-pool sequence, apparently found its inspiration in *Charlie Chan in Egypt*).

Rita then impersonated a Russian girl with dancing career aspirations in a Jane Withers Fox vehicle, *Paddy O'Day,* which allowed her to sing, in her own voice, dance, and have a romantic interlude with, of all people, Pinky Tomlin. Her next assignment was in *Human Cargo,* in which she was an illegal alien working as a nightclub dancer who was being blackmailed by the gang that had smuggled her into the country. It was less prestigious than *Paddy O'Day* but certainly better than her next film experience, a two-minute sequence, as Barbara Stanwyck's sister in *A Message to Garcia,* which eventually was deleted from the released film after just one preview; even Winfield Sheehan realized what a bit of incongruous casting it was.

In 1972, George Marshall, who directed *A Message to Garcia,* vaguely recalled the circumstances but told me:

"Well, if Sheehan hadn't ordered that sequence with Rita deleted, I would have done so myself. It was really extraneous to begin with and brought attention to the fact that Barbara Stanwyck was miscast as a Cuban noblewoman. And the film was much too long anyway. It's still too long. . . . The only other opportunity I had to work with Rita was many years later when she and her husband, producer James Hill, hired me to direct her in *The Happy Thieves,* which we filmed in Spain. We had one helluva good time making the film but I think it's one Rita would like to forget. I know I would!

"Even with Rita and Rex Harrison in it, I still couldn't make the damn thing play—at least not as a comedy. On paper the script seemed to have tremendous comedy potential. But, for one reason or another, I just couldn't bring it off. Maybe another director might have been able to . . . I don't know.

"But I do know that if somebody called me up tomorrow and asked me to direct another film with Rita I'd drop whatever I was doing for the opportunity. She's one helluva great gal and one of the most thoroughly professional actresses in the business."

Although *Human Cargo* and *A Message to Garcia* were both actually filmed under the supervision of Shee-

With her daughter, Rebecca Welles, and Lana Turner's daughter, Cheryl Crane, in 1946.

han, they were not released until 1936 under the trademark of the newly formed 20th Century-Fox Corporation, with Darryl F. Zanuck credited as executive producer. In 1935 Fox Films found themselves in serious financial difficulties. Their main star assets included Warner Baxter and Janet Gaynor, neither of whom were any longer in strong demand, Will Rogers, who died in an airplane accident in August of that year and Shirley Temple. Except for the Temple and Rogers films, and a few bread-and-butter programmers, such as the popular *Charlie Chan* series, most Fox products showed little or no financial returns and the studio was on the verge of bankruptcy when Darryl F. Zanuck took over.

Zanuck had made a hasty and somewhat stormy departure from Warners in 1933 where he had been Jack's most loyal and trusted executive in charge of production. Exiting Warners, Zanuck formed 20th-Century Pictures and made over twenty films in just about two years which were filmed at the Goldwyn Studios and which all made money. Joseph Schenck partly financed these films and released them through his United Artists Corporation. And it was Schenck, a Fox stockholder, who helped Zanuck effect a merger of 20th-Century Pictures and Fox Films, which Jesse L. Lasky and Win-

With her daughters Yasmin and Rebecca (aged three and eight), in their Las Vegas hotel suite where they remained under heavy guard after Miss Hayworth received two different death threats in the mail.

field Sheehan both opposed, but which, nonetheless, was a shrewdly-brought-off merger.

During the negotiations, while Sheehan was still in charge of Fox production supervision, he had a Technicolor test made with Rita and Gilbert Roland (and another with Don Ameche) which convinced him she could handle the title role in a proposed remake of *Ramona,* Helen Hunt Jackson's famous romantic tale of early California. Rita was elated with the prospects of this assignment which, if successful, could elevate her to stardom. She posed for gallery portraits, patiently spent hours at costume fittings and was never without a copy of the script, which she studied with absolute concentration. ("I think I can still recite my dialogue from memory," she said in 1972.)

But when 20th-Century and Fox did merge, Sheehan found himself unemployed. Taking over as executive producer, Zanuck wanted no part of any project to which Sheehan had given his interest and attention. After looking at Rita's Technicolor tests and some of her other Fox footage, he felt there was no justification whatever in gambling an expensive property on what he considered her dubious abilities. And, since it was the time to either take up her option, at a substantial salary increase or release her, he elected to let her go and gave Loretta Young, a personal contractee, the role of *Ramona.*

Rita, who had splurged a small fortune on a new

personal wardrobe on her prospects, learned of her misfortune from a Zanuck assistant who rather coldly telephoned the bad news, saying it was unnecessary for her to return to the studio as her contract had been canceled.

"Zanuck just didn't have the time, or so he later said, to meet me face to face and tell me his decision," Miss Hayworth said. "Naturally I cried and I screamed and I vowed I would show those people they had made a terrible mistake. I determined I would become successful and famous in films and they would be sorry."

It took her exactly five years to do just that and the occasion of her stardom, success and international acclaim were all a result of being cast as Doña Sol in Darryl F. Zanuck's expensive Technicolored remake of *Blood and Sand* when director Rouben Mamoulian, over Zanuck's protests, insisted that she have the role. Reluctantly, Zanuck arranged with Columbia Pictures, where she was under contract, to negotiate for her services at five times the salary she was then receiving.

"You don't have to be a revengeful person to taste the sweetness of that," said Rita.

There were times, however, between her initial departure from Fox and her triumphant return, when her vow of becoming a success seemed futile indeed. Along the way, however, she found someone to constantly renew her optimism and enough film work to give her the experience and ability to carry off an important assignment when it did come along.

Her early tenure at Fox automatically canceled all nightclub work, which left her father available to work at the same studio occasionally as either a dance instructor or assistant choreographer, and to rally his sister Elisa and other members of the dancing Cansino clan for an appearance in the 1936 RKO film *The Dancing Pirate.* Eduardo also reactivated his interest in his School, still being operated by his father, who had subsequently been joined by his uncle, José. The School relocated over a hardware store on South Vermont Avenue and changed enrollment policies so that youngsters with only aspirations of a professional dancing career were also eligible to benefit from instructions by the famous Cansinos. Before too long, the School was again a viable enterprise.

Years later, when Rita was the screen's reigning sex symbol, Padre, her grandfather, would sit at the downstairs entrance to the School, idly strum his guitar, which he also taught his granddaughter to play, and tell everybody who stopped to chat with him how he had once danced for King Alfonso of Spain.

But it was during Rita's early days at Fox that she met a man who was destined to play an important part in her life, personal and professional, and who had won the instant approval of her father. He was Edward C. Judson, a middle-aged Hollywood figure rumored to have been an ex-gambler, a sometimes salesman and agent for new and used Isotta-Fraschini cars and, sometime later it turned out, former husband of Chicago toothpaste heiress Hazel Forbes. In 1935, however, Judson was in Hollywood acting as a front man for a Texas oil promoter who had a short-term lease on an oil field in which he had high hopes and no cash to acquire the necessary equipment to begin drilling. It was Judson's function to find financial backers, and Winfield Sheehan was one of his prospective angels. The day Judson made his pitch to Sheehan, who had completely forgotten the appointment, the promoter was invited to come along to a projection room with the Fox vice president while he looked at Rita's color tests for *Ramona*. After the screening Judson was so impressed with Rita he almost forgot his own purpose for being there and enthusiastically asked Sheehan for an introduction to the potential star.

Eduardo Cansino took an immediate fancy to Judson and gave his wholehearted approval to his courting his daughter. After Rita lapsed into a state of depression when her contract was canceled, Judson was on hand to comfort and console her and squire her around town. He failed, however, to raise the required financing for the oil wildcatter, and reverted to earning a substantial salary selling foreign cars. He felt, however, that there were even bigger financial rewards to be gained by helping promote the screen career of Rita Cansino. Through manipulations and an acquaintance with Harry Cohn, he secured a small part for her in a Columbia film, *Meet Nero Wolfe,* and later, after selling Nat Levine a car, offered him a substantial "discount" if Levine could find a spot for Rita in one of his Republic films.

The spot she got was the feminine lead in one of the Three Mesquiteer series films, *Hit the Saddle.* Similar wheeling-and-dealing at Grand National got her the lead opposite Tex Ritter in *Trouble in Texas;* and a night of revelry with the casting director of the independent Crescent Pictures resulted in Rita's being used in two Tom Keene adventure films, *Rebellion* and *Old Louisiana.* While Rita was hardly overwhelmed with any of her roles, she was constantly working, gaining experience, continuously on-screen and thoroughly convinced that Judson had only her best interests at heart.

So, when the moment was right, Judson proposed to her and she accepted without hesitation. On May 29, 1937, they were married. Much later she learned she was the *third* Mrs. Judson. But Judson was too shrewd to allow his ego to forget the dangers of marrying a nineteen-year-old girl who could well have been his daughter. When Rita confronted him about former marriages he had neglected to mention, he merely snapped his fingers and said he had also forgotten to casually mention that he had arranged a screen test for her at Columbia Pictures which, if favorable, would guarantee her a long-term player contract. Neither Judson nor Harry Cohn, who hadn't been impressed much with her brief part in *Meet Nero Wolfe,* confided in anyone how Judson had induced him to do another test of her. The general consensus is, of course, that Cohn recognized a brother under the skin who, like himself, was a born gambler, psychologically unable to resist a long shot.

Judson also reminded Cohn that Rita was not exactly a neophyte in films and that he'd be a fool not to take advantage of the experience and knowledge she had gained at Fox and that she also had a solid theatri-

Orson Welles giving his estranged wife some lessons in seamanship off the coast of Mexico between scenes of *The Lady from Shanghai.* The photo was taken by the owner of the yacht, Errol Flynn.

With her three-month-old daughter, Rebecca Welles.

cal heritage. Under Judson's deluge of salesmanship, Cohn could find only one line of resistance: Latin-type actresses offering sultry insinuations and little else had become a glut on the film market at that moment and Columbia, least of any studio, couldn't afford to gamble on another of that type. Cohn therefore insisted Rita

change her last name and when it was suggested she use her mother's maiden name, he suggested adding the *y* to the spelling so she wouldn't be confused with her uncle, Vinton Haworth, who, at that time, was also under contract to Columbia. Judson grabbed Cohn's hand and started pumping it vigorously and simultaneously slapped the mogul on the back, exclaiming he drove a hard bargain but it would turn out to be the best deal he ever made. Before Harry Cohn knew what hit him, he found he had signed Rita Hayworth to a seven-year contract.

As a parting shot, Judson confided in Cohn that he was about to marry Rita and exclaimed: "What bride ever received a better wedding gift than a movie contract?"

Cohn, having regained his composure, looked at Judson with narrowed eyes and retorted, "It looks to me as if an old man has just found himself a seven-year meal ticket with free room and broad."

All connotations of Rita's partially Latin heritage slowly started disappearing although in her first film under her new Columbia contract, *Criminals of the Air,* she played a Mexican nightclub dancer in a below-the-border dive! After this film her hair was restored to its natural shade of brown and she underwent long and painful electrolysis treatments in order to broaden her forehead and temporarily accentuate a widow's peak.

But in 1938, in *Who Killed Gail Preston?,* she wore a black wig and temporarily became one of the many Hedy Lamarr imitations which glutted the screens after Miss Lamarr's sensational appearance in *Algiers*. Rita's raven tresses disappeared in *There's Always a Woman* and, except for about a thirty-second scene, so did Rita! It seems the subplot in which she was involved was eliminated from the final release version of that film

Errol Flynn, his wife, Nora Eddington, Orson Welles and crew members of the "Zaca," Flynn's yacht, surprise Rita with a birthday cake during the filming of *The Lady from Shanghai* (1947).

since Columbia had an idea of turning the husband-and-wife detective team into a series and the fewer running characters needed, the more economical the series would become if it caught on. Actually, however, there was only one sequel, *There's That Woman Again,* when the series idea was abandoned because William Powell and Myrna Loy and their zany *Thin Man* episodes proved to be too much box-office competition.

It was at this conjuncture that George Cukor was preparing his elegant remake of Philip Barry's *Holiday* and he tested Rita for the role of the younger sister. Although impressed with her grace, a decided éclat for wearing clothes with a flair, Cukor felt she still needed vocal seasoning and finally gave the role to Doris Nolan. He recommended to Rita that she take some additional diction lessons from a well-known vocal coach, a woman noted for achieving some remarkable results with actresses with slight speech impediments or an inability to fully master vocal projection. Kay Francis, noted for her lisp, was one actress helped to stardom by this woman's genius.

Rita, disappointed at not being awarded the prize, took Cukor's advice and now has fond memories of the experience:

"For one thing, I had the opportunity to rehearse and work on a scene with Katharine Hepburn, and I learned more from her in three days than I had in working for a year in B films. She was friendly, considerate and a complete professional. She went out of her way to put me at ease, and I've never forgotten her kindness.

"In later years, whenever I was asked to make a test with a newcomer I always forgot my 'star status' and tried to be as gracious and helpful as Miss Hepburn had been to me.

"About two years after I did the test for *Holiday* I ran into George Cukor and he remembered me and asked if I had taken his advice. When I told him I had, he smiled, nodded and said, 'Yes, I can hear the difference. Keep it up, you're doing splendidly.' I thought no more about it, but two days later I found out I had been loaned to MGM for a part in *Susan and God,* which Mr. Cukor was going to direct!"

In the interim of her *Holiday* test and her brief sortie at MGM, Rita was borrowed by RKO to play a female Robin Hood in *The Renegade Ranger.* She had a fairly expensive wardrobe in Columbia's *The Lone Wolf Spy Hunt* and, for the first time, the luxury of her own stand-in! A street-length silver lamé cocktail dress she wore in *The Long Wolf* film was unique enough for several magazines to use illustrations of her modeling it. For its time, the dress was quite fetching and Rita was shrewd enough to purchase it from Columbia with a very definite purpose in mind.

Studio scuttlebutt had it that Howard Hawks was testing actresses for a small but important role as a mantrap in a forthcoming aviation drama but Rita was not among the chosen girls summoned by Hawks. So,

One of the screen's great romantic teams, Rita Hayworth and Glenn Ford, between scenes of *The Loves of Carmen* on location in northern California.

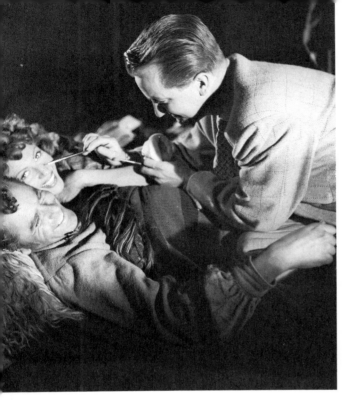

Sharing a private joke with Glenn Ford while makeup man Robert Schiffer adjusts her makeup for a scene in *The Loves of Carmen*.

although she seldom went in for the night-life circuit, she talked her husband into escorting her to all the Hollywood bistros Hawks was known to frequent, wearing her silver lamé dress. Eventually Hawks spotted her, wondered who she was, and soon learned she had been right under his nose at Columbia. A few days later a test was arranged and Rita was assigned the role of Richard Barthlemess's sexually tormenting young wife in the film which was eventually called *Only Angels Have Wings*. She worked in stiff competition with Barthelmess, attempting a comeback, Cary Grant and Jean Arthur, and most reviewers singled her out for her sensuous performance after the film was released.

Only Angels Have Wings was a box-office success, and fan mail for Rita Hayworth began pouring into Columbia's publicity department. Once this happened, Henry Rogers, her agent, and Judson attempted to convince Harry Cohn the time was ripe to promote Rita to better assignments and publicity saturation. After checking out the amount of fan mail Rita actually had received, Cohn decided to go along with the plan. The only actress at Columbia under a long-term contract who had any public following of consequence was Jean Arthur, and Miss Arthur, far from considering herself the queen of the lot, was uncooperative about doing

Compiling a photo album of her daughter, Rebecca.

publicity and was, in fact, thinking up ways to get out of her contract. Aware of this, Cohn knew it was time for Columbia to begin promoting its own stars instead of continuing to catch stars on their rebound from other studios, or merely using free-lance names, such as Cary Grant, on a one-, two- or three-picture deal.

Rita proved most cooperative about helping promote herself by spending long hours in Columbia's photo gallery posing for publicity stills which depicted her scantily costumed and labeled "Miss Thanksgiving," "St. Valentine's Special Sweetheart," "The Santa Claus Girl" and "July 4th's Hottest Firecracker." There was even a marked improvement in her film assignments. She got to co-star with Tony Martin in a modest musical and was then "showcased" in one of Columbia's *Blondie* films, their bread-and-butter series which found public approval. Her next assignment was to have been *Convicted Woman*, opposite Glenn Ford, but Rochelle Hudson replaced her because MGM borrowed her for *Susan and God*.

Rita was impressed with all the first-class MGM trappings—a specially designed wardrobe, her own dressing room and hairdresser and other luxury treatments. After seeing some of her footage in *Susan and God*, Louis B. Mayer considered using her again to play a mantrap in MGM's biggest budgeted film of the year, *Boom Town*. But Hedy Lamarr, who was under contract to MGM and had just suffered the indignity of

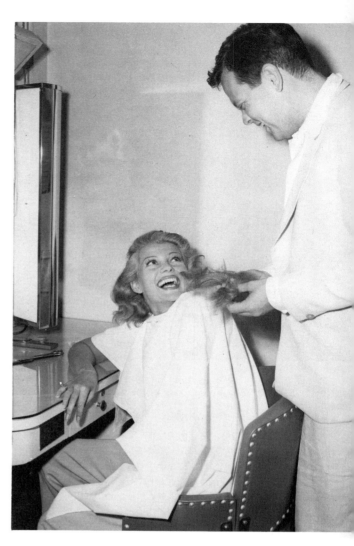

A sequence of three stills, showing the Hayworth transformation from redhead to "topaz blonde" for her role as *The Lady from Shanghai.*

appearing in two turkeys in a row, campaigned for the small mantrap role herself, and Mayer reluctantly gave it to her. It turned out to be a very shrewd move on Miss Lamarr's part and she regained all of her lost luster.

When I asked George Cukor about Rita and *Susan and God,* he said she was a decided asset to the film although he was totally unaware of any thoughts Louis B. Mayer may have had about using her in *Boom Town.* Said Mr. Cukor:

"I was never part of the inner circle of Louis B. Mayer's confidants and seldom had any dealings with him other than in connection with the film on which I was working. I know he was very pleased, as I was, with Rita's work in *Susan and God* and had questioned me at length about her. But that's all I know firsthand. Anything else I heard about her was merely studio gossip.

"Actually, Rita and I never again crossed paths in a professional sense. Harry Cohn had hired me to direct *Born Yesterday* and I more or less thought I had final word on who would play Billie Dawn. But when Cohn

insisted that Rita be given the role, I was ready to walk out. I wanted Judy Holliday to recreate her original Broadway role because she was exactly right for it and Rita would have been all wrong. I imply nothing derogatory by that, either. Rita was simply too elegant, too sophisticated and much too graceful to play anyone as crass as Billie Dawn was supposed to be.

"You hear and read so many stories, mostly unfounded gossip, about Hollywood stars that it's sometimes very difficult to get at the truth. Just recently some writer mentioned that Rita and I are very close friends who telephone each other every day! This just isn't true. We are friends, certainly, but she has never asked me for any advice, personal or professional, and I have never offered her any. And yet this same writer reported that Rita had rejected playing the leading role in *Heat* because I had advised her against doing it. I was not even aware she had been offered the part, if indeed she had, and any rejection of it was certainly her own decision.

"I *do* see Rita occasionally and I *do* talk with her on the telephone once in a while. Other than that, we have very little contact. We both have lots of friends but actually, except for an occasional large party, or an all-out industry effort, such as an Academy Award show, or something of that ilk, we orbit in different social circles. Of course, even now, at fifty-four, Rita is still a stunning creature. She also belongs to the grand tradition of glamorous movie queens who were not only beautiful and talented but who also generated excitement by always retaining a certain aura of mystery and allusion. Ava Gardner has these qualities too. In fact Rita and Ava are truly the last members of that very distinctive breed: genuine glamour stars.

"Unfortunately, we just don't have superstars like them anymore. Today actresses believe they must play down their beauty and be intellectual. But you have to be a Katharine Hepburn to get away with that. We now have 'instant' superstars who are all forgotten in a year or two. Once a woman forsakes her most cherished pos-sessions, glamour and mystery, she simply can't hold anyone's attention for very long. The industry doesn't seem to realize yet that the public still craves romance and glamour although this nostalgia thing for old movies has been going on for about ten years. I should think financiers and filmmakers would realize by now that glamour, mystery and the world of romantic intrigue and make-believe through which creatures like Rita Hayworth once moved are a necessary part of our fantasy world. Women's Lib may do a lot to advance a file clerk who hankers to be an executive, but it will never do anything for an actress or our waning film industry.

"Once a woman suppresses her allure and wants to be regarded only as an intellectual equal she automatically becomes a bore. I've never heard anyone talk about Rita Hayworth's intellect, although she has a very shrewd one—shrewd enough to know that wasn't what got her to the heights of superstardom."

After *Susan and God* one of the things which did

help Rita get to the top was her first screen encounter with Glenn Ford: *The Lady in Question,* a well-done, albeit modest, remake of the great Raimu's famous French film, *Gribouille,* which Brian Aherne contended for years contained his best screen performance. Critics also had kind words for Rita's subsequent film, *Angels over Broadway,* but the public found the film much too arty and literate and that Ben Hecht's script sacrificed action in favor of some excellent dialogue. Actually *Angels over Broadway* is a rather unique "character study" film such as *Our Town, The Long Voyage Home* and *Of Mice and Men,* which, coincidentally were all released about the same time, all lavished with critical praise and all ignored by the public. The reason for this may have been because the world was already in turmoil, draft conscription had begun in the United States, World War II appeared to be inevitable, and public interest seemed to be only in escapist film fare.

Rita's escapist film was *The Strawberry Blonde,* the nostalgic remake she then made of James Hogan's *One Sunday Afternoon* on loan-out to Warners. Good-natured vulgarity pervaded the script and the performances of Rita, James Cagney, Olivia de Havilland, George Tobias and Alan Hale. Warners were most pleased when Rita did so well with her role, as a last-minute replacement for Ann Sheridan, on suspension because of a salary dispute, that she remained to make *Affectionately Yours,* a comedy that she would have been better off refusing.

When the news broke that she had been awarded the role in *Blood and Sand,* for which no less than thirty-seven other actresses had tested, one columnist dubbed Rita "Lady Loan-out." And changing the color of hair for that film to the coppery red color it was to remain through the bulk of her career turned out to be the extra fillip which turned "Lady Loan-out" into "Lady Luck." For, after some thirty-one films, she suddenly was an "overnight" discovery and celebrity.

Her three loan-out films in a row had elevated her to international stardom strictly on her magnetic sexual appeal so when she returned to Columbia, Harry Cohn decided the time had come to remind everyone she had other assets which had never been fully exploited. Consequently, her much heralded return to her home studio, as a full-fledged star, with a new contract and a new dressing room, and a new regard for the studio's "hottest" property, resulted in her making *You'll Never Get Rich* with Fred Astaire that was so successful they reunited a year later in *You Were Never Lovelier.*

In his autobiography, *Steps in Time,* Fred Astaire recalls these two films as being among his happiest experiences. After meeting Rita the first time, he reminded her that he was an old friend of her father's and also wrote:

"Rita danced with trained perfection and individuality. She, of course, knew through experience what this dancing business was all about. That was apparent the moment I started working with her." Disappointed because their second film, *You Were Never Lovelier,* was not in Technicolor, Astaire said, "I looked forward to it mainly because Rita was so delightful to work with and I wanted very much to have a big hit with her. She had gained a lot of experience and was by then one of the top feminine stars on the screen."

Off the record Astaire has maintained Rita is his all-time favorite dancing partner and recently, in *Filmograph* magazine, the notable dance authority and film historian Glenn Shipley wrote:

"Of all the dance partners that Fred Astaire had, I think Rita Hayworth was the most suited to him. Miss Hayworth had grown up in the field of dancing, and in her two films with Mr. Astaire her every movement matched his, as was the case with none of his other partners."

During the question-and-answer part of the day devoted to a "Rita Hayworth Retrospective" during the 1972 San Francisco Film Festival, Rita said:

"I guess the jewels of my life were the pictures I made with Fred Astaire. When he came to do two films at Columbia he *asked* for me. Fred *knew* I was a dancer."

With two of the sailfish she caught during a day off from filming *The Lady from Shanghai.*

He knew what all those dumb-dumbs at Columbia didn't know, and if it hadn't been for him, I would never have been cast in either film!"

On another occasion, she also said:

"Dancing is my natural heritage, and I have always loved it. But I always hated to practice. But rehearsals with Fred Astaire were occasions I found myself looking forward to with an anticipation of pleasure.

"When I was younger I used to study ballet, Spanish and tap dancing for four or five hours a day and it was no cinch, especially having a father who was so very strict. It was hard and tedious work and there were times when I didn't think I could go on. But I did and, of course, as it turned out, the effort was worth it.

"Every girl who wants to dance should start training when she is young. I don't mean at four, as I did, but while she is still ambitious and able to 'take it.' Nor is dancing alone enough today. If she really wants to succeed she must broaden her background to include drama, music, singing, everything."

To coincide with the opening of *You'll Never Get Rich* at New York's famous Radio City Music Hall, Columbia sent her there on a publicity junket and Ed Judson, who remained very unobtrusive, accompanied his wife. For the first time in her life, Rita had the spotlight all to herself but because *You'll Never Get Rich* spotlighted pre–Pearl Harbor U.S. Army life and she didn't want anybody thinking she favored a single

On January 25, 1949, Rita Hayworth, with Prince Aly Khan, met her future-in-laws, the Aga Khan and his wife, the Begum Aga Khan, at their chateau in Cannes.

branch of government service, the government supplied her with a military escort consisting of a soldier, a sailor, a marine and a Coast Guardsman. The four GIs accompanied her to a horse show where, after presenting the owner of the winning horse with a trophy, she sold war bonds. And the GI quartet also went along when she appeared on four national broadcasts, plugging her new picture and pleading with everyone to buy bonds; attended a party for the Columbia employees who worked in New York; and they stood by while she beguiled theater exhibitors gathered for their annual get-together. Rita and her military quartet showed up at cocktail parties where she was honored by the press, fashion designers and even the New York Furriers Association. She also presided over two war bond rallies and dispensed kisses to every man who bought a bond.

Theodore Strauss, *The New York Times* columnist and film reviewer, assigned to accompany Rita and tell his readers about her successful conquest for publicity, finally cornered her for a few minutes and asked her if she didn't find the hectic pace of the short junket somewhat exhausting. Said Rita:

"Certainly not! Why should I mind? I like having my picture taken and being a glamorous person. Sometimes when I find myself getting impatient I just remember the times I cried my eyes out because nobody wanted to take my picture at the Trocadero. All women

Immediately following their wedding ceremony, Prince Aly Khan and his bride stroll among guests at their champagne reception at the sumptuous Chateau de L'Horizon.

like being fussed over and I'm no exception. I think it's damned nice!"

What Rita neglected to mention, however, was the fact that she had seldom gone to the Trocadero, or any other night spot for that matter, because her husband preferred spending their evenings at home. But all that changed after she returned to Hollywood and made *My Gal Sal,* on loan-out to Darryl F. Zanuck. Because if Ed Judson wasn't willing to show her off around the Hollywood nightspots, Victor Mature, her new co-star, was certainly more than anxious to do so. Consequently, nobody in the film colony was the least bit surprised when Rita announced that she and Judson had separated. Shortly afterward she filed suit for divorce and charged Judson with extreme mental cruelty and claimed that he tried to keep her in total seclusion when she was not working.

What she had hoped would be a very quiet court action turned out to be much more sensational than she had anticipated when Judson filed a counter-suit contesting her action and asking for a $10,000 settlement as partial payment for the time and effort he had devoted to promoting his estranged wife's film career. Columnist Erskine Johnson reported that Cohn did pay Judson off and he was satisfied enough to drop his counter-suit. By this time, however, the case had dragged on for days and each day Volga Cansino accompanied her daughter to Superior Court and when called to testify, she corroborated her daughter's complaints. Finally, on Friday, May 22, 1942, Rita was granted her first divorce. Her marriage to Judson had lasted just about five years.

Said Rita:

"He regarded me only as an investment and I had no fun—except on that trip to New York, which was the longest time Ed and I had spent away from home since we had eloped to Yuma and got married. But I'm not bitter now. I realize how much Ed has done for me. I never had to do any fighting for myself with executives and agents. He fought for me. After we got married, running my career was his only concern and he gave it everything he had and his efforts paid off. And although we had our domestic differences, he's entitled to a fair return."

During the period between her separation from Judson and her divorce, Rita completed her stanza in Julien Duvivier's all-star film, *Tales of Manhattan,* and became one of Hollywood's most sought-after girls about town. Victor Mature, who had publicly professed

his love for her, was away on active duty with the U.S. Coast Guard, but since Rita had not acknowledged that the feeling was mutual, she kept columnists in constant confusion speculating which of her current beaux, Howard Hughes, David Niven, Gilbert Roland, Tony Martin or Orson Welles, was the one she was most serious about. And she was no help whatever when the question was put directly to her. She merely smiled and shrugged and said:

"I like them all—for different reasons, of course. In Spain, where my father came from, and in Mexico, where I have lived, a girl's worth is judged by the number of suitors she has! I'm not out to corner the bachelor market in Hollywood but I do enjoy window shopping whenever I can."

Rita's romances and appearances at local niteries were always well covered in the gossip columns but few writers, with the exception of her loyal friend and staunch supporter, Louella Parsons, ever alluded to her war effort contributions. Just before her separation, she appeared on stage in a Hollywood edition of *Charlot's Revue* that played nightly for weeks at the El Capitan Theater with all proceeds being donated to the British War Relief Association of Southern California. She sang, in a surprisingly good voice, and danced in this star-studded entertainment. She did several "Command Performance" broadcasts recorded for replay overseas to entertain servicemen, toured with the USO, turned

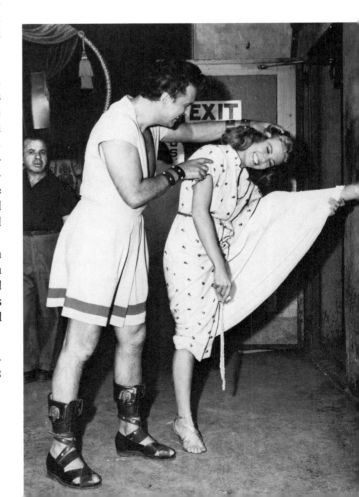

Clowning with co-star Stewart Granger between scenes of *Salome* during its 1952 filming.

With fourth husband, Dick Haymes, and daughters Rebecca and Yasmin.

up at military hospitals and training camps where she signed autographs, sang and played her own guitar accompaniment, danced, often with castanets and gave unstintingly of her time and talents. She also showed up often at the Hollywood Canteen, not merely on the nights designated for employees of Columbia Studios to come over and help—including part-time dishwasher-waiter Harry Cohn.

What more could any bug-eyed GI, who turned up at the canteen ask than to be approached by Rita Hayworth and asked if he would like to dance with her? During one unforgettable night, I personally danced with Rita, Betty Grable, Deanna Durbin, Kay Francis, Barbara Stanwyck and Bette Davis in a matter of a couple of hours.

It's hardly any secret that Louella Parsons loathed Orson Welles after the release of *Citizen Kane* but it remains a matter of wonderment that she and Rita remained on the same friendly and intimate terms after she married the man Miss Parsons referred to as "awesome Orson—the self-styled genius."

Rita first met Hollywood's wonder boy at a party hosted by the Joseph Cottens and soon afterward joined Welles and Cotten in a magic act performed in a tent, just off Hollywood Boulevard, for the entertainment of servicemen. Nightly, the man who helped conceive, co-author, star in and direct *Citizen Kane,* the most controversial film, most talked about and most written about production in the entire history of Hollywood, amused and amazed GIs by giving the illusion that he was actually sawing the gorgeous Rita Hayworth in half.

It was actually Joseph Cotten, not Rita, who first told an aghast Louella that Rita and Orson were in love and would probably marry. Miss Parsons wasted no time at all in printing her disapproval after Rita confirmed the possibility of her marrying Welles. So on the day Rita officially became eligible to marry, September 7, 1943, she became the second Mrs. Orson Welles. (The first had been a Chicago society beauty, Virginia Nicholson, who once had aspirations of becoming an actress and joined Welles's theatrical group.)

Rita soon reverted to type and became the dutiful wife of a domineering husband. This time, however, there was a difference: her new husband's chief interest was his own career and his advice to his second wife was merely suggesting what books she should read to improve her mind, which classical records she should listen to and what art galleries and museums she should visit. Welles found the going rough, as no one appeared very interested in financing any of his proposed film projects and the best he could do in Hollywood was to star in such vehicles as *Jane Eyre, Tomorrow is Forever* and *The Stranger,* none of which did very much toward furthering his "wonder boy" image.

It was a different story with Rita. By the time *Cover Girl* was in production, a lush Technicolor musical that co-starred her with Gene Kelly, she had become known as The Love Goddess of the screen. *Cover Girl* was a smash hit and Columbia, which had just purchased a short-lived Broadway play called *Heart of a City* and intended starring Merle Oberon and Ida Lupino in it, had a sudden inspiration to musicalize it for Rita and

A 1953 publicity pose of her torrid number "The Heat Is On" for *Miss Sadie Thompson*.

retitle it *Tonight and Every Night*. While it was in production Rita discovered she was pregnant and when filming completed she went into seclusion until December 17, 1944, when she and Orson Welles became the parents of a daughter, Rebecca. Rita's euphoria at becoming a mother was short-lived, About a month after her daughter's birth, her own mother, Volga Haworth Cansino, died tragically at the age of forty-five of generalized peritonitis following a ruptured appendix.

Soon after *Tonight and Every Night* had opened, in 1945, Rita's brothers, Vernon and Eduardo, Jr., came home from military duty with the U.S. Army. Vernon worked in a few Columbia films and Eduardo became a taxicab driver. Neither seemed interested in following the Cansino family dancing tradition.

After Rebecca's birth, and Rita's mother's sudden death, Rita talked of retiring and Orson Welles, anxious to get out of Hollywood, was not overly opposed to her plans. So, in collaboration with Broadway producer Mike Todd, he involved himself in a mammoth stage production, based on Jules Verne's *Around the World in 80 Days,* to which Cole Porter contributed the songs. But the necessary money to bring it to Broadway ran out while its creators' enthusiasm was still at a peak. Consequently, because his wife's new film, *Gilda,* was

setting all-time Columbia box-office records, he appealed to Harry Cohn for a loan. Cohn advanced the money after guaranteeing himself repayment (no matter how the show fared) by having Welles agree to write, direct and co-star in a Columbia film. But even the most carefully calculated plans of geniuses and executives can have disastrous results.

Welles finally opened *Around the World* on Broadway on May 31, 1946, where it remained, after curiously mixed reviews, ranging from just bad to very bad, for seventy-five performances. Said critic Burns Mantle:

"Mr. Welles built up a loose but lively entertainment featuring everything from two or three Cole Porter songs to a full-stage circus, with tumblers, wire-walkers and a magic show doing some violence to a crateful of ducks, geese, rabbits and Mr. Welles. The critics didn't like it, but neither did Mr. Welles like the critics' comments . . . 'Wellesapoppin' they called it."

When the show folded Welles took off for Europe and made a film called *Black Magic* while his wife wisely remained in Hollywood and resumed her career with *Down to Earth*. At first she tried ignoring the gossip which linked her husband romantically with Italian actress Lea Padovani.

At that juncture Rita and Columbia received the

Awaiting instructions from director Curtis Bernhardt (raised arm) during the filming of *Miss Sadie Thompson* in Hawaii.

With Dick Haymes immediately after their wedding at the Sands Hotel, Las Vegas.

kind of international publicity money can't buy. Her famous World War II pinup picture was pasted on the first atomic bomb denotated on Bikini Atoll and named *Gilda!*

Down to Earth, a tailor-made Harry Cohn concoction was a musical sequel to one of Columbia's biggest all-time money-making comedies, *Here Comes Mr. Jordan,* that gave Rita, the screen's Love Goddess, an opportunity to play the goddess Terpsichore and co-star her with Columbia's hottest male star of the moment, Larry Parks, fresh from his triumphs in *The Jolson Story.* Film critics were no kinder to it than their Broadway brothers had been to Welles's staged fantasy but the filmgoing public is seldom discouraged by the critics and the box-office returns on *Down to Earth* were astronomical, so much so that when Rita's contract came up for renewal, she told her agents to advise Harry Cohn she wanted part of the action.

Rita, Harry Cohn and her agents finally reached what appeared to be a feasible agreement which would allow her to form her own production company, named Beckworth, in honor of her daughter, and henceforth receive a salary and a percentage of the gross on all her subsequent films made and released by Columbia. Before signing on the dotted line, however, Cohn did a bit of wheeling-and-dealing to collect the money owed him by Welles, by getting Rita to agree to co-star with her now-estranged husband in the promised film he was to deliver as repayment. This film, Cohn added, would not be included in her Beckworth Corporation set-up. And before Rita could protest, he casually reminded her that Columbia had given *Down to Earth* the most extensive and expensive prerelease and sales promotion publicity campaign in the studio's history!

Full-page ads, in glowing or garish color, depending on the quality of the newspaper or magazine in which they appeared, told the world of the film's virtues: "Larry Parks Sings It *His* Way" was the slogan alloted to Rita's co-star; but of Rita herself, the campaign centered around such searing questions and statements as "Who is She? Where Does She Come From? They Say She Kissed 2,000 Men! She's Out of This World and Down to Earth in Technicolor with Music. She Sings! She Dances! She's Terrific! But Who is She?"

The answer, it soon turned out, was the ex-Mrs. Orson Welles. After obtaining a legal separation from her husband, Rita proceeded to file suit for divorce. Because of this, Harry Cohn readied a western script, *Lona Hanson,* that was to have co-starred her with William Holden and Randolph Scott in a lavish Technicolor spectacle to be directed by Norman Foster. Rita, however, rejected the idea and elected to fulfill her bargain to appear opposite Welles in the film he had concocted and eventually titled *The Lady from Shanghai.* Asked if this meant a reconciliation, Rita said, "Of course not! I made an agreement and I'll stand by it! I owe it to Orson."

Based loosely on Sherwood King's novel, *If I Should Die Before I Wake,* Welles filmed his screenplay, *The Lady from Shanghai,* on locations in Mexico and San Francisco. He also co-starred with his estranged wife and insisted her world-famous red hair to be trimmed to a feather bob and bleached a champagne blonde. And although Columbia hair stylist Helen Hunt did the actual cutting, Welles was on hand to supervise every snip of her scissors. The resulting publicity had the studio deluged with requests from all over the world for strands of Rita's shorn hair.

Harry Cohn was anything but elated with Rita's "new look" and appeared to be in no hurry to release *The Lady from Shanghai* after its completion in mid-1947. And during filming, Rita quickly dispelled any and all rumors that a reconciliation was in the offing and quickly filed for her divorce once the film was completed. And when Cohn finally did release it, in 1948, reviews were unduly harsh, to the point where *The Lady from Shanghai* turned out a gigantic box-office failure.

But Rita has always maintained that it is a good film and audiences merely failed to appreciate its virtues. Welles himself called it "an experiment—in what *not* to do." Time, however, has proved Rita to be right since telecasts of *The Lady from Shanghai* and its inclusion on retrospectives of Welles's films have been successful.

While awaiting her final divorce decree, and while Harry Cohn waited for her hair to grow back, Rita was given a Columbia-sponsored vacation in Europe. In France, accompanied by her daughter, Rebecca, she was mobbed by reporters at Le Havre when her ship docked and again in Paris after she arrived there by train. A few days after her arrival, she was felled by a virus infection and hospitalized. Her condition worsened and she was given daily blood transfusions for better than a week. She rallied slowly but her recuperation, on the Riviera, turned out to be the beginning of an era when her name would appear, almost daily, in headlines all over the world throughout the next three years!

It was one of Rita's former co-stars of her *Charlot's Revue* days, international party giver, Elsa Maxwell, who ran into her on the Riviera at this time and took it upon herself to try and cheer her up. Miss Maxwell's

With co-star Jack Lemmon enjoying a break while filming *Fire Down Below* on location in the Bahamas (1957).

solution to Rita's depression was giving a small party in her honor, inviting a few witty friends and famous personalities to make the occasion an event to remember. Included was Prince Aly Khan, the royal playboy, who lived nearby in a villa that had once belonged to Maxine Elliott.

Handsome, wealthy, and one of the Continent's most sought-after men, Prince Aly, estranged from his wife, Joan Yarde-Buller, the British heiress to the Guinness Brewery millions, so played the role of bachelor-playboy-at-large to the hilt that gossips found it impossible to keep track of his romances. His first encounter with Rita engendered the same kind of off-screen romantic chemistry that she had engendered on-screen with Glenn Ford in *Gilda.* The prince and the Love Goddess soon became known as inseparable companions. Aly began his romantic campaign by giving weekly and elaborate parties in Rita's honor that were soon replaced by smaller bi-weekly soirées, eventually culminating in daily tête-à-têtes. Then, when Prince Aly motored to Spain to attend the bullfights at Madrid, Rita went with him.

Elsa Maxwell, instigator and close-hand observer of

With Robert Mitchum between scenes of *Fire Down Below*.

the romance, later said, "It was my notion that Rita, in the beginning, intended her friendship with Prince Aly as a come-on to intrigue Orson Welles and get him away from Lea Padovani. Orson arrived in Cannes just after Rita had left for Spain with Prince Aly. He told me Rita had telephoned him and said she wanted to see him. I guess he waited just too long to turn up. I think Rita originally came to Cannes because it was Orson's stamping ground. Perhaps she hoped they might patch up their differences. Their daughter Rebecca will always be a bond between them and Rita's love for her is great. And Orson adores her more and more. However, he's also a loving father to Christopher, his daughter by his first marriage. But whatever Rita's original intentions were, she's now certainly intrigued by Prince Aly."

So were the news wire services, which flashed daily reports of Rita's adventures in Spain to the entire world. When he could no longer ignore them, Harry Cohn cabled Rita and ordered her to return to Hollywood to begin a new film. When no reply came back, Cohn flew to Spain to talk to her. Whatever it was he had to say proved effective, and Rita soon came back to Hollywood to commence filming *The Loves of Carmen*. When she arrived, local newsmen queried her about her future and inquired about her plans to marry Prince Aly.

Glaring icily at one reporter, Rita retorted, "I'm not yet legally free to marry and he has a wife—or haven't you heard?"

It turned out the prince's wife *had* heard, or read, about his romance. And when he visited her personally to request his freedom in order to remarry, she immediately started divorce proceedings.

And Rita started filming her first production for her newly formed Beckworth Corporation. In true tradition of Hollywood nepotism, Eduardo Cansino was hired to stage the gypsy dances which replaced the ballet of the operatic version of *Carmen*. And Columbia further advertised that the film was not based on the Bizet work but would be a straight dramatic version of the Prosper Mérimée novel, the opera's original source. Much of it was filmed on location in Northern California and lushly photographed in Technicolor. Included were heavy-breathing romantic interludes, hand-to-hand knife fights, duels, stagecoach robberies and a somewhat authentic gypsy atmosphere pervaded, in spite of the fact that Glenn Ford was a very miscast Don José.

By the time the *Carmen* company returned to Columbia to complete interiors, Prince Aly turned up in Hollywood too. And when *The Loves of Carmen* reached the theater screens, critics were somewhat less than enthusiastic about it but the general public couldn't be dismayed from seeing it and, apparently, reveling in every moment of it. The Love Goddess had not lost her box-office appeal. When she got her final divorce decree from Orson Welles, the marriage had lasted approximately four years.

After vacationing in pre-Castro Cuba with her daughter, Rebecca, where, by sheer coincidence, Prince Aly was also vacationing, Rita arrived in New York with her daughter in December 1948 just in time to sail aboard the *Britannica*, in order to spend the Christmas holidays in Switzerland. A fellow passenger on that voyage turned out to be Prince Aly Khan, who told reporters he, too, by sheer coincidence intended spending the Yule season in Switzerland with his two sons.

Coincidence, however, was stretched beyond credulity when Rita and Aly both arrived at the same Swiss hotel on the same day. The incident made international

Posing with co-star Gig Young for promotion of *The Story On Page One* (1959).

headlines and when a newsman finally managed to talk to Prince Aly, all he said was, "My two sons and Miss Hayworth's daughter, Rebecca, have become playmates and they appear to be having a wonderful holiday together."

By early January 1949, newspaper readers throughout the world had an opportunity to pore over daily accounts of Rita's royal romance. But various columnists, whom she had not taken into her confidence, began censuring her behavior, as did five million members of the General Federation of Women's Clubs in America, who all voted to boycott Rita Hayworth films on the grounds that her behavior was unbecoming to the image of American womanhood.

When news of the boycott broke, Rita's father was interviewed and asked about his reactions. "I advised her once," said Eduardo Cansino. "I told her to go back home to Orson Welles for the sake of the baby. It didn't work. Now I keep my advice to myself."

Rita and Aly continued to deny there was any truth in the rumors of an impending marriage until she met and had been approved by the prince's father, the Aga Khan. Soon after that meeting it was officially announced that America's Love Goddess of the Screen would soon become a princess. After this news broke, Rita agreed

to meet the press and answer questions. Among the first ones asked was if she had been nervous about meeting the Aga Khan. Rita laughed and said:

"Nervous! My heart was in my mouth for fear that I would not please him. But he was kind and so charming, I was at once at ease. No one could have welcomed me more warmly into his family."

Not since Britain's King Edward abdicated his throne to marry American divorcée Wallis Simpson had any romance of modern times captured quite the fancy and furor of the Hayworth-Khan alliance. Even in Hollywood—where it had been years since Gloria Swanson, Mae Murray and Constance Bennett had married titled noblemen—talk of the royal romance and the wedding plans dominated all other gossip of the time.

And much to the chagrin of Hedda Hopper, who steadfastly maintained in her column that the Hayworth-Khan nuptials would never occur, rival columnist Louella Parsons announced to her readers that she had received a personal invitation to attend the wedding as both guest and official reporter. To which Miss Hopper wrote, "I don't believe a word of it. She won't get within a mile of the wedding."

But, true to her word, Miss Parsons attended the ceremony and Hearst newspapers carried her daily stories of the wedding preparations at L'Horizon, the Prince's fabulous villa at Cannes, and of the double-ring civil ceremony that occurred in the city hall of Vallauris, a small French town, on May 27, 1949 which united Rita and Aly in marriage. The ceremony was performed by the Communist mayor whom Miss Parsons had bribed a day earlier to allow her exclusive use of his telephone so she could be the first reporter to have an eye witness story on the wire services.

A week after their marriage, when over two hundred policemen and security guards were needed to keep order among the more than ten thousand joyous curiosity seekers, the newlyweds turned up unexpectedly in England to attend the races at Epsom Downs and then a few days later they arrived in Paris. For a charity benefit at the Chatelet Theater, Prince Aly was among the spectators who applauded the longest and loudest for an amusing little skit performed by Rita and her former co-star, Charles Boyer. The bulk of the audience was amazed to discover that Rita projected beautifully and spoke flawless and fluent French. Later that summer, Rita and Aly curtailed their tour of rural France when the news leaked out that she was pregnant. The royal couple retreated to Switzerland and took up residence at the palatial Lausanne-Palace Hotel, which the Aga Khan owned.

They remained there, in virtual seclusion, but a few days before Christmas Rita appeared in public to do some Christmas shopping and her outing made international headlines. Wire services soon set up around-the-clock operations in the hotel lobby to keep an appar-

ently anxious world informed of any trivial event connected with Rita and her prince. Arrangements had already been made in advance for the birth of their child at the world renowned Clinique Mont-Choisi, where, outside, another contingent of newsmen began what turned out to be a very long vigil.

On Christmas Eve, all the newsmen standing by chipped in and sent Rita a bouquet. Then, on Christmas morning, Prince Aly appeared to thank them personally for their thoughtfulness and gifted them with several cases of Scotch, telling them to "live it up," as no change was expected in Rita's condition for at least another twenty-four hours. It was actually 3 A.M. December 28, 1949, the seven-month anniversary date of their marriage, that Prince Aly rushed his wife to a waiting limousine for a hasty journey to the clinic, some two miles away. Some eight hours later Prince Aly appeared outside the clinic and told the waiting newsmen that the much-anticipated heir, a beautiful baby girl, later named Yasmin, had just been born, without complications, and the mother and child were both sleeping.

On New Year's Day 1950, a Lausanne photographer, delegated by Prince Aly, was permitted to take pictures of the newly born Yasmin and her royal parents which were to be shared by all news media. Ten days later Swiss authorities issued the parents a birth certificate for their daughter that avoided mention of her royal status. To confounded newsmen it was explained that the child and her parents were ecclesiastical dignitaries and it would be incorrect, by Swiss law, to denote Yasmin or her parents as royal personages on any official documents issued by that country.

Instead of returning to the Lausanne-Palace Hotel as expected, the royal couple and their daughter retreated to the luxurious Chateau Dorigny, where they stayed as guests of Jane Andree, one of the Aga Khan's former wives (who was also the mother of Prince Aly's half-brother, Sadruddin). At the end of that January, however, Prince Aly and his two sons, his wife, newborn daughter and stepdaughter, Rebecca, took up residence in the resort town of nearby Gstaad, where they remained, in virtual seclusion, until spring.

Late in May of 1950, sans offspring, Rita and Aly went on a long tour of the Continent before visiting Africa, where they were acclaimed with much fanfare and celebration by the resident Moslems. Rita invited film

With Edgar Bergen, Charlie McCarthy and bandleader Ray Noble, as a guest on the "Bergen-McCarthy" radio show. Miss Hayworth sang on this broadcast.

Being kissed by her fifth husband, producer James Hill, immediately after their wedding in her Beverly Hills home on February 2, 1958.

producer Jackson Leighter and his wife along on what she termed her "second honeymoon" and Leighter was permitted to take color photographs of the royal couple on their romantic safari. But, after just a few weeks in Africa, Rita suddenly departed, and later turned up in Paris with both her daughters. Although she ostensibly was on a shopping excursion for an entire new wardrobe for herself, rumors immediately started circulating that all was not well with the marriage of the royal couple.

Gossip, later proved gospel, alluded to the prince's penchant for all-night gambling sessions, his more than casual attentions to other women and the fact that he had announced, without consulting his wife, that their daughter Yasmin would be reared as a Moslem, were some of the reasons for the estrangement. Rita neither confirmed nor denied any of this speculation but when she unexpectedly returned to Hollywood with her daughters, her action appeared to confirm the truth of the situation.

Once back on home ground, she consulted her at-

torney, Bartley Crumm, and, she announced at a press conference that she had legally separated from Prince Aly and intended filing for an immediate divorce and then resuming her film career. Hearing of this, Prince Aly, accompanied by a brace of attorneys, arrived in New York and confirmed to newsmen that he was indeed enroute to Hollywood to see his wife in the hope of effecting a reconciliation.

During August 1950, the prince and Rita met at her Beverly Hills home on three successive days to discuss their problems. There were rumors that the royal couple had settled their differences and Rita's demands, which her attorney would not divulge, would be agreed to. But the predicted reconciliation was of very short duration and early in 1951 Rita established residence in Lake Tahoe, Nevada, and filed suit for divorce. She charged her royal husband with mental anguish and cruelty and requested a $3,000,000 settlement to be placed in trust for the welfare and education of their daughter, Yasmin.

"If Rita makes her demands stick and actually gets

Chatting between scenes of *Circus World* with Claudia Cardinale, filmed in Europe during 1964.

her pretty little hooks into the three million clams, she'll be the first American in generations to snatch any real money out of a foreign country," a reporter for the New York *Daily News* wrote, and added: "Thus, Rita will be a national heroine!"

When the case came up in the Nevada courts, Rita testified that Prince Aly's solo social life, his addiction to gambling, which often kept him away from home for days at a time, and his rank in the world, which caused him to have utter disregard for her own celebrity status, had caused her mental anguish. When the Nevada judge trying the case ascertained that she had been financially satisfied with the arrangements privately agreed to concerning Yasmin, her divorce was granted. Consequently, her third marriage, including separations, reconciliations, and legal maneuvering, had lasted less than two years.

But Rita, who had remained constant headline news for three solid years, soon discovered her ability to remain a top newsworthy personality had far from ended, although her romance, marriage and divorce from Prince Aly, had already made her the most publicized woman in the world. But her three-year spree of hogging international headlines was merely a warm-up for the banner newspaper stories about her that were yet to come.

When Rita had first returned to Hollywood in 1950 and announced she intended resuming her film career, Harry Cohn gave serious consideration to several potential vehicles for her. She had been suspended from salary during the latter days of her courtship by Prince Aly but that had ended when she made *The Loves of Carmen.* But it was reactivated when she refused to remain in Hollywood after its completion to make the long-

postponed *Lona Hanson,* which was to be turned over to director Charles Vidor. Rita's departure and ultimate marriage caused Harry Cohn to look around for a personality he felt he could build up in the image and the results of his search appeared for a while to culminate when he put dancer Valerie Bettis, who had created a sensation on Broadway the previous theatrical season, under personal contract. Cohn had already bought the screen rights to *Born Yesterday* for Rita, and her marriage caused him to consider Miss Bettis as a potential Billie Dawn, the dumb-blonde heroine of that Broadway hit. George Cukor, already signed to direct the film, viewed Miss Bettis's various screen tests but was unimpressed with the results. Cukor had already directed Judy Holliday in an MGM film, *Adam's Rib,* and since she had originated the stage role, he, along with Katharine Hepburn, actively campaigned on her behalf that she re-create the part on screen. With much trepidation, Cohn finally agreed to using Miss Holliday and she rewarded his wavering faith by winning a "Best Actress" Academy Award for her performance. In reciprocation, Cohn rewarded her with a long-term Columbia contract. But, nevertheless, Miss Holliday still was not the actress Cohn sought to groom as a glamour-star threat to Rita.

But she ended suspension, against her better judgment, when she finally agreed to star in *Affair in Trinidad,* a script concocted by Virginia Van Upp which bore more than a faint resemblance to *Gilda,* right down to using Glenn Ford as co-star. Because of daily script revisions, *Affair in Trinidad* had a long shooting schedule and by late November 1951, it was still being revised and refilmed. By early December the film was still in production and the situation unaltered when Rita decided it was all an impossible mess and walked off the production.

Harry Cohn immediately put her on suspension and filed a damage suit against her which, if she had lost, would have meant she would have been required to pay all production costs involved, including the salaries of coworkers who had remained on salary during the time she was on suspension and off-salary. Consulting her agents and her attorney, Rita discovered she had two choices: return and complete the film; or, make Harry Cohn an offer for her contract. The price Cohn put on her contract made the latter choice an impossibility so, somewhat reluctantly, she returned to Columbia and completed the film.

To further complicate Rita's celluloid situation, Jackson Leighter, having edited his color film of Rita's second honeymoon into a four-hour documentary, tried to interest Cohn in distributing it. Cohn rejected the plan, but a small New York independent distributor, Defence Films, agreed to release the documentary if Leighter could edit it down to a feasible, feature-length running time. Hearing of this, Cohn tried to get an injunction against Leighter and prevent the release of the product which was tentatively titled *Safari So Good* (but ultimately released as *Champagne Safari)*. Much to *his* surprise, Cohn discovered he didn't have a case since Rita's contract made allowances for outside film appearances and there was no way he could prevent Leighter or anyone else from releasing the film as long as Miss Hayworth voiced no objection. It eventually had its first theatrical booking December 31, 1951, when several theaters in key cities booked it as an added attraction on their New Year's holiday program. The film, however, remained in obscurity until some four years later when, after a lurid exploitation campaign, it turned up on the grind-house circuits which operated in large U.S. cities, such as those which deface West 42nd Street in New York's Times Square area. According to Leighter, the film never even recovered its prints and advertising expenses, although he did later recover some money from a television sale. As far as I can determine, however, it had just a single telecast, although a few minutes of the deleted footage turned up in David L. Wolper's *The Odyssey of Rita Hayworth,* one of his "Hollywood and the Stars" TV series shown in the early 1960s.

Any doubts Harry Cohn may have had that Rita's public had abandoned her were quickly dispelled when *Affair in Trinidad* went into release and soon outgrossed *Gilda,* the film it more than faintly resembles. But it was less dramatically complicated and certainly showcased Rita's best physical assets without straining her dramatic abilities.

The financial success of Rita's first feature film in almost four years did not prevent Harry Cohn's continuing his quest to discover a new sex symbol for Columbia, as he had long ago learned that the public can indeed be fickle. The actress subsequently selected was Kim Novak, a somewhat bovine blonde beauty who never appeared all *that* anxious to be a glamour star. But Cohn was quite taken with her and screened some of her tests for his top-notch publicity man. When the screening concluded, Cohn leaned forward and asked his valued publicity man what he thought of Miss Novak. The man looked Cohn squarely in the eyes, as-

With co-star John Wayne and their youngest daughters on the set of *Circus World.*

Presenting Gene Barry with a scroll honoring him as the best male TV personality of 1964.

sumed an "Oh-what-the-hell" attitude, and gave a frank answer.

"Harry," he said, "you've achieved the impossible. You've just discovered a girl who, with exactly the right buildup, can become the last of the great silent screen personalities."

Cohn removed the cigar from his mouth, stared at his trusted publicity man, and finally asked, "Do you think it will take you more than ten minutes to get your desk cleaned out and get your ass off the lot?"

The story made the Hollywood rounds and when Rita heard it she quipped, "Some people have all the luck."

To some, Miss Hayworth's next film, *Salome,* may have seemed a curious choice of vehicles. But it merely proved just how astute a producer Cohn really was. Aware of the amount of money 20th-Century Fox was lavishing on their forthcoming Biblical spectacle, *The Robe,* of how well MGM's *Quo Vadis?* was doing in

general release and that Paramount had just made a killing with *Samson and Delilah,* he rightly felt it was the ideal time for Columbia to put some new life in the Old Testament. And since many of Rita's biggest successes had been new interpretations of classic screen sirens, casting her as the world's first acknowledged stripper, via her "Dance of the Seven Veils," in lush Technicolor, Cohn had no qualms about announcing and advertising the fact that *Salome* would be "The Screen Achievement of 1953."

Many critics, however, suddenly devoutly religious took exception to Columbia's tampering with the Testament and had few kind things to say about the film. The public, curiosity piqued, decided for themselves to count how many veils Rita shed during her big dance number and *Salome* was a box-office achievement, but hardly a spiritually enlightening one.

Having decided classic screen sirens reimpersonated à la Rita was one surefire way of keeping her box-office, Cohn continued his quest and found just what he wanted in Somerset Maugham's sultry, sensuous and highly volatile *Miss Sadie Thompson,* which was partly filmed on one of the Hawaiian Islands and released in both wide screen and 3-D versions. Efforts were exerted to keep clergymen from protesting by changing the all-important Reverend Davidson, played by José Ferrer, into a board member of an international mission group. And instead of *Sadie* remaining the parasol-swinging, parakeet-carrying prostitute of the Polynesian pleasure palaces, she became a girl more sinned against than sinning whose sole departure from virtue was taking it on the lam when the San Francisco police became interested in knowing what connection she had with a mysteriously murdered underworld gambler.

In spite of these apparently necessary changes, *Miss Sadie Thompson* was still something of a challenge for Rita's considerable dramatic abilities. Much to the surprise of everyone, critics included, she turned the film into a personal triumph. Looking every minute of her actual age (thirty-five), she simulated singing a few sultry songs, engaged in some energetic and remarkably well-staged dance numbers, and proved more than a match for Academy Award winner Ferrer in their dramatic encounters. Whether dancing uninhibitedly in the atmosphere of a jerry-built island joy joint, smoke-filled and seething with humidity, she performed with a joie de vivre as her face and body glistened with perspiration, as seldom encountered in a Hollywood product of the time. Never once did Rita resort to relying on her glamour-girl screen image to bring off what was unquestionably her best screen performance to date.

She later said to one columnist, "This was really the first chance I had to show Harry Cohn I could be more than just a sex symbol. I considered myself an actress, too, and I'd be damned if I'd let him screw me out of the opportunity of proving it."

Her clashes with Cohn over how *Sadie* should be interpreted cost her the role of Karen in *From Here to Eternity*. There's no argument here that Deborah Kerr gave her best screen performance to date in a U.S.-produced film in that coveted role but Rita would, nonetheless, have been a more ideal choice.

By electing to play *Miss Sadie Thompson* with such realistic gusto, in what many considered a brave departure, Rita found she had more partisans than Harry Cohn, who felt the film would destroy her, did.

José Ferrer, aware his performance would add no laurels to his credits, said:

"When Rita is called before the camera, she illuminates the whole scene, and she herself lights up with the flashing personality that her fans know. As for her beauty which has won her such all-encompassing titles as 'The Love Goddess,' since I do a little painting perhaps I can analyze it from a painter's point of view Her features are not perfectly symmetrical, but there is an organization in the elements in her face, and a wonderful proportion, which makes it a delight to study. The balance of head and neck and shoulders is perfect, particularly in profile. She has the long, shapely legs of a dancer, and, like a dancer, moves and holds herself well. *Miss Sadie Thompson* will also prove just what a fine performer she is, without anyone to 'carry' her. *She* carries the picture."

Her other co-star, Aldo Ray, said:

"She was never out to make an impression on anybody. To her the measure of whether she was a success didn't depend on anything except that her performance would be worth the money an audience paid to see it. *Miss Sadie Thompson* gave them more than their money's worth. It's one of the best things she ever did.

"It's easy for me to go into raves about her. But you can ask anybody else who has worked with her! José Ferrer, Glenn Ford, Stewart Granger, Charles Boyer, Fred Astaire. All of 'em feel the same as I do."

After seeing *Miss Sadie Thompson,* author Somerset Maugham, who seldom had very high opinions of any screen translation of his work, said:

"Of all the actresses in Hollywood I can think of no better choice than Miss Hayworth to play the part of *Sadie*. She has everything to disturb a man's senses, and whatever she does to Davidson in the film of my story, she will do to all men in the audience. I couldn't be more delighted that it was in a screen version of one of my stories that she proved just how superb an actress she really is."

The critics also paid her homage and the film was a personal triumph. Oddly enough, however, it didn't turn out to be one of her box-office bonanzas. Although in-

On the set of *The Money Trap* with Yasmin in 1965.

itially premiered in the 3-D version, the novelty of that process had already passed its peak and the "flat" version is the one Columbia put into general release. The reason usually offered that the film didn't do as well as expected is that during its filming Miss Hayworth was personally involved in making some unflattering headlines and the public used the opportunity to silently voice their disapproval.

Between completing *Salome* and beginning *Miss Sadie Thompson,* a new romance began in Rita's life with actor-singer Dick Haymes, a veteran of radio, television, records, movie musicals and three previous marriages (to singer Joan Marshall; actress Joanne Dru; and, Nora Eddington, the ex-wife of Errol Flynn, who had been a friend of Rita's since 1947 when *The Lady from Shanghai* was partly filmed aboard the *Zaca,* the Flynn yacht). At first, Haymes seemed an ideal suitor who, more or less, had the sanction of Rita's devotees. And Rita had redeemed herself in the public mind by rejecting Prince Aly Khan's alimony offers and asking only that their daughter Yasmin's financial future be assured. Khan's ultimate romance with another screen glamour star, Gene Tierney, starting before his divorce

With Carol Burnett.

from Rita was final, appeared to be further proof that on all counts it was Rita who had been wronged.

But when Haymes turned up in Hawaii during the filming of *Miss Sadie Thompson* to profess to Rita and the world she was "the only woman I have ever loved," some startling facts about the crooner, of which even Rita had not been aware, came to light, and public approval turned to dismay. Dick Haymes, the all-American farmboy-type of musicals like *State Fair*, it turned out, was not a U.S. citizen, although he had been a U.S. resident since he was a teenager. But, by never applying for U.S. citizenship, although his parents were both American-born, and maintaining his status an as Argentine citizen, he avoided serving with the U.S. armed forces during World War II, declaring allegiance to a country ostensibly neutral but actually pro-Nazi. And by visiting Rita in Hawaii, which had not then achieved statehood, the U.S. Department of Immigration decided to make him the subject of a test case of the newly adopted McCarran Act which decreed that any alien working in the United States for any duration who leaves the country without special government permission was subject to deportation to his native country whenever he returned to the United States.

But since Hawaii was a U.S. possession, a question arose as to whether or not Haymes had actually violated the McCarran Act. He was therefore permitted to re-enter the United States until the U.S. Supreme Court made its decision about the legality of the act and whether or not Haymes had violated it. The disclosure that Haymes had lived in the United States and earned a great deal of money without ever applying for citizenship lost him many allies during his dilemma. The one Haymes partisan to remain loyal, however, was Rita Hayworth.

Consequently, when she returned to the United States, she took her daughters with her to Las Vegas, where Haymes was appearing at the Sands Hotel and there, on September 24, 1953, married him. Hotel owner Jack Entratter was best man and Rita's daughters, Rebecca and Yasmin, served as flower girls. More than a few close associates felt Rita married Haymes out of a sense of loyalty, and that by so doing she averted any chance of his being deported since no matter what decision the Supreme Court now reached as the spouse of a U.S. citizen he was entitled to legal residency. The day of their wedding was the date Haymes's divorce from Nora Eddington Flynn became final.

On the strength of Haymes's new marriage, and the fact that Rita agreed to star in *Joseph and His Brethren*, a Biblical spectacle based on a Clifford Odets screenplay that Louis B. Mayer would personally produce under the aegis of Columbia Pictures immediately after

attending to some last-minute details involved with his inimical MGM departure, Harry Cohn advanced Haymes $50,000.

After a one-day Las Vegas honeymoon, Rita and her fourth husband went East, where she had made arrangements to leave her daughters in charge of a housekeeper in a house she had leased in Greenwich, Connecticut. She then proceeded with her husband to Florida, where he fulfilled a nightclub engagement at a Miami Beach hotel. It wasn't too long afterward that some of her darkest days occurred. Unmerciful headlines reported she had been publicly accused of child neglect by the woman she hired to look after her daughters. All that had actually occurred was that the worried housekeeper had panicked when one of the girls caught a slight virus infection and she could not immediately make telephone contact with Miss Hayworth. Orson Welles and Prince Aly Khan, reached overseas by over-eager newsmen, were quick to come to Rita's defense and each of them called the charges utter nonsense. Both described her as a mother who always put the welfare and well-being of her daughters ahead of her own happiness.

No sooner had this story broken when Dick Haymes became enmeshed in a long legal hassle, which entailed many court appearances, but which finally won him the right to remain in the United States whether the spouse of a citizen or not. During these trying times, Rita received threatening letters which warned her that Yasmin would be kidnaped or permanently injured unless Rita returned to Prince Aly and restored her daughter to the Moslem faith. Rita and her daughters barricaded themselves in a New York City hotel and private security guards were hired. But several scandal sheets published her whereabouts and in a fit of panic she switched hotels, hired additional security guards and applied for police protection. The FBI soon came into the case and disclosed that the letters were legitimate but the work of a crank and were in no way connected with any Moslem plot. A few newsmen were unkind enough to accuse Rita of merely seeking publicity. But insiders were quick to squash such talk, especially after Rita suffered a nervous collapse and required hospitalization after her ordeal.

When she returned to Hollywood with Haymes, they rented a modest Westwood apartment although Haymes's attempts at masterminding his wife's career turned out to be anything but modest. He convinced her to dissolve her Beckworth Corporation and form a new producing company with himself as the majordomo. And as president of the new Crystal Bay Productions, Haymes's first endeavor was an attempt to reactivate production on *Joseph and His Brethren* with himself playing the title role! But Louis B. Mayer wanted no

Attending a sneak preview of *The Money Trap* with Glenn Ford.

But producer Jackson Leighter was of another mind, and being a close friend of Rita's, told columnists and friends Haymes had physically abused her on more than one occasion and in point of fact she was fearful of him and his tempestuous behavior.

Rita confirmed Leighter's statement by filing for divorce in Reno and then departing for Europe with her children. In December 1955 she was granted an "in absentia" divorce. She and Haymes had lived as husband and wife less than two years.

At the time her divorce was granted, she was in England and when newsmen confronted her for a statement she was polite and apologetic as she said, "Things just didn't work out the way I had hoped they would." Following her usual out-of-court custom, Rita made no public statements about Haymes, just as she had been evasive about discussing her causes of separation from former husbands, before, during or after their divorce, which would ever denigrate their public image. In 1960, however, learning of Prince Aly Khan's accidental death in a motor accident, she collapsed in shock. And on one occasion when asked about Orson Welles, she said:

"I saw him in Spain a few years ago. He had gotten so fat! And he was such a handsome man when I married him. He's a genius, there's no doubt about that. But I don't think living with a genius is any more difficult than living with me! Orson never had any respect or regard for money, that's always been his biggest problem. And, believe it or not, I do worry a lot about him."

When Rita later left England for Mexico, she managed the trip without any fanfare in the press and seemed relieved to realize that as long as she wasn't romantically involved with a man with a certain public image, newsmen tended to ignore her. Even a rumor that she planned to marry Freddie Stauffer, the orchestra-leader-turned-restaurateur, merely appeared as a gossip-column item. And dates with former leading men and close friends like Gilbert Roland caused little or no comment from the press.

But she was still under contract to Columbia and obliged to make two films for them and settle the debt incurred at the time of her marriage to Haymes. She returned to work in late 1956 in *Fire Down Below*. A British-Columbia Pictures venture filmed partly in England but mostly on location in the Bahamas. But an extensive advertising campaign for the film and saturation booking failed to generate much interest in the film and it appeared that Rita's reign as the Love Goddess of the screen was over. The public had turned their attention and adoration to Ava Gardner, Marilyn Monroe, Elizabeth Taylor and Kim Novak. When confronted with these circumstances, Rita said:

"I've always maintained I wanted to be an actress,

part of such a deal and Harry Cohn was even more adamant. As a result, Rita filed a damage suit against Columbia for not fulfilling their contractual obligations and eventually won an out-of-court settlement.

Neither Rita nor Haymes worked professionally for a long period and when a columnist inquired about how she managed financially, she retorted:

"My husband supports me and my children and still manages to fulfill his alimony obligations. Do I look as if I've reached the point where I have to support a husband?"

It wasn't too long after she made that statement that Rita and her daughters arrived in New York, ostensibly incognito, but quickly recognized. Without beating it around the bush, she frankly admitted she had separated from Haymes and confided to a friend, "I stood by him as long as he was in trouble, but I can't take it anymore."

Confronted with Rita's published admission, Haymes attempted to laugh it off and dismiss it as one of his wife's whims. "She's just taking a little holiday from love," he said. "We'll work things out."

not a sex symbol. Now maybe I'll have that opportunity. But, nevertheless, it's comforting to know it took a quartet of dames to replace me!"

Rita's opportunity to prove herself a capable actress came much sooner than even she anticipated when, much to everyone's surprise, Columbia cast her as the society matron willing to support a nightclub heel in *Pal Joey*. Her musical numbers were exceptionally well-staged and dubbed and even the few minutes screen time she shared with Kim Novak proved that at thirty-nine, she could still physically and professionally hold her own. When further announcements about *Pal Joey* included the interesting fact that Rita would receive top billing, a few columnists asked Frank Sinatra, at the apex of his new-found popularity, how he allowed it. Said Sinatra:

"Who else but Rita should get top billing? After all, in my mind, she always was and always will be Columbia Pictures! The studio may have built her into a star but just remember it was Rita Hayworth who gave Columbia status!"

Soon after completing *Pal Joey*, Rita began dating James Hill, a forty-one-year-old bachelor, who was the middle man of the Hecht-Hill-Lancaster producing combine. Hill, who had made the annual Hollywood "most eligible bachelor" list for many years, was handsome, well-educated, wealthy and a person whose main interests always appeared to be amassing an art collection, avidly reading the more profound books and appreciating and promoting interest in classical music. Rita was the first woman to whom he gave more than casual attention. He also gave her the role of Burt Lancaster's sexually tormenting wife in his coproduction of *Separate Tables*.

Instead of rejecting the role, as Hill thought she would, Rita accepted the assignment with alacrity and later said, "It was the kind of role I'd been waiting a professional lifetime to be offered!"

Top-billed over Deborah Kerr, David Niven, Wendy Hiller and Burt Lancaster, Rita rewarded Hill's belief in her abilities by turning in the best performance of her career to date. And *Separate Tables* turned out as one of 1958's most memorable films, with David Niven's and Wendy Hiller's both winning Academy Awards for their brilliant performances.

In a quiet ceremony in her Beverly Hills home, Rita married James Hill on February 2, 1958. Returning to work to complete *Separate Tables,* the Hills then honeymooned extensively and Rita appeared and looked happier than she had in years. By the time *Separate Tables* opened, she had negotiated a one-picture deal with Columbia to play the only feminine role in a $4,000,000 production of *They Came to Cordura,* which was filmed on some rugged desert locations. She played her role with an uncompromising honesty and without any makeup and in spite of some strong male competition (Gary Cooper, Van Heflin, Tab Hunter, Michael Callan, Richard Conte, Dick York and Robert Keith), she gave the film's best performance. When it was released and reviewed everyone agreed that the only thing about the film that was worthwhile was Rita. Nonetheless, *They Came to Cordura* was a financial disaster.

Clifford Odets, author of the ill-fated *Joseph and*

With hosts Dan Rowan and Dick Martin on her "Laugh-In" TV appearance.

His Brethren, then wrote and directed Rita in *The Story on Page One,* which Jerry Wald produced. Again Rita managed, against overwhelming odds, to give another first-rate performance. But when she formed a production company with her husband and made *The Happy Thieves,* on location in Spain, neither Rita, co-star Rex Harrison nor director George Marshall could inject any life in what looked as if it might be a worthwhile Technicolor comedy about art thieves and forgers.

Rita and Hill returned to Hollywood and started preproduction work on *I Want My Mother!* in which she was to play the mother of a young psychopathic killer slated for execution in California's gas chambers. Then, on the day principal photography was scheduled to commence, the project, for reasons never fully elucidated, was canceled. That cancellation, which Rita's friends called a major disappointment in her life, and the fact that *The Happy Thieves* proved to be a financial fiasco, are usually the reasons cited as the major cause of the breakup of the Hayworth-Hill marriage.

In September 1961, Rita sued Hill for divorce in Santa Monica Superior Court and testified her husband "was more concerned with his career than he was with our marriage and our family life." She rejected an alimony settlement, stating that she wanted only her freedom. A divorce was granted, and Rita's fifth marriage ended a little over three years after it started.

Said Rita, "I didn't want five husbands, but it happened that way and that's all there is to it." But when an interviewer prodded her about how many husbands a career woman should limit herself to, Rita revealed once again that she was a past mistress at handling loaded questions. "At least six, I would imagine, but it's really difficult for me to say since seventeen has always been my lucky number." Of future film plans, she alluded to a possible screen version of James Kirkwood's *There Must Be a Pony,* which the author had dramatized and in which Myrna Loy was touring the country in a pre-Broadway production which closed before reaching New York. Of her immediate plans, she confided, "I'm going to Europe for a while to look over the situation. I may even decide to live there. That's what Ava [Gardner] has done. But she's smart, she knows the score."

After she arrived in Madrid she announced she would make a film called *On the Carousel,* co-starring with Bette Davis' ex-husband, Gary Merrill. The project never materialized, but Merrill became her constant escort and they caroused around Spain, eventually retreating to Venice, where they cavorted around that Italian city barefooted in outfits best described as "pre-hippie" style. On several occasions they became involved in bistro brawls with photographers, autograph seekers and newsmen, who all censured them in print for their behavior.

Rita and Merrill then returned to the United States and she agreed to co-star with him in a three-act stage comedy, *Step on a Crack,* slated for a Broadway opening during October 1962. But after weeks of rehearsal, she realized the play still needed a great deal of rewriting and decided against continuing with it. A day after making this disclosure, she was hospitalized with a severe case of influenza, complicated by the fact that she was also suffering from fatigue and anemia. Before news of her illness reached the newspapers, however, columnists hinted that she walked out of the play for any number of professional reasons: she was overweight; she was suffering stage fright; she was no longer in rapport with Gary Merrill; and that she lacked the vocal projection necessary for a successful stage performance. But after *Step on a Crack* reached Broadway and closed after a single performance (on October 17, 1962), it appeared that Rita could add another asset to her long list of abilities: astute drama critic.

She had, meanwhile, returned to Hollywood and told columnist Vernon Scott:

"Apart from anemia and fatigue, there is nothing wrong with my health or my outlook. It is ridiculous for anyone to say I am at the end of my rope.

"I'm looking for a good script. So far I haven't found one and I don't feel like doing television, but I may do a few things in the future. If you love making pictures and enjoy the medium, it is difficult to go into television and then try and return to films. I'm not especially interested in doing a variety show, which is what I'm generally offered, or a half-hour situation comedy that you rehearse and shoot in three to five days. That would be like going back to my early film career when I first worked at Columbia and made a B picture in a week. And a couple of them looked as if they didn't take that long to shoot!"

Rita remained professionally inactive until 1964. That year she presented the "Best Director" Academy Award on the annual telecasting of that event and soon afterwards replaced Lilli Palmer in *Circus World,* a John Wayne film made abroad. After winning acclaim as giving that film's best performance, producer Max Youngstein gave her a strong but small role in *The Money Trap,* which was produced at the MGM studios, and which reunited her with Glenn Ford, although Elke Sommer had the romantic feminine lead. Youngstein offered Rita a top role in a subsequent film, *Welcome to Hard Times,* which she accepted but later bowed out when production was postponed. So instead of making that offbeat Western, she donated her services as an actress to the all-star Telsun production of *The Poppy is Also a Flower,* which Terence Young directed on European locations and which was originally conceived as a United Nations effort, slated for telecasting only.

Presenting the "Best Director" Academy Award to Dame Edith Evans who accepted it for Tony Richardson for his film *Tom Jones.*

But critical and public reaction was so favorable to its TV premiere that Comet Films undertook a theatrical release of it, which turned out to be a financial coup. *Poppy* also gave Rita the opportunity to appear on-screen with her long-time friend, and the co-star of her early *Ramona* color test, Gilbert Roland.

In late January 1966, Rita went to Fort Lauderdale to star in a film tentatively called *The Grove,* but which was ultimately released some five years later, very

briefly, as *The Naked Zoo.* Later, known as *The Hallucinators,* it had a one-week booking in Chicago after which it was withdrawn from distribution.

Rita says she has never seen the completed film and says her participation in it was "a dreadful mistake." But Stephen Oliver, her handsome co-star, saw a rough-cut screening of it in Hollywood some months after it was completed.

Unable to get any information on the film from

With Gary Merrill during rehearsals of *Step On A Crack*.

other sources, I asked Oliver about it. He said:

"The original screenplay was written by Ray Preston, which everyone who had read it thought it had lots of potential. Dustin Hoffman was originally interested in doing it, but *The Graduate* came along and he very wisely chose that. I'm not sure how Rita became interested in it, probably through Curtis Roberts, or whoever happened to be her agent at that time. She too realized the possibilities of it and that if properly made it could be another *Sunset Boulevard*. Her role was a strong one and called for the talents of a really first-rate actress.

"I was offered the role originally offered to Hoffman and after reading the script and learning Rita would be in it, I accepted. William Grefe, who directed it, apparently put up part of the money to finance it. I've been told he owned or operated an automobile agency and was interested in getting into film work. The film was shot at the Film World Studios in Florida and Fay Spain, Fleurette Carter and Ford Rainey were also cast in it.

"When I arrived in Fort Lauderdale, Grefe had re-

written the script and seemed quite pleased with himself. What he had actually done was to make it over into a rather ludicrous sexploitation type of film. Rita didn't say anything about the changes but I knew she wasn't too happy with them.

"Some scenes were shot at a ranch some distance from the studio but close to an airport so that the noise of airplane and helicopter motors drowned out the dialogue in these scenes. Grefe seemed to be totally unaware of just how sensitive sound equipment is, and those scenes shot at the ranch are worthless because of the faulty sound track. It would really take an extensive and expensive looping job to make them worthwhile, but I don't think the film deserves any further expenditure.

"I found working with Rita a real pleasure. She's a true professional. Only on one occasion did she say anything to Grefe, and she did attempt it with great tact and discretion. Instead of listening to her advice, which, incidentally, was very good, Grefe treated her very rudely in front of the entire company. She excused herself and walked off the set and disappeared into the kitchen of the ranch house. A few minutes later I followed her in and found her crying quietly to herself. When she saw me, she said, 'I'm terribly sorry, I didn't mean to hold everybody up.'

"That's the kind of actress and woman she is. I talked to her for a few minutes and told her to forget it, that she had forgotten more about making films than Grefe would ever learn. She smiled, wiped her eyes and was ready to resume work.

"The whole experience was a sort of two-month nightmare for the whole cast but at least I had the pleasure of meeting and working with Rita Hayworth. I think she was in Europe when Grefe had a rough cut of the film screened in Hollywood some months later. I'm glad, for Rita's sake, that film hasn't had very much theatrical exposure. It should never have had any. It should have been buried somewhere."

Rita also claims she has never seen the two subsequent films she made after *The Naked Zoo.* One is *L'Avventuriero (The Rover),* which reunited her with Anthony Quinn for the first time since they had made *Blood and Sand* and the other is one that was also filmed abroad and originally called *The Cats.* Under the title, *I, Bastardi,* it had a brief release in Italy and was ultimately imported by Warner Bros.-7 Arts, which decided it had little or no theatrical potential so they sold it to CBS-TV, but it has rarely been shown on network television.

Rita cannot understand why the film was never released. Says she:

"My role was one of the most challenging I had ever done. The character I play is sympathetic, tragic, sad, warm, poignant, amusing. It's a story of a very human being who can't see her life as it really is."

The next film Rita made was the very unusual *Road to Salina,* which was filmed in the Canary Islands and which had a very limited U.S. showing during late 1971 and early 1972 after receiving generally good reviews.

It was also during 1971 that Rita was offered the Lauren Bacall role in the Broadway musical *Applause.* Rita saw the show several times in New York, and at first seemed eager to do it. "But," she says, "I changed my mind when I realized I couldn't be ready by the time they wanted me to go on. There wasn't enough rehearsal time. I wouldn't have had more than five days of working on stage with the company before my opening, and the staging was far too intricate to learn in so little time."

A little later in 1971 Bob Mitchum, Rita's *Fire Down Below* co-star, telephoned her and asked if she would be interested in doing another film with him, to be shot on location in Mexico and directed by Ralph Nelson. Without even asking what the film was about,

or what her part consisted of, Rita accepted on the spot. The film turned out to be *The Wrath of God,* which opened in mid-1972 to less-than-enthusiastic reviews and below-average business. The film is actually a superior product, every bit as brilliant as John Huston's *Beat the Devil,* which took seventeen years to finally receive its just due.

Rita's sorties into television have been rather minimum. In 1969 she allowed herself to be interviewed on the premiere stanza of the NBC show *First Tuesday,* a monthly two-hour roundup of news events presented in a sort of magazine format. In 1971 she appeared with mixed results on "Rowan and Martin's Laugh-In," "The Carol Burnett Show" and on the "Merv Griffin Show" that was dedicated to "An Evening with Rita Hayworth."

She announced, in 1972, that she had agreed to make a television pilot film in Rome for a series to be called "The Deadly Species" but nothing came of that. Later that year she also accepted the leading role in a British horror film, *Tales That Witness Madness,* but four days after filming commenced, she failed to show up for work. Three doctors confirmed her story that she had fallen ill with the flu and was confined to her bed in her suite at the Dorchester Hotel in London. The following Sunday the film company's insurance doctor examined her and announced she was fit to return to work.

Fred Hift, publicist for the film, said:

"She wasn't due to appear on the set then until Tuesday but when the studio limousine arrived to pick her up at 6:30, her manager, Mr. Curtis Roberts, informed the chauffeur that Miss Hayworth had no intention whatsoever of working that day.

"It was only later on that we learned that Miss Hayworth had, in fact, packed her bags, booked out of the Dorchester the previous day, and had flown back to the States. Her exact whereabouts are still unknown to us."

A secretary who takes messages for Miss Hayworth at her Beverly Hills home was contacted from overseas but she stated she had not seen or heard from Miss Hayworth since her departure for England. In desperation, director Freddie Francis contacted Kim Novak at her Carmel, California, home, explained the situation and asked if she would be willing to take over the role that Miss Hayworth had apparently vacated. Miss Novak arrived in England a few days later, but when asked if she could account for Rita's unusual behavior, she said:

"I can tell you nothing whatever. I suggest that you contact Miss Hayworth and ask her about the circumstances."

Just before her departure from England, Rita attended the San Francisco Film Festival on the day a Rita Hayworth Film Retrospective was held, After some six hours of films and clips, Miss Hayworth came onstage and was greeted with a standing ovation. At first, she appeared to be ill-at-ease but soon after she started answering questions, she relaxed and answered audience questions with remarkable candor and a sense of humor.

She stated that she had no particular favorites among her leading men. "They were all professionals and I got along with all of them," she said.

Her dislike of Harry Cohn has never been a secret, but on this occasion she appeared to have mellowed a little and admitted she would never have been a star without his backing.

"I signed a contract with Harry Cohn when I was about eighteen and I went on suspension so many times I can't really remember them all. And although I can't prove it, I think Harry had all the dressing rooms bugged so he always knew what was going on. And even while I was his biggest box-office star I still had to punch a time clock! But you want to know something about him? I think if he could ever have been in love with anyone, he was secretly in love with me."

A question from a young man in attendance brought a gasp from the audience when he asked Rita how she felt about looking at herself in the morning and then recalling she had once been the screen's Love Goddess.

Rita laughed good-naturedly. "That's one problem I don't have, honey, I never get up until the afternoon." That response brought her a second standing ovation. And a woman who admitted being one of her fans since the late 1930s, asked, somewhat timidly, if there was any man in her current life and if she thought of marrying again. Said Rita:

"There's always some man in my life. But marriage? Me? Again? Well, I'd have to think about that a long time."

The Wrath of God turned out to be her final film. Rita Hayworth was seen less frequently in public after that, and it sooned turned out that she had developed Alzheimer's disease. In 1981, a Los Angeles court declared her incompetent, and daughter Yasmin took over her mother's affairs. (Daughter Rebecca had married an artist and was living in Washington State.)

After bringing her mother to New York to live with her, Yasmin became increasingly active in the Alzheimer's Disease and Related Disorders Association, Inc., as vice president of that organization, while drawing international attention to the disease which now afflicted the movies' one-time love goddess. In her mother's name, Yasmin several times testified before congressional committees concerned with appropriating funds for research of the disease and, in 1985, helped organize Alzheimer's Disease International and became its president.

In 1983, David Susskind brought Rita's life to the screen in a harmless television movie called *Rita Hayworth: The Love Goddess*, with Lynda Carter in the title role.

Rita Hayworth died in Yasmin's Central Park West apartment on May 14, 1987, at age sixty-eight. "[She] was one of our country's most beloved stars," President Ronald Reagan said on learning of her death. "Glamorous and talented, she gave us many wonderful moments on the stage and the screen and delighted audiences from the time she was a young girl."

Her obituary in *The New York Times* summed it up simply: "Rita Haworth was the epitome of Hollywood glamour and allure, a stunningly beautiful actress and dancer."

With Gary Merrill in Venice, 1961.

The FILMS
of RITA CANSINO

Previous to appearing in her first U.S. feature film, Miss Hayworth, as Rita Cansino, appeared in a ten-minute short subject, produced by the Vitagraph Corporation and filmed in New York in 1926. This short presented demonstrations of the dances performed in various foreign countries. Along with her father, her aunt and other members of The Dancing Cansino Family, she came on for a few brief moments at the end of their portion. This short was part of the program used to introduce the Warner Bros. production of *Don Juan* at its premiere engagement in New York City.

The Columbia quota quickie film she often alludes to having worked in while living in Mexico was, in all probability *Cruz Diablo (The Devil's Cross),* which was partly filmed in Caliente and Tijuana and directed by Fernando de Fuentes. It had a limited U.S. release in 1935.

Her other prefeature film debut in the United States was a Fox short subject, in Spanish, made as a promotional exhibit for forthcoming Spanish language Fox productions in 1935. Except for those U.S. theaters devoted entirely to presenting all-Spanish-language programs (in 1935), it had no other U.S. release.

As Rita Cansino, Miss Hayworth's "official" screen debut was in *Dante's Inferno,* although two subsequent Fox Films that she made were released first. Her feature films made in the United States are therefore listed in the order of release.

Under the Pampas Moon

A Fox Film   1935

Produced by B. G. De Sylva. Directed by James Tinling. Screenplay by Ernest Pascal and Bradley King. Additional dialogue by Henry Jackson. Based on a story by Gordon Morris. Photographed by Chester Lyons. Musical Direction by Arthur Lange. Songs: "The Gaucho," by B. G. De Sylva and Walter Samuels; "Querida Mia," by Paul Francis Webster and Lew Pollack; "Zamba," by Arthur Wynter-Smith; "Love Song of the Pampas," "Veredita" and "Je t'adore," by Cyril J. Mockridge and Miguel De Zarraga. Dance Direction by Jack Donahue. Gowns by René Hubert.

Makeup by Ernest Westmore. Chief Sound Engineer, E. H. Hansen. Edited by Alfred DeGaetano. 78 minutes.

CAST:

Cesar Campo, WARNER BAXTER; *Yvonne LaMarr,* KETTI GALLIAN; *Tito,* J. Carrol Naish; *Graham Scott,* John Miljan; *Rosa,* Armida; *Madame LaMarr,* Ann Codee; *Bazan,* Jack LaRue; *Don Bennett,* George Irving; *Carmen,* Rita Cansino; *Dancers in Cafe,* Veloz and Yolanda; *Cafe Singer,* Tito Guizar; *Pietro,* Chris-Pin Martin; *Big José,* Max Wagner; *Little José,* Philip

Warner Baxter, a disillusioned gaucho who has come to Buenos Aires to find his stolen horse, is given a tip on the day's big sweepstake race by cantina girl Rita Cansino.

Warner Baxter, Rita Cansino and Paul Porcasi discuss the possibilities of a long shot entry winning the sweepstakes in which a featured favorite horse has been predicted to win.

Cooper; *Bartender,* Sam Appel; *Rosa's Father,* Arthur Stone; *Aviator,* George Lewis; *Headwaiter,* Paul Porcasi; *Girl,* Lona André; *Magistrate,* Lucio Villegas; *Court Clerk,* Martin Garralaga; *Cesar's Gauchos,* Frank Amerise, Tommy Coates, John Eberts, Enrique Lacey, Charles Ramos, Vinegar Roan, Antonio Samaniego, Manuel Valencia, Mariano Valenzuala; *Bazan's Gauchos,* Mariano Betancourt, Frank Cordell, Antonio Manifredi, Joseph Rickson, Paul Perodi; *Stenographer,* Jean De Briac; *Hairdresser* Jacques Vanaire; *Maid,* Catherine Cotter; *Groom,* Charles Stevens; *Jockeys,* Bobby Rose, Pedro Regas; *Doormen,* Fred Malatesta, Francesco Maran; *Barber,* Rafael Storm; *Valet,* Ambrose Barker; *Police Sergeant,* Juan Ortiz; *Newsboy,* Joe Dominguez; *Waiters,* Nick Thompson, Manuel Perez; *Señora Campo,* Soledad Jiminez.

NOTES:

In *Under the Pampas Moon,* Rita's part consisted of a few lines of dialogue exchanged with Warner Baxter and a dance, called the "Zamba," which she performed while ostensibly a waitress-entertainer in an Argentine cafe sequence.

Recalls Miss Hayworth:

"I remember somebody asked the dialogue director what kind of accent we were supposed to simulate for our characters and he said, 'Standard Hollywood-Mexican—nobody will know the difference!' I guess maybe he was a better critic than dialogue coach since I don't believe too many people saw the picture."

Although *Under the Pampas Moon* did open at New York's Radio City Music Hall, it wasn't exactly received with critical enthusiasm or public approval. Its star, the handsome, versatile and very accomplished Warner Baxter, won an Academy Award some years earlier for his portrayal of the O. Henry character "The Cisco Kid" in *In Old Arizona* and being one of Fox Films's biggest drawing male stars, and one of their highest salaried performers under a long-term contract, he played variations of his O. Henry characterization whenever Fox had no other type of story suitable for him. Unfortunately, impersonating a Spanish (or South American gaucho) outdoorsman was far from Baxter's most accomplished characterizations, and this film probably contained the nadir of such roles for him.

In his *New York Times* review, André Sennwald said:

"*Under the Pampas Moon* is so bad that after a while you stop resenting it and begin to be amused by its antique humors. . . . Everyone in the picture assumes a phony Spanish accent and the consequence is such a bombardment of picturesque verbiage as has not been unloosed from a sound track in many months. Mr. Baxter himself is very quaint and makes love in the my-heart-is-on-fire-for-you tradition."

Weekly Variety reported:

"*Pampas Moon* is a new background for the same old glorified Western character Warner Baxter created years ago. He wears a wider belt, is given the use of a knife instead of a six-gun and he carries a bolas instead of a lariat but he's still the Cisco Kid."

Inspecting a mummy case prop between scenes.

Charlie Chan in Egypt

A Fox Film   1935

Produced by Edward T. Lowe. Directed by Louis King. Screenplay by Robert Ellis and Helen Logan, based on the character created by Earl Derr Biggers. Photographed by Daniel B. Clark. Musical Score Arranged and Conducted by Sammy Kaylin. Costumes Supervised by Arthur M. Levy. Art Direction Supervised by William Darling. Makeup Supervision by Ernest Westmore. Chief Sound Engineer, E. H. Hansen. Edited by Alfred DeGaetano. 72 minutes.

CAST:

Charlie Chan, WARNER OLAND; *Carol Arnold,* PAT PATERSON; *Tom Evans,* THOMAS BECK; *Nayda,* Rita Cansino; *Professor Thurston,* Frank Conroy; *Edfu Ahmad,* Nigel de Brulier; *Barry Arnold,* James Eagles; *Fouad Soueida,* Paul Porcasi; *Dragoman,* Arthur Stone; *Snowshoes,* Stepin Fetchit; *Professor Arnold,* George Irving; *Snowshoes's Girlfriend,* Anita Brown; *Chemist,* John Davidson; *Bit Girl,* Gloria Roy.

NOTES:

Charlie Chan in Egypt was the eighth entry in the successful Fox series (two earlier Chan films had been made by other studios) and one of the very best entries. Once again Warner Oland excelled as the Oriental detective famous for spouting aphorisms ("Hasty conclusion easy to make, like hole in water"; "Theory, like mist on eyeglasses, sometimes obscures fact.") during his unraveling of a murder puzzle.

Charlie Chan in Egypt is also Rita's first appearance

in a "series" film and during her apprenticeship days, even when she occasionally doubted her eventual super-stardom, she made one-time appearances in such other film series as *Blondie, The Lone Wolf, Nero Wolfe* and *The Three Mesquiteers*. She also appeared in the "inspiration" film *(Human Cargo),* from which Fox studios eventually evolved another series dealing with exposé newsmen known as "The Roving Reporters," all of which should establish for her some sort of record for one-time appearances in various films of the series genre.

Customarily for the era, Fox produced their money-making Chan films well and gave them special production values not ordinarily bestowed on such type of programmers. As always, Warner Oland was absolutely ideal in his role, solving three murders and the disappearance of rare artifacts from an ancient tomb, but critics also singled out Stepin Fetchit, who brightened literally hundreds of films, for his delightful performance. In addition to his unique comedy talents, Mr. Fetchit was also an accomplished songwriter. In fact, one of his songs, "Misunderstanding Moon," was used in another 1935 Fox film, *One More Spring,* in which he also appeared.

Of *Charlie Chan in Egypt, Photoplay* reported:

"Warner Oland, as the Chinese philosopher-detective, goes to the tombs of the Pharaohs this time, to encounter murder and unravel the mysteries. Grand atmosphere and unique settings plus some hilarious comedy with Stepin Fetchit puts this one way up top in the Charlie Chan series. Oland is A-1."

With Warner Oland.

And in his *New York Times* review, André Sennwald said:

"Lifts the sage of Honolulu several notches above the Philo Vances and the Perry Masons. Where these eminent sleuths are curiously helpless until the fifth or sixth assassination has removed most of the suspects from active competition, Charlie require only two murders for a good running start . . . the eighth in the series is a lively and entertaining if somewhat minor mystery work . . . Warner Oland, of course, is quite perfect in his most famous screen characterization. The cast includes Stepin Fetchit, the master of slow motion, who manages as usual to be both hilarious and unintelligible."

In *Weekly Variety,* "Odec" wrote:

"Combines a suavely sustained concept of drama, another surehanded interpretation of the central role by Warner Oland and an effective interplay of background color."

With Thomas Beck, Pat Paterson, Frank Conroy and Warner Oland.

Dante's Inferno

A Fox Film   1935

Produced by Sol M. Wurtzel. Directed by Harry Lachman. Screenplay by Philip Klein and Robert Yost, suggested by Cyrus Wood's story, as adapted originally by Edmund Goulding. Photographed by Rudolph Mate. Musical Score by Hugo Friedhofer, Sammy Kaylin, R. H. Bassett and Peter Brunelli. Musical Direction by Sammy Kaylin. Art Direction Supervised by William Darling. Allegorical Sets Designed by Willy Pogany. Dance Sequence Choreographed by Eduardo Cansino. Makeup Supervision by Ernest Westmore. Chief Sound Engineer, E. H. Hansen. Edited by Alfred DeGaetano. 88 minutes.

CAST:

Jim Carter, SPENCER TRACY; *Betty McWade,* CLAIRE TREVOR; *Pop McWade,* Henry B. Walthall; *Alexander Carter,* Scotty Beckett; *Jonesy,* Alan Dinehart; *Baseball Concessionaire,* Joe Brown; *Tony,* George Humbert; *Dean,* Robert Gleckler; *Madame Zucchini,* Maidel Turner; *Mrs. Hamilton,* Nella Walker; *Mrs. Martin,* Lita Chevret; *Mr. Hamilton,* Richard Tucker; *Clinton,* Edward Pawley; *Girl in Stokehold,* Ruthelma Stevens; *Man in Stokehold,* Don Ameche; *Captain Morgan,* Morgan Wallace; *Second Officer Reynolds,* Harry Woods; *Specialty Dancers,* Rita Cansino, Gary Leon; *Mrs. Gray,* Ruth Clifford; *Ticket Seller,* Dorothy Dix; *College Boys,* Hal Boyer, Jack Lloyd; *College Girl,* Jayne Regan; *Radio Operator,* Gardner James; *Spieler,* Jerry Gamble; *Professor,* Edward McWade; *Sailor's Girl,* Patricia Caron; *Ticket Buyer,* Ron Randell; *Concessionaires,* Harry Schultz, John Carpenter, George Chan; *Concessionaire's Wives,* Gertrude Astor, Tiny Jones; *Photographer,* Frank Austin; *Mike,* Frank Moran; *Assistant Purser,* Kenneth Gibson; *Engine Room Crew,* Harold A. Miller, Barret Whitelaw; *Engine Room Visitor,* Jean Fenwick; *Bozo,* Warren Hymer; *Cleopatra,* Lorna Lowe; *Sappho,* Elinor Johnson; *Borgia,* Leone Lane; *Salome,* Andre Johnson; *Catherine de Medici,* Juana Sutton; *Eve,* Marion Strickland; *Little Bo-Peep,* Gale Goodson; *Oriental Maid,* Eve Kimberly; *Trumpeters,* Margaret McCrystal, Dorothy Stockmar; *First Bidder,* Jay Eaton; *Second Bidder,* Reginald Sheffield; *Dowager,* Maude Truex; *Williams,* Oscar Apfel; *Inspector Harris,* Willard Robertson; *Police Inspector,* Charles C. Wilson; *Wireless Operator,* John H. McGuire; *His Assistant,* Bob McKee; *Wallace,* Hale Hamilton; *Drunks,* George Meeker, Barbara Pepper, Lloyd Pantages, Jack Norton, Robert Graves; *Page Boy,* Eddie Tamblyn; *Jolly Fat Man,* Harry Holman; *Ship's Officers,* Harry Strang, George Magrill, Paul Palmer; *Park Attendant,* But Geary; *Maid,* Antoinette Lees (Andrea Leeds); *Husband and Wife,* Paddy O'Flynn, Billie Huber; *Court Clerk,* Robert Ross; *Prosecuting Attorney,* Russell Hicks; *Judge,* George Irving; *Defense Attorney,* Frank Conroy; *Fortune Teller,* Georgia Caine; *Devils,* Noble Johnson, Ray Bernard, Paul Schwegeler, Aloha Porter; *Bits in New Inferno,* Mary Ashcraft, Paul Power, Marion Ladd.

NOTES:

Fox, using a much different story-line, had filmed *Dante's Inferno* in 1924 as a top-notch feature of which the highlight was an approximately six-minute-long "Inferno" sequence depicting the awesome fate of those who live profligate lives. Much of the earlier sequence, with added sound effects, was reused in this updated version which changed the main story-line from a penny-pinching tenement-house owner who must face the consequences when some of his buildings collapse to that of a carnival barker who hits the big time with a

With Gary Leon.

pleasure-gambling ship, which he allows to be over-loaded on its maiden voyage so that it meets with disaster. Produced in this new version as nothing more than a routine B film by Sol Wurtzel, the lifted footage, which was adroitly matched to the new film, gave the film the appearance of having much higher production values than, in point of fact, it really did.

The production, however, still went over the original schedule and budget and part of the delay was an accident which occurred while filming the shipboard dance sequence with Rita Hayworth and her partner, Gary Leon, who suffered a sprained ankle. The film, however, exploited the near-nude "Inferno" sequences and its other sensational elements and made a packet of money in original release. And although it was Rita's first U.S. feature film appearance and her footage was minimal, 20th Century-Fox had no reservations about reissuing it during World War II and elevating Rita Hayworth to star billing on the new advertisements!

In 1948 Spencer Tracy said:

"Rita Hayworth's first film was *Dante's Inferno,* the last one I made at Fox under my old contract and one of the worst pictures ever made anywhere, anytime. The fact that she survived in films after *that* screen debut is testament enough that she deserves all the recognition she's getting right now."

In a 1935 *Weekly Variety,* a review by-lined "Bige" said:

"Insertion of a ten-minute scenic and photographic flash in the middle of the story gives this picture a wallop where it needs it the most, and a selling title to boot. Immediately following the brief, stirring picturization of Hollywood's conception of Dante's version of Hell, the story reverts to its native dullness."

André Sennwald, in his *New York Times* review, said:

"All in all, *Dante's Inferno* is a pretty blistering assortment of sound and fury, and the chances are that no picture of the season has beaten its audiences into quite so abject a state of self-conscious terror."

Paddy O'Day

A Fox Film, Distributed by 20th Century-Fox   1935

Produced by Sol M. Wurtzel. Directed by Lewis Seiler. Original Story and Screenplay by Lou Breslow and Edward Eliscu. Photographed by Arthur Miller. Musical Direction and Supervision by Sammy Kaylin. Songs: "Keep a Twinkle in Your Eye" and "I Like a Balalaika" by Sidney Clare, Edward Eliscu and Harry Akst; "Changing My Ambition," by Pinky Tomlin. Dance Direction by Fanchon. Makeup Supervision by Ernest Westmore. Edited by Alfred DeGaetano. 73 minutes.

CAST:

Paddy O'Day, JANE WITHERS; *Ray Ford,* PINKY TOMLIN; *Tamara Petrovitch*, RITA CANSINO*; Dora,* Jane Darwell; *Mischa,* George Givot; *Immigration Offi-*

With Pinky Tomlin and George Givot in one of the film's funniest sequences.

Moppet Jane Withers plays cupid for timid Pinky Tomlin and Russian dancer Rita Cansino.

cer, Francis Ford; *Aunt Flora,* Vera Lewis; *Aunt Jane,* Louise Carter; *Benton,* Russell Simpson; *Popushka,* Michael Visaroff; *Momushka,* Nina Visaroff; *First Class Passengers,* Selmer Jackson, Ruth Clifford, Larry Steers; *Ship's Doctor,* Harvey Clark; *Immigration Women,* Jessie Pringle, Evelyn Selbie; *Matron,* Myra Marsh; *Maid,* Jane Keckley; *Street Boys,* Tommy Bupp, Sherwood Bailey, Harry Watson; *Policeman,* Russ Clark; *Truck Driver,* Larry Fisher; *Motorist,* Hal K. Dawson; *Brewster,* Clarence Wilson; *Taxi Driver,* Richard Powell; *Russian Musicians,* Egon Brecher, Leonid Snegoff, Demetrios Alexis.

NOTES:

Fox Vice President Winfield Sheehan, who also functioned as general manager of all studio productions, cast Rita, his discovery, in her first important role in *Paddy O'Day* to convince himself, as well as corporation skeptics, that she was capable of handling a leading role before announcing he intended starring her in a Technicolor remake of *Ramona.* But between the completion of *Paddy O'Day* and its release, Fox Films merged with 20th-Century Pictures and Darryl F. Zanuck, who did not share Sheehan's enthusiasm for Rita, took over as executive vice president in charge of all productions. (And cast personal contractee Loretta Young in *Ramona.*)

Since Rita's contract had some weeks to run, Zanuck cast her in an unimportant bit, as Barbara Stanwyck's chapel-praying sister, in *A Message to Garcia.* But when that film ran overlong, Rita's footage, completely extraneous, was deleted after a sneak preview and before the film went into general release. And when it came time for Zanuck to renew her option, he opted for letting her go.

Rita consequently ended the first phase of her Hollywood film career with one short subject, one film which required her to speak no dialogue at all and four films which required that she simulate foreign accents. Although still inexperienced and somewhat untrained, the very fact that she survived such casting should have given Zanuck an inkling of her potential. But it was not until some five years later that he fully realized her true value. Much to Zanuck's chagrin, *Paddy O'Day,* a product of the old Fox regime and therefore a property to be sloughed off without too much exploitation, proved a moderately entertaining film which the critics and the public liked.

In *The New York Times,* Bosley Crowther said:

"A lilt of Irish laughter runs a bit forcedly through *Paddy O'Day,* in which that consummate little showman, Jane Withers, displays her numerous talents. As a little Irish immigrant who sings and dances her way into everybody's affections, except possibly those of an occasional grouch in the audience, she proves herself to be a veritable Shirley Temple of her age group. . . . The picture roars along at a good pace."

In *Weekly Variety,* a review signed by "Chic" said:

"Rita Cansino comes along nicely in this, though she is better known as a dancer than a player. She has two dance bits, both Russian, the last in a tasteful production number that actually fits the stage on which it's supposed to be played!"

And *Photoplay* alerted its readers with:

"Jane Withers brings plenty of laughs and some tears in this homely little story of an Irish orphan's kaleidoscopic adventures in New York. . . ."

Rita Cansino, an illegal alien, is willing to testify and help district attorney Ralph Morgan break up the smuggling ring preying on such people, as reporter Claire Trevor takes notes.

Human Cargo

A 20th Century-Fox Picture   1936

Produced by Sol M. Wurtzel. Directed by Allan Dwan. Assistant Director, Samuel Schneider. Screenplay by Jefferson Parker and Doris Malloy, based on Kathleen Shepard's novel, *I Will Be Faithful*. Photographed by Daniel B. Clark. Musical Direction by Sammy Kaylin. Art Direction by Duncan Cramer. Costume Supervision by Gwen Wakeling. Makeup Supervision by Ernest Westmore. Sound Engineers, Alfred Bruzlin and Harry Leonard. Edited by Louis Loeffler. 66 minutes.

CAST:

Bonnie Brewster, CLAIRE TREVOR; *Packy Campbell*, BRIAN DONLEVY; *Lionel Crocker*, Alan Dinehart; *D. A. Cary*, Ralph Morgan; *Susie*, Helen Troy;

In a publicity still used in conjunction with this action programmer dealing with the exploitation of illegal aliens, Rita Cansino was presented as, of all things, the Easter Madonna!

Carmen Zoro, Rita Cansino; *Gilbert Fender,* Morgan Wallace; *Fritz Schulz,* Herman Bing; *Spike Davis,* John McGuire; *Tony Sculla,* Ralf Harolde; *Bob McSweeney,* Wade Boteler; *Ira Conklin,* Harry Wood; *Detectives,* Wilfred Lucas *(Lieutenant),* Pat Hartigan, Edward Cooper, Tom O'Grady, Stanley Blystone, Ivan (Dusty) Miller; *Ship's Officer,* Paul McVey; *Reporter,* Tom Ricketts; *Barreto,* Harry Semels; *Butler,* Edward Cooper; *Captain,* Fredrik Vogeding; *Gangsters,* Lee Phelps, Alonzo Price; *Copy Boy,* Eddie Buzard; *Sob Sister,* Claudia Coleman; *Italian,* Hector V. Sarno; *German Cook,* Otto A. Fries; *German Couple,* Arno Frey, Rosalie Hegedus; *Other Germans,* Hans Fuerberg, Milla Davenport.

NOTES

In Rita's final Fox feature of phase one of her career, she died before the climax, playing an illegal alien blackmailed by a smuggling ring. The film was turned out by the prolific Sol Wurtzel and his unit, which churned out machine-made programmers with agility, rapidity and, occasionally, surprising entertaining results. The uncontested queen of Wurtzel's "B" hive was Claire Trevor, and *Human Cargo* was one of her better honeypots. So much so that Wurtzel continued to produce newspaper-exposé stories and eventually evolved a minor but short-lived series which featured a group of hotshot newspapermen called "The Roving Reporters." But by then (1938), Miss Trevor had graduated to second leads in A pictures, and Rita Hayworth, ironically enough, was under contract at Columbia where, for quite a time, she reigned as that studio's queen of the quickies.

Human Cargo, therefore, has a minor niche in the cinema hall of fame as a film which inspired a series and also an occasion when two overworked B queens appeared together.

Motion Picture Herald reported:

"The picture is acted with vigorous realism and conviction. It is so directed that there is always movement, suspense and punch to maintain unflagging interest. Performances on the part of the principals are uniformly good."

And *Photoplay* enthused with:

"Brian Donlevy and Claire Trevor give robust performances in this exciting exposé of one of the flourishing rackets of the day—the smuggling of aliens into this country. He is a reporter assigned to disclose the head of a vicious ring and she is a bored heiress turned sobsister who is working on the same assignment for a rival newspaper. Good!"

Meet Nero Wolfe

A Columbia Picture   1936

Produced by B. P. Schulberg. Directed by Herbert Biberman. Assistant Director, George Rhein. Screenplay by Howard J. Green, Bruce Manning and Joseph Anthony, based on Rex Stout's novel, *Fer de Lance*. Photographed by Henry Freulich. Musical Direction by Howard Jackson. Sound Recording by George Cooper. Costumes by Lon Anthony. Sound Recording by George Cooper. Edited by Otto Meyer. 73 minutes.

CAST:

Nero Wolfe, EDWARD ARNOLD; *Ellen Barstow,* JOAN PERRY; *Archie Goodwin,* LIONEL STANDER; *Claude Roberts,* VICTOR JORY; *Sarah Barstow,* Nana Bryant; *Mazie Gray,* Dennie Moore; *Manuel Kimball,* Russell Hardie; *E. J. Kimball,* Walter Kingsford; *Professor Barstow,* Boyd Irwin, Sr.; *Olaf,* John Qualen; *O'Grady,* Gene Morgan; *Maria Maringola,* Rita Cansino; *Dr. Bradford,* Frank Conroy; *Carlo,* Juan Toreno; *Anna,* Martha Tibbetts; *Golf Starter,* Eddy Waller; *Mike,* George Offerman, Jr.; *Johnny,* William Benedict; *Tommy,* Raymond Borzage; *Bill,* William Anderson; *Butler,* Eric Wilton; *Attendant,* Al Matthews; *Kimball's Chauffeur,* David Worth; *Messenger Boy,* Roy Bliss; *Bit Men,* Arthur Stewart Hull, Jay Owen, Henry Roquemore, Arthur Rankin.

NOTES:

Intending to make a series, Columbia acquired the screen rights to three Rex Stout novels and one magazine story, all featuring the exploits of Nero Wolfe, the recluse sleuth. Edward Arnold was the ideal choice to impersonate the beer-swilling, orchid-growing detective, but after just one film his aspirations were for more plush assignments *(Come and Get It; The Toast of New York,* et al.) Since Columbia did not yet have him under contract, it was necessary to find a replacement and he turned out to be a Columbia contractee, Walter Connolly, who, at this juncture, was being considered for the role of the High Lama in Frank Capra's *Lost Horizon.* Connolly appeared only once as Wolfe (in *The League of Frightened Men)* and Lionel Stander repeated his Archie Goodwin role.

Connolly's health, however, was not good—he suffered from severe asthma attacks—and Columbia, reluctantly, abandoned what promised to be a very worthwhile series. So Rex Stout's character remained a reader's pleasure until the early days of television when he reappeared briefly on the tube.

Rita's contribution to *Meet Nero Wolfe* was negligible and merely the first of five films she made freelancing before returning to Columbia as a contract player. But the film's leading lady, the very beautiful Joan Perry, later became the wife of Rita's Columbia boss, mentor, and nemesis, Harry Cohn.

In *Weekly Variety*, "Odec" said:

"Edward Arnold's characterization of the Falstaffian private dick who solves 'em without leaving his easy chair should strike the general fancy favorably and rate well at the box office. The comedy and the guessing elements have been deftly mixed, the well-knit narrative precludes any drooping in interest and the cast disports itself in crack whodunit fashion."

And *The New York Times* reported:

"A most comforting sort of detective for these humid days is Nero Wolfe, a sedentary sleuth given to drinking great quantities of homemade beer in his cool, shade-drawn brownstone and solving murder mysteries therefrom by means of remote control and the extremely helpful hand of the screen's Archie Goodwin, whose voice is the voice of Lionel Stander. Mr. Wolfe is, of course, the rotund Edward Arnold whose characterization of Rex Stout's fairly recent fictional figure presages brisk competition for such current screen masterminds as Philo Vance and Perry Mason, both in matters of deduction as well as esthetically."

Motion Picture Herald added:

"Melodrama and comedy are adroitly balanced under Herbert Biberman's direction and B. P. Schulberg's production is wholly adequate to story requirements as to settings, cast and technical aspects. Now that we've met Mr. Wolfe, we hope to see more of him."

In her first Columbia programmer, Rita Cansino appeals to detective Edward Arnold for help in locating her missing brother as his chef, John Qualen, looks on.

With Tom Keene.

Rebellion

Distributed by Crescent Pictures   1936

Produced by E. B. Derr. Associate Producer, Bernard Moriarty. Directed by Lynn Shores. Assistant Director, Fred Spencer. Original Story and Screenplay by John T. Neville. Production Supervisor, Frank Melford. Photographed by Arthur Martinelli. Musical Supervision by Abe Meyer. Art Direction by Edward C. Jewell. Costumes Supervised by Lou Brown. Makeup Supervision by Steve Corso. Chief Sound Engineer, J. S. Westmoreland. Edited by Donald Barratt. 62 minutes.

CAST:

Captain John Carroll, TOM KEENE; *Paula Castillo,* RITA CANSINO; *Ricardo Castillo,* DUNCAN RENALDO; *Harris,* William Royle; *Pablo,* Gino Corrado; *Honeycutt,* Roger Gray; *Judge Moore,* Robert McKenzie; *President Zachary Taylor,* Allen Cavan; *Hank,* Jack Ingram; *Marquita,* Lita Cortez; *General Vallejo,* Theodore Lorsch; *Dr. Semple,* W. M. McCormick.

NOTES:

Tom Keene, whose best-known screen role was probably the lead in King Vidor's *Our Daily Bread* (1934), started working in films under the name of George Duryea, and still later under the name of Richard Powers. Handsome and virile, but a less-than-expert horseman and actor, Keene appeared in a plethora of westerns and pseudohistorical costumers during the 1930s and appears to belong to that minor league of western players now all but forgotten, but which once included

such luminaries of their sphere as Kermit Maynard (Ken's brother), Rex Lease, Rex Bell, Monte Montana, Wally Wales, Edmund Cobb, Jack Perrin and Jack Luden.

Jack Ingram, who had a small role in *Rebellion,* and was a fixture in countless other westerns, worked at Columbia during the 1940s in several minor programmers and serials when Rita Hayworth was the studio's reigning star. He ran into her there once and was surprised she had remembered him. Later, when asked if he thought she had changed much, he said, "She's much more beautiful now but quite as unaffected and still just as shy as she was when I knew her."

Strictly a programmer intended for the action-house circuit, the release of *Rebellion* was ignored by most metropolitan newspapers.

In *Weekly Variety,* "Barn" ended his brief review with:

"Film has enough of the tried and true western ingredients to get it by in the overall trade, and it's just long enough not to tire."

In *Motion Picture Herald,* McCarthy said:

"Production values of the film are of a high caliber, as is the quality of the acting contributed by the principals. Essentially a romance-tinged thrill drama, it is of the kind that appeals to those patrons who appreciate the value of a logical story and at the same time like to see their pictures move."

Trouble in Texas

A Grand National Picture   1937

Produced by Edward F. Finney. Executive Producer, Edward L. Alperson. Directed by R. N. Bradbury. Screenplay by Robert Emmett. Original Story by Lindsley Parsons, Production Supervisor. Photographed by Gus Peterson. Musical Supervision by Frank Sanucci. Tex Ritter's Songs: "Down On the Colorado," "Song of the Rodeo," "Cowman's Lament," "Headin' For the Rio Grande" and "The Looney Cowboy Band." Art Direction Supervised by Ralph Burger. Costume Supervision by Maizie Lewis and Lou Brown. Chief Sound Engineer, A. E. Kaye. Edited by Fred Bain. 64 minutes.

CAST:

Tex Masters, TEX RITTER; *Carmen,* RITA CAN-

After averting a stagecoach holdup, Tex Ritter wins the grateful thanks of passenger Rita Cansino.

Yakima Canutt gets the drop on rodeo star Tex Ritter and undercover agent Rita Cansino who has been investigating a series of mysterious hold-ups of rodeo prize money.

SINO; *Lucky,* Horace Murphy*; Barker,* Earl Dwire; *Squint,* Yakima Canutt; *Pinto,* Charles King; *Duke,* Dick Palmer; *Announcer,* Tom Cooper; *G-Man,* Hal Price; *Sheriff,* Fred Parker. Other players: Chick Hannon, Oral Zumalt, Fox O'Callahan, Henry Knight, Bob Crosby, Jack Smith, Shorty Miller, Milt Morndi, George Morrell; appeared as *Themselves.*

NOTES:

Grand National Pictures, an independent film company formed in 1936 by Edward L. Alperson, began inauspiciously by distributing low-budget independent products under their trademark but the first star of the new company was Tex Ritter, a country and western singer new to films. The studio also got some additional publicity when, in 1936, after a contractual and salary dispute with Jack L. Warner, James Cagney made *Great Guy* at Grand National, followed by a second film, *Something to Sing About.* Neither film, however, was top-grade Cagney and he was soon back at Warners.

Grand National produced Tex Ritter's first twelve films, all of which had moderately good budgets and production values. All of them made money. Each followed a decided pattern of having sound scripts, musical interludes and just enough action to make them

popular enough on the action-house circuit to where motion-picture exhibitors named Tex Ritter one of the five top money-making western stars within a year of his screen debut in *Trouble in Texas.*

Weekly Variety, which usually ignored the actresses who played the heroines in westerns, said:

"Perhaps the best looker of any of the girls working in hoss pics to date is Grand National's latest recruit, Rita Cansino. She was on the Fox lot for a while, and classes up the company she's in here."

Motion Picture Herald reported:

"This picture has more action sequences than is common even to these outdoor dramas. The action includes an attempted holdup of a stagecoach, two man-to-man struggles, a rodeo that is part acting and part genuine, and a bank robbery that culminates in a wild ride as Ritter and the bandits struggle on a dynamite laden buckboard drawn by runaway horses."

Trouble in Texas is actually the last film Rita made using the name Cansino, but the two films she made prior to this film, *Old Louisiana* and *Hit the Saddle,* were not released until after this film premiered.

With Tom Keene.

Old Louisiana

Distributed by Crescent Pictures   1937

Produced by E. R. Derr. Associate Producer, Bernard A. Moriarty. Directed by Irvin V. Willat. Assistant Director, Raoul Pagel. Screenplay by Mary Ireland, based on John Neville's original story. Production Supervisor, Frank Melford. Photographed by Arthur Martinelli. Musical Direction by Abe Meyer. Art Direction by Edward C. Jewell. Costume Supervision by Lou Brown. Makeup Supervision by Steve Corso. Chief Sound Engineer, Karl Zint. Edited by Donald Barratt. 60 minutes.

CAST:

John Colfax, TOM KEENE; *Angela Gonzales,* RITA CANSINO; *Gilmore,* Robert Fiske; *Flint,* Ray Bennett; *Thomas Jefferson,* Allan Cavan; *Steve,* Will Morgan; *Kentucky,* Budd Buster; *Governor Gonzales,* Carlos DeValdez; *Davey,* Wally Albright; *James Madison,* Ramsay Hill.

NOTES:

Although *Old Louisiana* was Rita's ninth U.S. feature film released, it was actually made immediately after *Rebellion* was completed, and although she ostensibly has the feminine lead, her footage was much less than it been in her previous vehicle with Keene, and her performance was somewhat more self-conscious.

Tom Keene and two guns, Rita Cansino and two nuns standing off two guards whose orders are to detain them.

Western star Tom Keene romances ingenue Rita, who had little inkling then that just five years later she would be called the "World's Most Famous Redhead."

Rita Cansino played the dark-haired daughter of the Governor of the Louisiana Territory during the days of the political struggle for its recognition and U.S. purchase.

Film Daily said:

"A satisfactory action programmer, made doubly interesting, inasmuch as it touches upon history and events leading up to the Louisiana Purchase . . . Rita Cansino is decorative as the love interest."

Weekly Variety, however, had a different opinion:

"Poorest of the Tom Keene series for this company [Crescent] *Louisiana* will fare moderately and worse whenever booked. Even scenes of utmost intensity are

passed in the spirit of relaxation by the cast. . . . Femme nicety is Rita Cansino, whose tamale accent fits her well for the part of the daughter of the Spanish governor."

An astute distributor unearthed *Old Louisiana* in the mid-1940s, at the apex of Rita's wartime popularity and retitling it *Louisiana Gal* gave Hayworth top billing. In reissue, the film played made large metropolitan areas, such as New York City, where, when new, the film never even had an official release.

With Tom Keene, surrounded by good guys and bad guys, Budd Buster, Carlos DeValdez, Robert Fiske and Will Morgan.

Hit the Saddle

A Republic Picture   1937

Produced by Nat Levine. Associate Producer, Sol C. Siegel. Directed by Mack V. Wright. Assistant Director, George Blair. Screenplay by Oliver Drake, based on an original story by Drake and Maurice Geraghty, adapted from a William Colt MacDonald novel. Photographed by Jack Marta. Musical Supervision by Alberto Colombo. Songs by Oliver Drake and Sam H. Stept. Art Direction by John Victor Mackay. Chief Sound Engineer, Dan Bloomburg. Edited by Lester Orleback. 61 minutes.

CAST:

Stony Brooke, ROBERT LIVINGSTON; *Tucson Smith,* RAY CORRIGAN; *Lullaby Joslin,* MAX TERHUNE; *Rita,* RITA CANSINO; *Buck,* Yakima Canutt; *MacGowan,* J. P. MacGowan; *Miller,* Edward Cassidy; *Tim,* Sammy McKim; *Harvey,* Harry Tenbrooke; *Hank,* Robert Smith; *Pete,* Ed Boland.

NOTES:

Stony, Tucson and Lullaby, a cowboy triumvirate known as The Three Mesquiteers, were the creation of William Colt MacDonald and made their first screen appearance in *Powdersmoke Range* (RKO; 1935). The same year, two of the trio, Tucson and Stony, appeared in a Normandy film, *Law of the .45's* and reappeared the following year in Normandy's *Too Much Beef,* which the newly formed Grand National Pictures distributed. These features were all based on MacDonald books.

But also in 1936, the newly formed Republic Pictures released *The Three Mesquiteers,* based on the MacDonald characters and incidents from several books. Ultimately fifty additional Mesquiteer films comprised a profitable series. At the time of its release, *Hit the Saddle,* the eighth Republic entry, was considered the weakest one turned out by that studio. Robert Living-

With Max Terhune, Robert Livingstone and Ray Corrigan in a scene from one of the least popular of the very popular "Three Mesquiteers" film series.

ston, Ray Corrigan and Max Terhune, who started out together in the Republic series, made fifteen of the Mesquiteer adventures. However, Livingston played Stony in twenty-nine films; Corrigan played Tucson in twenty-four; and, Terhune played Lullaby twenty-one times. John Wayne, Ralph Byrd, Bob Steele, Tom Tyler, Rufe Davis, Jimmy Dodd, Raymond Hatton and Duncan Reynaldo also worked intermittently as one or another of the trio.

Edward Connor wrote in *Screen Facts* magazine (in 1964):

"As in their serials of that time, Republic showed they also had the secret of making slick, fast-paced, action-packed westerns, running an average of fifty-five minutes each, filled with wonderful feats performed by top stuntmen like Yakima Canutt and Cliff Lyons. There was also a strong undercurrent humor in the series: the byplay between Livingston and Corrigan being, on the whole, somewhat funnier than ventriloquist Max Terhune's sallies with dummy Elmer.

"Plots were strong and unusual . . . it was sad when The Three Mesquiteers at the close of the 1943 *Riders of the Rio Grande* turned to wave at the audience (traditional ending to their films) and then rode off—to be seen no more."

In his *Weekly Variety* review of *Hit the Saddle*, "Shan" said:

"Its speedy popgun routine should help fit this horse opera on the multiple screens for interest to the inveterate buckshot dans and the juveniles. Mixed up in here is a crude bit of romance between one of the Mesquiteers and a fandango dancer. The girl (Rita Cansino) is highly deficient in terps and as an actress, but it is of no consequence. . . . Picture offers some nice outdoor scenics and the Mesquiteers themselves are a likable trio."

Although in all the Republic Mesquiteer films the costumes of the male characters remained consistently standard Hollywood western garb of no particular period, it was quite another matter with women's costumes. In *Hit the Saddle,* for instance, Rita's clothes were contemporary to the year of the film's release but in other series entries the women were often garbed in period costumes.

RITA HAYWORTH
Starlet

B films were a wonderful training ground for fledgling players, and Rita Hayworth was no exception. In the late 1930s, in supporting roles in A films and secondary and starring roles in B films, she played every kind of good and bad woman imaginable. When stardom came in the early 1940s, she starred in a number of lavish Technicolor musicals which emphasized her vibrant beauty. Between musicals she was a sultry *Gilda,* a fiery *Carmen,* a flamboyant *Salome,* the best *Sadie Thompson* ever, and one of our servicemen's favorite pin-ups.

Off-screen, too, she played many roles—housewife, mother, princess—and was, at the height of her stardom, one of the most publicized women in history. Yet she was cooperative, self-effacing and shy, and had a completely honest heart.

With Charles Quigley and menace Marc Lawrence in a publicity still.

Criminals of the Air

A Columbia Picture   1937

Produced by Wallace MacDonald. Executive Producer, Irving Briskin. Directed by Charles C. Coleman, Jr., Assistant Director, Thomas Flood. Screenplay by Owen Francis, based on a Jack Cooper original story. Photographed by George Meehan. Musical Director, Morris Stoloff. Gowns by Kalloch. Makeup Supervision by Johnny Wallace. Art Direction Supervised by Stephen Goosson. Chief Sound Engineer, John Livadary. Edited by Dick Fantl. 61 minutes.

CAST:

Nancy Rawlings, ROSALIND KEITH; *Mark Owens,* CHARLES QUIGLEY; *Rita,* RITA HAYWORTH; *Ray Patterson,* JOHN GALLAUDET; *Blast Reardon,* Marc Lawrence; *Mamie,* Patricia Farr; *Captain Wallace,* John Hamilton; *Williamson,* Ralph Byrd; *Camera-Eye Condon,* Walter Soderling; *Kurt Feldon,* Russell Hicks; *Bill Morris,* John Tyrell; *Trigger,* Lester Dorr; *Contact,* Frank Sully; *Hot Cake Joe,* Herbert Heywood; *Ruby,* Lucille Lund; *Ronnie,* Crawford Weaver; *Ronnie's Wife,* Ruth Hilliard; *Arnold,* Matty Kemp; *Groom,* Robert Fiske; *Bride,* Martha Tibbetts; *Harrison,* Howard Hickman; *Chafin,* Sam Flint; *Simmons,* Eddie Fetherstone; *Harry-the-Actor,* Jay Eaton; *Harry's Wife,* Jane Weir; *Field Porter,* Norma Pabst; *Bartender,* Sammy Blum; *Mike,* Richard Botiller.

NOTES:

Among aficionadoes of B films, *Criminals of the Air* is generally considered to be one of Columbia's more tolerable efforts produced during the latter half of the 1930s. Aside from its modest entertainment values, there are a few trivial cinema facts associated with it on which B film devotees usually dote.

Originally titled *Guardians of the Air,* but previewed under the title *Honeymoon Pilot,* it was the third Columbia programmer to team Charles Quigley and Rosalind Keith. But Miss Keith, who began her film career at Paramount under the name of Rosalind Culli (unbilled in 1934's *Murder at the Vanities* but featured in 1935's *The Glass Key),* soon lost Quigley, once voted "one of the five handsomest men in movies" by the Women's Clubs of America, to Rita Hayworth. *Criminals of the Air* was the first of five Columbia quickies to team Miss Hayworth and Quigley, an appearance record with the same leading man she later duplicated with Glenn Ford.

The name-changing penchant associated with this film also included Miss Hayworth, as the preview version billed her as Rita Cansino. That version also had its direction credited to C. C. Coleman, Jr. *and* Folmer Blangsted. Release prints only mention Coleman as director and credit Thomas Flood as his assistant and make no allusion whatever to Blangsted; *Criminals of the Air* is also the first Columbia film to feature Miss Hayworth, a smuggling gang's decoy in a below-the-border nightclub, dancing. That facet of Miss Hayworth's talents was subsequently ignored by the studio for a few years but later exploited—with spectacular results.

In *Weekly Variety,* "Barn" reported:

"Rita Hayworth, charming and voluptuous brunette, dances and plays up to Quigley from the lower side of the border. She does one Spanish terp number, which shows her off well, even if it's nothing fancy. Gets liberal footage on it, and she seems to have possibilities for straight talking roles."

Motion Picture Herald said:

"Criminals of the Air winds itself up as it goes along and races to an exciting climax. . . . The production gives promise of appeal both to those who appreciate the value of thrilling action and semimystery and those who find interest in a refreshing love story."

And *Boxoffice* added its approval:

"A picture that should hold its own on any bill. It is an unpretentious tale of the Mexican border patrol, aided by some good acting, with sufficient action to please the most exacting patron."

Rosalind Keith appears very disinterested in Rita Hayworth's dance.

In one of her most expressive and explosive screen scenes thus far in her career, Rita Hayworth verbally abuses and disapproves of a decision by an umpire against a member of her softball team.

Girls Can Play

A Columbia Picture   1937

Produced by Ralph Cohn. Executive Producer, Irving Briskin. Direction and Screenplay by Lambert Hillyer, based on "Miss Casey at Bat," an original screen story by Albert DeMond. Photographed by Lucien Ballard. Musical Supervision by Morris Stoloff. Costume Supervision by Ray Howell. Women's Costumes by Kalloch. Art Direction Supervised by Stephen Goosson. Chief Sound Engineer, John Livadary. Edited by Byron Robinson. 59 minutes.

CAST:

Ann Casey, JACQUELINE WELLS;* *Jimmy Jones,* CHARLES QUIGLEY; *Sue Collins,* RITA HAYWORTH; Foy *Harris,* JOHN GALLAUDET; *Sluggy,* George McKay; *Peanuts,* Patricia Farr; *Lieutenant Flannigan,* Guinn "Big Boy" Williams; *Brophy,* Joseph Crehan; *Danny Maschio,* John Tyrell; *Cisto,* Richard Terry; *Bill O'Malley,* James Flavin; *Infielders,* Beatrice Curtis, Ruth Hilliard; *Coroner,* Lee Prather; *Dugan,* Harry Tyler; *Mae,* Beatrice Blinn; *Anna,* Fern Emmett;

*Later known as Julie Bishop.

Rita Hayworth and John Gallaudet as a romantic duo that one critic claimed was as unbelievable and false as Rita's eyelashes.

Mann, Michael Breen; *Mr. Raymond,* Richard Kipling; *Doctor,* Bruce Sidney; *Jane Harmon,* Lucille Lund; *Fortune Teller,* Evelyn Selbie; *Captain Curtis,* Lee Shumway; *Secretary,* Ann Doran.

NOTES:

Originally known as *Miss Casey at Bat,* then previewed as *Fielder's Field,* it appears that *Girls Can Play* struck out after batting three titles around. The contrived script has an ex-convict, who could never be legally licensed to operate a chain of drug stores that sell liquor (at least not in California where the action ostensibly occurs), invite exposure to his counterfeit liquor racket by advertising it via the sponsorship of a girls' softball team! The film's virtues were few indeed, one being, of course, Lucien Ballard's first-rate photography. Another an exchange of dialogue in which one of the character actors, observing the obvious assets of one girl player, remarks, "You can play in my ball park anytime." To which the player retorts, "Yeah, I'll bet I can. You'll even supply the bat."

In its review, *Weekly Variety* cited the film's other sole virtue:

"Rita Hayworth, as the moll of the crooked druggist, furnishes the smartest female portrayal of the picture. She shows potentialities."

Rita Hayworth, member of a girls' soft-ball team, is the concern of coach, manager and players as she is suddenly taken ill.

The Shadow

A Columbia Picture   1937

Associate Producer, Wallace MacDonald. Executive Producer, Irving Briskin. Directed by Charles C. Coleman, Jr. Assistant Director, Bob Farfan. Screenplay by Arthur T. Horman, based on Milton Raison's original screen story. Photographed by Lucien Ballard. Musical Direction by Morris Stoloff. Costume Supervision by Ray Howell. Women's Costumes by Kalloch. Art Direction by Stephen Goosson and Lionel Banks. Chief Sound Engineer, John Livadary. Edited by Byron Robinson. 59 minutes.

Arthur Loft questions Charles Quigley, Rita Hayworth and Marjorie Main in connection with a murder at their circus.

With Dwight Frye.

CAST:

Mary Gillespie, RITA HAYWORTH; *Jim Quinn,* CHARLES QUIGLEY; *Kid Crow,* MARC LAWRENCE; *Sheriff Jackson,* Arthur Loft; *Carlos,* Dick Curtis; *Dutch Schultz,* Vernon Dent; *Hannah Gillespie,* Marjorie Main; *Peter Martinet,* Donald Kirke; *Vindecco,* Dwight Frye; *Marianne,* Bess Flowers; *Mac,* Bill Irving; *Woody,* Eddie Fetherston; *Dolores,* Sally St. Clair; *Rosa,* Sue St. Clair; *Mr. Moreno,* John Tyrell; *Mrs. Moreno,* Beatrice Curtis; *The Shaw Sisters,* Ann Doran, Beatrice Blinn; *Ticket Sellers,* Bud Jamison, Harry Strang; *Mr. Shaw,* Francis Sayles; *Circus Doctor,* Edward Hearn; *Bascomb,* Edward LeSaint; *Knife Throwing Act,* Mr. and Mrs. Clemens; *Watchman,* Harry Bernard; *Messenger Boy,* Ernie Adams; *Masked Figure,* Ted Mangean.

NOTES:

Although the denouement of *The Shadow* involved a bit of subterfuge on the part of the writer in revealing the identity of a murderous maniac loose in a small-time company, which some mystery film addicts felt wasn't exactly cricket, the total surprise of the killer's identity more than compensated for this petty complaint. And a second, very careful scrutiny of the film certainly does pinpoint the climax. *The Shadow,* which had no relation whatever to the famous radio program of that era, must also have impressed screenwriters Aben Kandel and Herman Cohen because, some thirty years later, they devised an almost identical "original" story, *Berserk,* which, filmed in England by Columbia Pictures, starred a ludicrously miscast Joan Crawford. Granted they expanded the plot and changed the killer's identity but other similarities between the films are too numerous to have been totally coincidental.

The Shadow is notable for another reason: it was the first film to give Rita Hayworth top billing!

In *Weekly Variety,* "Barn." said:

"Rita Hayworth, the manager of the show, and Quigley, her press agent, both turn in good performances, the Hayworth girl turning in better work all the time. Even gets away with a show of high emotion occasionally, which is something for these femmes assigned to leads in films which consume less than a month from brain to can."

With Charles Quigley.

The Game That Kills

A Columbia Picture   1937

Produced by Harry L. Decker. Executive Producer, Irving Briskin. Directed by D. Ross Lederman. Assistant Director, Sam Nelson. Screenplay by Grace Neville and Fred Niblo, Jr., based on J. Benton Cheney's original story. Photographed by Benjamin Kline. Musical Supervision and Direction by Morris Stoloff. Costume Supervision by Ray Howell. Art Direction Supervised by Stephen Goosson. Edited by James Sweeney. 55 minutes.

CAST:

Alec Ferguson, CHARLES QUIGLEY; *Betty Holland,* RITA HAYWORTH; *Sam Erskine,* JOHN GALLAUDET; *Joe Holland,* J. Farrell MacDonald; *Rudy Maxwell,* Arthur Loft; *Eddie,* John Tyrell; *Dick Adams,* Paul Fix; *Bill Drake,* Max Hoffman, Jr.; *"Leapfrog" Soule,* Dick Wessel; *Jeff,* Maurice Black; *Steven Morean,* Clyde Dilson; *Walter,* Harry Strang; *Whitey,* Dick Curtis; *Bronson,* Lee Prather; *Policemen,* Jack Dougherty, Edmund Cobb; *Detective,* Ralph Dunn; *Cab Drivers,* Ethan Laidlaw, Eddie Fetherston; *Waiter,* George Cheseboro; *Motorcycle Cops,* Bud Weiser, Lloyd Ford; *Jack,* Sammy McKim.

NOTES:

The Game That Kills, which previewed under the title *Flashing Skates,* was the sixth of eight Columbia films released during 1937 and the first in which noticeably careful attention was given to Rita Hayworth's grooming and makeup. She had started taking electrolysis treatments to have her hairline raised, and this subtle alteration gave audiences an indication of the glamour evolution she would accomplish.

Still dark-tressed, although no longer raven-haired, she was now being publicized on cheesecake stills with national holiday motifs: for the Fourth of July, she was depicted straddling a giant firecracker; for Thanksgiving, she was posed as a Pilgrim maiden carving a turkey; and, for Christmas, she was dressed in a mini-Santa suit, perched beside a cardboard chimney amidst a glitter of artificial snow. Such were the photographic results of Harry Cohn's orders to his publicity department to promote her as an all-American girl—which, of course, is exactly what she was!

But at that period in her career, no one, least of all Harry Cohn, gave any thought to promoting her chance of stardom with a strong role in a first-rate film. But Rita remained cooperative, although not without a sense of humor. While posing as the pilgrim, she told the still photographer, "This should be an easy session. I'm getting quite adept at carving a niche in cardboard turkeys!"

Nonetheless, "Barn." of *Weekly Variety* remained one of her champions and also singled her out in his reviews. Of *The Game That Kills,* he said:

"Film features Charles Quigley on top, but sharing with Rita Hayworth, who broke in recently with a small dancing role in one of his pictures. Brunette is a looker and talks the role well; we will probably see her more often in the Columbia prints of the future."

Paid to Dance

A Columbia Picture   1937

Produced by Ralph Cohn. Executive Producer, Irving Briskin. Directed by Charles C. Coleman, Jr. Assistant Director, Cliff Broughton. Screenplay by Robert E. Kent, based on Leslie T. White's original story. Photographed by George Meehan. Musical Direction by Morris Stoloff. Art Direction Supervised by Stephen Goosson. Gowns by Kalloch. Sound Engineer, George Cooper. Edited by Byron Robinson. 56 minutes.

CAST:

William Dennis, DON TERRY; *Joan Bradley,* JACQUELINE WELLS; *Betty Morgan,* RITA HAYWORTH; *Jack Miranda,* ARTHUR LOFT; *Charles Kennedy,* Paul Stanton; *Nifty,* Paul Fix; *Phyllis Parker,* Louise Stanley; *Nickels Brown,* Ralph Byrd; *Frances Mitchell,* Beatrice Curtis; *Suzy,* Bess Flowers; *Lois,* Beatrice Blinn; *Evelyn,* Jane Hamilton; *Mike Givens,* Dick Curtis; *Joe Krause,* Al Herman; *Governor,* Thurston Hall; *Barney Wilson,* John Gallaudet; *LaRue,* Horace MacMahon; *Sanders,* George Lloyd; *Ruth Gregory,* Ruth Hilliard; *Rose Trevor,* Ann Doran; *Lieutenant of Police,* Bud Jamison; *Salesman,* Bill Irving; *Skipper,* Eddie Fetherston; *Magistrate,* Edward LeSaint; *Francine,* Ernest Wood; *McDonald,* Lee Prather; *Mrs. Daniels,* Georgie Cooper; *Butler,* Edward Hearn; *Attendant,* Harry Strang; *News Vendor,* Walter Lawrence; *Newsboy,* Bud McTaggart; *Conductor,* Edward Peil, Sr.; *Sailor,* George Lollier; *Radio Cop,* Jack Cheatham; *Policemen,* Bill Lally, Dan Wolheim; *Dance Hall Customers,* Ethan Laidlaw, Jay Eaton, Stanley Mack, Arthur Stuart Hall.

NOTES:

After advancing to a leading role in the moderately tolerable *The Game That Kills,* Rita returned to a supporting role, albeit the second feminine lead, in the wholly intolerable *Paid to Dance,* which seemed to suggest that her status at Columbia was none too solid. It's impossible to imagine what assignment could have been more unfortunate than this one at this point in her career.

Rushed into production a month after Warner Bros. released their crackling exposé of racketeers who use and abuse clip-joint hostesses, *Marked Woman,* this programmer was such an obvious, shoddy and cheap imitation it hardly deserves the dignity of comparison. Running a scant fifty-six minutes, its sole virtue, film economy was evident everywhere in *Paid to Dance!*

Screen characters elucidated on off-screen events of which they could have no possible knowledge and even discussed events which had not yet transpired as having already occurred! One sequence really stretched credulity when audiences were asked to believe a scene in which the chief racketeer contacts the mastermind of the mob by the simple expediency of picking up a telephone and without dialing a number, or getting operator assistance, or even offering a salutation to his employer to ascertain whether or not he's speaking to the right person, begins by asking his boss for advice on a situation that transpired only moments earlier and of which the mastermind could not possibly have any knowledge. Early in the film the distance from one location to another is established by what appears to be about a twenty-minute automobile ride. This distance is considerably shortened later in the film when someone goes from the second destination to the point of departure merely by crossing a room and opening a door! A montage of action sequences depict the following events which is later established as all having taken place in less than one hour: an undercover agent attempting to prove to a racketeer that he, too, is a mobster able to

bribe police officials has a clip-joint raided and padlocked, the hostesses arrested, arraigned and bailed out after a payoff is effected, newspaper headlines, depicting each development and then having the scene end with the girls back at work, dancing to a crowd of pleasure-seekers while one hostess complains that her feet hurt and bemoans the fact that she still has an additional four hours to work!

In their review, *Daily Variety* summed up *Paid to Dance* in one succinct sentence:

"It has all the earmarks of being churned out with a minimum of expense and effort."

A nameless reviewer on the *Los Angeles Daily News* said:

"This is the first film of recent memory which, instead of being exhibited, should be sentenced to a life term without any chance of parole in a merciful effort to keep the unsuspecting public away."

Rita Hayworth, underpaid dance hall hostess, who has been heard voicing her complaints to undercover policewoman Jacqueline Welles (later known as Julie Bishop), encounters the wrath of their employer Arthur Loft who is unaware that Don Terry, posing as a shady agent, is also an undercover police agent.

Hayworth's singing of "It's Twelve O'Clock and All Is Not Well" was a mixture of her own voice and that of Gloria Franklin, but the film's other song, "The Greatest Attraction in the World," was completely dubbed. Robert Paige is the orchestra leader.

Who Killed Gail Preston?

A Columbia Picture   1938

Produced by Ralph Cohn. Executive Producer, Irving Briskin. Directed by Leon Barsha. Screenplay by Robert E. Kent and Henry Taylor, based on Taylor's original screen story, "Murder in Swingtime." Photographed by Henry Freulich. Songs: "The Greatest Attraction in the World" and "Twelve O'Clock and All's Not Well," by Milton Drake and Ben Oakland. Musical Direction by Morris Stoloff. Art Direction Supervised by Stephen Goosson. Gowns by Kalloch. Chief Sound Engineer, John Livadary. Edited by Byron Robinson. 61 minutes.

CAST:

Inspector Kellogg, DON TERRY; *Gail Preston,* RITA HAYWORTH; *Swing Traynor,* ROBERT PAIGE; *Ann Bishop,* WYN CAHOON; *Cliff Connolly,* Gene Morgan; *Frank Daniels,* Marc Lawrence; *Jules Stevens,* Arthur Loft; *Charles Waverly,* John Gallaudet; *Patsy Fallon,* John Spacey; *Mike,* Eddie Fetherston; *Hank,* James Millican; *Maid,* Mildred Glover; *Mr. Owen,* Dwight

Frye; *Curran,* John Dilson; *Arnold,* Bill Irving; *Watchman,* Vernon Dent; *Cigarette Girl,* Ruth Hilliard; *Hat Check Girl,* Jane Hamilton; *Radio Technicians,* Allen Brook, Jack Egan; *Head Waiter,* James Burtis; *Society Woman,* Nell Craig; *Policemen,* Larry Fisher, Charles Hamilton, George Magrill, Bill Lally; *Motorcycle Cop,* Hal Craig; *Marshall,* Ralph McCullough; *Elevator Operator,* Malcolm McTaggart; *Radio Announcer,* Lee Shumway; *Society Man,* Bruce Sidney.

NOTES:

Although top-billed, Rita's footage was limited to about twenty minutes but she made every on-screen moment count. Sleekly gowned and coiffed and glamorously turned out, she made Gail Preston a properly sensual but hateful creature with dramatic economy rather than an acting excess. In an effort not to tip off audiences to the fact that she is murdered early in the proceedings, the publicity department posed her with cast members

With Wyn Cahoon and Robert Paige in a posed publicity still depicting the romantic triangle elements of the murder mystery plot.

in photographs it distributed who otherwise shared no scenes with her.

Anticipating that Hedy Lamarr, the most promoted and publicized film personality of the season, would be the rage of the country with the release of *Algiers,* Columbia's makeup department put Rita in a dark wig and designed her makeup so she had a vague resemblance to the Viennese import. Columbia's coup, having a Lamarr look-alike on screen before the release of *Algiers* in no way dismayed almost every other studio from designing one of their standard stars into the Lamarr mold. Some three years later, after her appearance in *Blood and Sand,* Rita herself became a star subjected to the flattering but dubious distinction of having other studios attempt to turn out a reasonably exact Hayworth facsimile. But these efforts were no more fruitful than the Hedy Lamarr look-alike sweepstakes had been (except in the case of Joan Bennett's sudden switch from blonde to black tresses which she continued to use for her entire career during which she out-Lamarred Hedy and outlasted her too!).

Realizing Rita's singing, pleasantly melodious and on-key but an otherwise small and untrained talent was unsuitable for the voice of a professional songstress, Columbia's music and sound departments dubbed her songs with the voice of Gloria Franklin, a not-particularly-ideal choice. But on the soundtracks of her later films, except *Blood and Sand,* Rita's "voice ghosts" were more carefully selected and specially trained to match her speaking voice with almost uncanny results. Of the first Columbia film to feature the dubbed singing of Rita, Bosley Crowther, in *The New York Times,* said:

"Even as Class B melodrama, *Who Killed Gail Preston?,* boils down to a rhetorical question. The obvious reply is, 'Who cares?' "

Rita Hayworth as a blackmailing songstress attempts to extort money from her nightclub employer, John Spacey.

There's Always a Woman

A Columbia Picture   1938

Produced by William Perlberg. Directed by Alexander Hall. Assistant Director, William Mull. Screenplay by Gladys Lehman (Joel Sayre, Philip Rapp and Morrie Ryskind, uncredited contributors), based on William Collison's short story. Photographed by Henry Freulich. Musical Direction by Morris Stoloff. Art Direction by Stephen Goosson and Lionel Banks. Gowns by Kalloch. Chief Sound Engineer, John Livadary. Edited by Viola Lawrence. 81 minutes.

CAST:

Sally Reardon, JOAN BLONDELL; *Bill Reardon,* MELVYN DOUGLAS; *Lola Fraser,* MARY ASTOR; *Anne Calhoun,* FRANCES DRAKE; *Nick Shane,* Jerome Cowan; *Jerry Marlowe,* Robert Paige; *District Attorney,* Thurston Hall; *Mr. Ketterling,* Pierre Watkin; *Grigson,* Walter Kingsford; *Walter Fraser,* Lester Matthews; *Mary,* Rita Hayworth.

NOTES:

An admittedly blatant attempt at hoping to cash in on the success of the very popular *Thin Man* films, *There's Always a Woman* was the spin-off film of what Columbia hoped would be a popular series. There was a second Sally and Bill Reardon mystery adventure, *There's That Woman Again,* which had Melvyn Douglas repeating his original role but with Virginia Bruce replacing Joan Blondell as the lovable and scatterbrained Sally. In some respects the sequel was more soundly constructed, but it was not as popular as the first film and the series was abandoned. Columbia later reteamed Blondell and Douglas in another mystery comedy, *The Amazing Mr. Williams,* which had some delightful sequences, but which was too episodic in construction for Columbia to continue with a second *Mr. Williams* film as was first planned.

There's Always a Woman was a top-budgeted production with an adequate shooting schedule but in-production script problems demanded daily on-the-set revisions and Rita's modest role, as Joan Blondell's confidante and spy in the district attorney's office, was all but deleted from the released film. Her footage, in fact, lasted less than thirty seconds, and you had to be keen of eye to catch her at all!

Curious about this unusual Hayworth film credit, I discussed it with director Alexander Hall before his death. He told me that although Gladys Lehman received solo credit for the screenplay, Joel Sayre, Phil Rapp and Morrie Ryskind had all been called in to "juice up" the comedy elements of the story (their contribution included Miss Blondell's hilarious police grilling sequence) but keep in mind that the finished film was to be first in a series and that, except for the two leads, there should be no other characters necessary to additional stanzas for the sake of economy. And since Rita's role was important enough that her disappearance from a second film might be questioned, she was all but deleted from the original.

Nevertheless, Rita was not exactly a complete loser. Columbia's publicity department consoled her by seeing to it that she had good exposure in the fan magazines modeling costumes worn by Frances Drake, Miss Blondell and Mary Astor. A subsequent consolation was being awarded the second feminine lead in *The Lone Wolf Spy Hunt,* a role originally intended for Mary Astor who, instead, went on loan-out to MGM.

Of the first Sally and Bill Reardon mystery-comedy, *Motion Picture Herald* reported:

"The market for *There's Always a Woman* should be wide and enthusiastic. It is an amusing show in which tomfoolery, mystery, melodrama, suspense and surprise have been welded in expert fashion."

Alexander Hall directing a rehearsal with Thurston Hall, Rita Hayworth (standing in for Frances Drake, whose costume she is wearing), Robert Paige, Mary Astor and Melvyn Douglas.

With Charles Quigley.

Convicted

A Central Film Distributed by
  Columbia Pictures   1938

Produced by Kenneth J. Bishop. Directed by Leon Barsha. Assistant Director, George Rhein. Screenplay by Edgar Edwards, based on Cornell Woolrich's story, "Face Work." Photographed by George Meehan. Musical Direction by Morris Stoloff. Sound Engineer, Gary Harris. Edited by William Austin. 58 minutes.

CAST:

Burns, CHARLES QUIGLEY; *Jerry Wheeler,* RITA HAYWORTH, *Milton Militis,* MARC LAWRENCE; *Kane,* George McKay; *Mary Allen,* Doreen MacGregor; *Cobble-Puss Coley,* Bill Irving; *Berger,* Eddie Laughton; *Chick Wheeler,* Edgar Edwards; *Ruby Rose,* Phyllis Clare; *Rocco,* Bob Rideout; *Pal,* Michael Heppell; *Aggie,* Noel Cusack; *Frankie,* Grant MacDonald; *District Attorney,* Don Douglas.

NOTES:

Convicted was Rita's first programmer at Columbia not churned out by the Irving Briskin B unit, famous for being more prolific than the competing Sol M. Wurtzel B unit at 20th Century-Fox, although much less successful and adroit.

Charles Quigley was again restored to top billing, and Edgar Edwards, who plays Rita's brother, a condemned murderer she believes to be innocent, also wrote the screenplay, based on one of mystery writer Cornell Woolrich's least-successful magazine stories.

Boxoffice said:

"What makes the proceedings tolerable is the beauty of Rita Hayworth that graces the screen in an altogether attractive style."

And, in *The New York Times,* Bosley Crowther said:

"There are some frankly unimportant pictures the memory of which, nevertheless, we shall always cherish, and from now on one of them is going to be *Convicted.* . . . For us, its one really timeless feature is that dramatic instant when the medical examiner (an anonymous gentleman not even mentioned in the cast of characters), after having examined the body of the murdered woman, walks up to Detective Charles Quigley while pocketing his stethoscope, clears his throat with professional dignity and mutters in clipped, confidential tones: 'Strangulation, collapse of the larynx.' It is moments like this which convince you that movies really are your best entertainment."

With Doreen MacGregor.

The worried sister of Frankie Darro, leader of a street gang in trouble with the police, appeals for help from public defender Paul Kelly in courthouse corridor.

Juvenile Court

A Columbia Picture   1938

Produced by Ralph Cohn. Executive Producer, Irving Briskin. Directed by D. Ross Lederman. Assistant Director, Wilbur McGaugh. Original Screenplay by Michael L. Simmons, Robert E. Kent and Henry Taylor. Photographed by Benjamin Kline. Musical Direction by Morris Stoloff. Art Direction Supervised by Stephen Goosson. Edited by Byron Robinson. 60 minutes.

CAST:

Gary Franklin, PAUL KELLY; *Marcia Adams*, RITA HAYWORTH; *Stubby*, FRANKIE DARRO; *Lefty*, Hally Chester; *Mickey*, Don Latorre; *Pighead*, David Gorcey; *Ears*, Dick Selzer; *Davy*, Allan Ramsay; *Squarehead*, Charles Hart; *Governor Stanley*, Howard Hickman; *Judge*, Joseph DeStephani; *Dutch Adams*, John Tyrell; *Detective*, Dick Curtis; *Policemen*, James Blaine, George Cheseboro, Edward Hearn, Tom London, Harry Strang, Lee Shumway, Edmund Cobb, Kernan Cripps, Charles Hamilton, Ethan Laidlaw; *Bradley*, Kane Richmond; *Mr. Lambert*, Edward LeSaint; *Mr. Allen*, Lee Prather; *Gary's Secretary*, Gloria Blondell; *Bit Women*, Cleo Ridgley, Dorothy Vernon, Eva McKenzie, Helen Dixon; *Davey's Mother*, Tina Marshall; *Bit Men*, Harry Bailey, Steve Clark, Stanley Mack, Dan Wolheim; *Drunk*, Nick Copeland; *Postman*, Al Herman; *Driver*, Bud Osborne; *Druggist*, Lester Dorr; *Hick*, Harry Bernard; *Schultz*, Vernon Dent; *Truck Driver*, Jack Long; *Joe*, Buster Slaven; *Referee*, Cy Schindell; *Kid*, George Billings; *Bit Boy*, Reggie Streeter; *Box-Office Boy*, Eddie Brian; *Butler*, Ed Cecil; *Bartender*, Bob Perry; *Reporters*, Reginald Simpson, Sam Ash, Don Reed; *Al*, John Fitzgerald.

NOTES:

Except for some tolerably amusing slang delivered by Frankie Darro and other cast members playing juvenile delinquents (all acting as if they were unaware that Warner Bros. and the Dead End Kids were much more adept at graphic gutter talk), *Juvenile Court*, in spite of its lofty but fictional salute to the Police Athletic League, had little to recommend it since it was treading on very familiar screen territory.

If, however, you are induced to losing sleep and catching a late-night telecast of it, don't be too surprised if it turns out to be a 1932 Capital Films Exchange programmer with Bette Davis and Pat O'Brien which was originally titled *Hell's House*. And although the films have identical themes and titles, and equally sleazy production values, the 1938 *Juvenile Court* is not a remake of the earlier film which played as often under that title as it did its original one!

But what "Hobe." wrote in *Weekly Variety* about the Columbia film, could also have been written about the earlier one:

"It's mostly a rehash of a familiar theme, hurried through the production mill. Nothing of interest in the script, direction or performances—all threadbare stuff."

Paul Kelly, Rita Hayworth, Howard Hickman and Charles Hart attend award presentation to P.A.L. members in climactic moments.

With Tim Holt, Guy Usher, Cecilia Callejo, Lucio Villegas, George O'Brien and Ray Whitley in the climactic scene when the outlaws have all been brought to justice and the immediate future appears to include a wedding.

The Renegade Ranger

An RKO-Radio Picture   1939

Produced by Bert Gilroy. Directed by David Howard. Assistant Director, Sam Ruman. Screenplay by Oliver Drake, based on Bennett Cohen's original story. Photographed by Harry Wild. Musical Direction by Roy Webb. Sound Recording by Hugh McDowell, Jr. Art Direction by Van Nest Polglese and Lucien Croxton. Edited by Frederic Knudtson. 60 minutes.

CAST:

Captain Jack Steele, GEORGE O'BRIEN; *Judith Alvarez,* RITA HAYWORTH; *Larry,* TIM HOLT; *Happy,* Ray Whitley; *Juan,* Lucio Villegas; *Sanderson,* William Royle; *Tonia,* Cecilia Callejo; *Sheriff Rawlings,* Neal Hart; *Monty,* Monte Montague; *Idaho,* Bob Kortman; *Manuel,* Charles Stevens; *Hank,* Jim Mason; *Red,* Tom London; *Major,* Guy Usher.

NOTES:

Beginning with Fox's 1931 remake of *The Rainbow Trail* and concluding with RKO's 1940 *Triple Justice,* David Howard directed western star George O'Brien in two dozen films. Each was a fast-moving, well-scripted hour of action—fisticuffs, fast-and-fancy riding, expert stunt work and horsemanship—and, with only a few notable exceptions, a minimum of distaff diversion.

The Renegade Ranger, one of the exceptions, gave Rita, cast as a sort of female Robin Hood of the Old West, almost as much footage as O'Brien. She proved quite adept at horseback riding and more than adequately able to handle the few dramatic demands of the script. Unlike many actresses who slip into western togs and strap on six-guns, Rita also managed to comport herself with a maximum of feminine charm and remain a very appealing creature quite capable of deal-

Rita Hayworth as a sort of female Robin Hood who has organized homesteaders into a vigilante group to fight off rustlers and politicians preying on them.

ing with tough men in a basically masculine milieu on their own terms.

O'Brien, who has a long list of leading ladies who all appeared in his very successful westerns (Myrna Loy, Cecilia Parker, Linda Watkins, Conchita Montenegro, Maureen O'Sullivan, Claire Trevor, Mary Brian, Irene Hervey, Dorothy Wilson, Irene Ware, Polly Ann Young, Heather Angel, Beatrice Roberts, Constance Worth, Laraine Day [then known as Laraine Johnson], Virginia Vale [formerly known as Dorothy Howe], and Sheila Ryan) said that Rita Hayworth's subsequent superstardom had not surprised him.

During the filming of *The Renegade Ranger,* O'Brien said Rita never failed to ask for advice when she was uncertain about the best way to achieve an effect or that she ever pretended to know more about filmmaking than she actually did. He also said she never assumed the attitude that working in a B western was below her usual standards, as some actresses did in similar situations because they were never exactly in the center of things. O'Brien also said:

"Rita carried herself beautifully. She walked and moved with *such* grace! Cliché though it might be, she was poetry in motion."

Said *Daily Variety:*

"Best of RKO's George O'Brien starrers to date, *The Renegade Ranger* will delight western addicts everywhere. Given an even more elaborate presentation than any of its predecessors, the picture is weighted with values—production and entertainment alike—and will no doubt top bills in the majority of nabes in which it is screened. . . . Rita Hayworth, playing opposite O'Brien, turns in one of the finest femme sagebrush performances seen in a long while. Ideally cast, she displays both acting and riding skill."

Hollywood Reporter said much the same thing:

"The type of picture which has kept George O'Brien one of the top ranking western stars through the years, is here seen at its best, packed with plenty of action, hard riding and thrills that should more than please the western fan. . . . Rita Hayworth, the girl falsely accused of murder, is a pretty eyeful who turns in an endearing performance."

Robert Paige, a crusading newspaper-man, and Bruce Cabot, a tough detective, await Rita Hayworth's findings.

Homicide Bureau

A Columbia Picture   1939

Produced by Jack Frier. Executive Producer, Irving Briskin. Directed by Charles C. Coleman, Jr. Assistant Director, Cliff Broughton. Original Screenplay by Earle Snell. Photographed by Benjamin Kline. Musical Direction by Morris Stoloff. Art Direction Supervised by Stephen Goosson. Edited by James Sweeney. 58 minutes.

CAST:

Jim Logan, BRUCE CABOT; *J. G. Bliss,* RITA HAYWORTH; *Thurston,* ROBERT PAIGE; *Chuck Brown,* MARC LAWRENCE; *Hank,* Richard Fiske; *Captain Haines,* Moroni Olsen; *Briggs,* Norman Willis; *Blake,* Gene Morgan; *Jamison,* Lee Prather; *Specks,* Eddie Fetherston; *Police Commissioner,* Stanley Andrews; *Pool Hall Attendant,* John Tyrell; *Henly,* Charles Trowbridge; *Boat Captain,* George Lloyd; *Nurse,* Ann Doran; *Miller,* Joseph DeStephani; *Stewardess,* Beatrice Curtis; *Bit Woman,* Beatrice Blinn; *Radio Broadcaster,* Dick Curtis; *Police Photographer,* Stanley Brown; *Trigger,* George De Normand; *Joe,* Harry Bernard; *Committee Women,* Nell Craig, Georgie Cooper; *Mug,* Kit

Guard; *Casey,* Ky Robinson; *Policeman,* Dick Rush; *Switchboard Operator,* Lee Shumway; *Gangster,* Lester Dorr; *Committee Man,* Wedgewood Nowell; *Bit Man,* Gene Stone.

NOTES:

Almost devoid of any romantic interest, and giving Rita only very limited footage in a rather thankless role as a lab expert for the police department, *Homicide Bureau* was the last of her Columbia programmers made by the Irving Briskin unit.

Briskin, who started in the industry in 1923 as a sales manager for Banner films, a low B company that also employed his brothers, Samuel and Barney, he moved with them to Sterling Productions and later to Chesterfield Pictures. In the early 1930s the Briskin brothers formed Meteor Pictures and produced the Tim McCoy westerns that Columbia released until 1933 when they bought out Meteor and gave Irving a producer's berth and his own low-budget film unit.

For more than a decade Irving Briskin produced B

films almost uniformly void of distinction but products which always earned back production costs and even showed a profit. His brother Barney worked at Columbia's booking exchange in New York during these years. Irving carried a vault of information in his head and always knew every standing set and prop on the Columbia lot that he could, sometime or other, put to use and he always knew when some technician or other, whose salary was being charged to another production, could do a few hours work for him without his film being charged for the services. He kept track of every Columbia costume that was already charged off to another film that he might use and also had no qualms about instructing his writers to fashion a low-budget film in the same genre as a successful A film, even to the point of copying some of Columbia's better products!

Amiable, and surprisingly well-liked, he was a model producer of the tight-fisted financial school and he used the same bit players and extras over and over in his films because he felt they knew what he was like and knew what was expected of them. Such onetime "names" as Edmund Cobb, Charles Ray, Cleo Ridgley, Lee Shumway, Vernon Dent, Edward LeSaint and Nell Craig, were employed by Briskin on an almost regular

Publicity stills such as this, depicting Miss Hayworth as a policewoman equipped with a snub-nosed .38 revolver, helping detective Bruce Cabot to break up a smuggling ring, have them involved in a scene never used in the film. For that matter, it wasn't even in the script!

basis and minor contract players like Beatrice Curtis, Beatrice Blinn, John Tyrell, Ann Doran, Eddie Fetherston, Lee Prather, Dick Curtis, Bud Osborne, Ruth Hilliard, Edwin Hearn, Harry Strang, Bill Irving and Bud Jamison were considered part of Briskin's personal stock company and any and sometimes all of them would at least have a walk-on or bit in a Briskin B. And everyone associated with the Briskin unit, directors, players, writers and technicians remained in his good graces as long as they followed his one rule that was not to be violated—"Do it in one take."

That policy often resulted in trade papers, such as *Weekly Variety,* saying of films like *Homicide Bureau:*

"Hits new low in cycle of crimewave opuses, with every department of production way below—par for this type of picture."

Bosley Crowther, in *The New York Times* was equally derisive:

"There are limits to what even a professional tolerator can stand. Take, for instance, *Homicide Bureau* (at the Rialto); in our humble opinion, the word 'homicide' in the title is grievous, pettifogging understatement. It's murder, folks, cold-blooded, premeditated murder."

Rita Hayworth as a police laboratory technician known only as "J. G. Bliss."

The Lone Wolf Spy Hunt was the first Columbia film for which Rita Hayworth had a specially designed wardrobe and her own stand-in.

The Lone Wolf Spy Hunt

A Columbia Picture   1939

Associate Producer, Joseph Sistrom. Directed by Peter Godfrey. Assistant Director, Cliff Broughton. Screenplay by Jonathan Latimer, based on Louis Joseph Vance's novel, *The Lone Wolf's Daughter.* Photographed by Allen G. Siegler. Musical Direction by Morris Stoloff. Art Direction by Lionel Banks. Gowns by Kalloch. Edited by Otto Meyer. 67 minutes.

CAST:

Michael Lanyard, WARREN WILLIAM; *Val,* IDA LUPINO; *Karen,* RITA HAYWORTH; *Patricia,* Virginia Weidler; *Spiro,* Ralph Morgan; *Sergeant Devan,* Tom Dugan; *Inspector Thomas,* Don Beddoe; *Jameson,* Leonard Carey; *Jenks,* Ben Welden; *Senator Carson,* Brandon Tynan; *Marie Templeton,* Helen Lynd; *Big Cop,* Irving Bacon; *Little Cop,* Dick Elliott; *Drunk,* Jack Norton; *Waiter,* Marek Windheim; *Marriage License Clerk,* Alec Craig; *Spiro's Henchmen,* Marc Lawrence, Dick Curtis, Lou Davis, John Tyrell; *Guests,* Stanley Brown, Beatrice Curtis, Lola Jensen, James Craig; *Bartender,* Tony Hughes; *Footman,* Eddie Laughton; *Palmer,* Forbes Murray; *Policeman,* James

Blaine; *Evans,* Russ Clark; *Thatcher,* Landers Stevens; *Police Broadcaster,* Lee Phelps; *Fat Man,* Vernon Dent; *Bit Girl,* Lorna Gray;* *Second Bartender,* But Jamison; *Man,* Eddie Fetherston; *Cab Driver,* James Millican; *Police Sergeant,* Edward Hearn; *Police Clerk,* Edmund Cobb; *Doorman,* Frank Baker.

NOTES:

Michael Lanyard, better known as *The Lone Wolf,* was the inspiration of Louis Joseph Vance and the retired safecracker was first featured in a 1914 story published in *Munsey's Magazine.* Films soon discovered the character's appeal and possibilities and by 1939 he had been impersonated on the screen by Thomas Holding, Jack Holt, Bert Lytell and Melvyn Douglas, among others, including Francis Lederer. Columbia starred Warren William in a resurrected series which lasted long after World War II and William's death when Columbia replaced him with Gerald Mohr and then Ron Randell. After that Columbia lost interest in the series and another B studio made a few subsequent films before abandoning the character. Warren William, who had already played Philo Vance and Perry Mason on the screen, was the best *Lone Wolf* of sound films.

    The Lone Wolf Spy Hunt, the only Michael Lanyard adventure to feature, unexplicitly, his daughter, had been filmed twice before, in 1919 and 1929, under its original title, *The Lone Wolf's Daughter.* For the 1939 version, mystery writer Jonathan Latimer updated the plot and substituted international spies for international jewel thieves. *The Lone Wolf Spy Hunt* is also

*Later known as Adrian Booth.

Host and master spy Ralph Morgan, and his sirenish assistant catch Warren William in the act of rifling a safe ostensibly containing stolen government documents.

notable as the first film Rita made which allowed her the luxury of a stand-in (Ellen Duffy).

In their review of it, *Motion Picture Herald* said:

    "Picture hits the level of fundamental slapstick in many spots, but has a moderate amount of laugh content. It's the first picture-directing chore for Peter Godfrey, English stage director who handled *Shadow and Substance,* New York legit presentation. Godfrey is handicapped by the script provided him."

Henchmen Ben Weldon, John Tyrell (top of stairs) and Richard Curtis (on landing) appear to have control of Rita Hayworth and Warren William in this tense scene.

Rita Hayworth and Charles Quigley come face to face with Bill Irving and Vincent McKenna, masterminds of a hijacking racket which preys on unwary truck drivers.

Special Inspector

A Central Film
Distributed by Columbia Pictures   1939

Produced by Kenneth J. Bishop. Directed by Leon Barsha. Assistant Director, George Rhein. Original Screenplay by Edgar Edwards. Photographed by George Meehan. Musical Direction by Morris Stoloff. Art Direction by Lionel Banks. Edited by William Austin. 65 minutes.

CAST:

Tom Evans, CHARLES QUIGLEY; *Patricia Lane,* RITA HAYWORTH; *Silver,* George McKay; *Bill,* Edgar Edwards; *David Foster,* Eddie Laughton; *Dapper,* Bob Rideout; *Skip,* Grant MacDonald; *Pete,* Bill Irving; *Mother Jones,* Virginia Coomb; *Ralph Collins,* Fred Bass; *Hendricks,* Vincent McKenna; *Williams,* Don Douglas.

NOTES:

Two of Rita's Columbia films, *Convicted* and *Special Inspector,* were both scripted by Edgar Edwards, who also played a minor role in each and produced by Kenneth Bishop and distributed as Central Films. This label alerted exhibitors to the fact that these films, made back-to-back, incidentally, were of even poorer quality than those of the Irving Briskin unit, although Briskin was executive producer on the first *(Convicted)*.

Completed late in 1937, *Special Inspector* played in England in 1938 and was released as a "Syndicate Production distributed by Warwick Films." Officially, it never had a release date in the United States!

When it played one downtown Los Angeles theater, co-billed with a reissue of *Old Louisiana,* then retitled *Louisiana Gal,* both films were offered as first-run attractions and ads featured a very glamorous pose of Rita, taken for one of her subsequent films, *Angels over Broadway,* to help exploit this double bill.

An annoyed but nameless critic on the *Los Angeles Mirror* said:

"There's no way I can think of to console myself for having had the misfortune of remaining wide awake during the unreeling of *Special Inspector.* Nobody else in the theater audience seemed to be so unlucky as to be suffering from insomnia."

While working undercover to expose a gang of highway thieves, Edgar Edwards and Charles Quigley encounter Rita Hayworth, a woman with a similar mission, at a highway truck stop.

A surprised Cary Grant discovers that his old flame is now the wife of a disgraced pilot, Richard Barthelmess, to whom he's willing to give a fresh start. Other pilots Allyn Joslyn, John Carroll and James Millican also resent her husband who once panicked during a flight, causing others to lose their lives.

Only Angels Have Wings

A Columbia Picture   1939

Produced and Directed by Howard Hawks. Assistant Director, Arthur Black. Screenplay by Jules Furthman (William Rankin and Eleanore Griffin, uncredited contributors), based on Howard Hawks's original story idea. Photographed by Joseph Walker. Aerial Photography by Elmer Dryer. Original Guitar Solo Music Composed and Conducted by Manuel Maciste. Musical Score and Direction by Morris Stoloff. Art Direction by Lionel Banks. Gowns by Kalloch. Special Effects Created by Roy Davidson and Edward C. Hahn. Technical Advisor and Chief Stunt Pilot Paul Mantz. Edited by Viola Lawrence. (Prints for first-run exhibition processed in Sepia-Tone.) 121 minutes.

CAST:

Geoff Carter, CARY GRANT; *Bonnie Lee,* JEAN ARTHUR; *Bat MacPherson,* RICHARD BARTHELMESS; *Judy MacPherson,* RITA HAYWORTH; *Kid Dabb,* THOMAS MITCHELL; *Les Peters,* Allyn Joslyn; *Dutchy,* Sig Ruman;* *Sparks,* Victor Kilian; *Gent Shelton,* John Carroll; *Tex,* Donald (Don "Red") Barry; *Joe Souther,* Noah Beery, Jr.; *Guitarist,* Manuel Maciste; *Lily,* Melissa Sierra; *Doctor,* Lucio Villegas; *Mike,* Pat Flaherty; *Pancho,* Pedro Regas; *Baldy,* Pat West; *Musician,* Candy Candido; *Mechanics,* Lew Davis, Al Rhein, James Millican, Curly Dresden, Ed Randolph, Ky Robinson, Eddie Foster; *Purser,* Rafael Corio; *Servant,* Charles Moore; *Lily's Aunt,* Inez Palange; *Harkwright, Sr.,* Forbes Murray; *Junior Harkwright,* Stanley Brown; *Cook,* Sam Tong; *Plantation Overseer,* Francisco Maran; *Assistant Purser,* Wilson Benge; *Ship's Captain,* Vernon Dent; *Planter,* Victor Travers; *Banana Foreman,* Jack Lowe; *Second Foreman,* Tex Higginson; *Tourists,* Enrique Acosta, Raoul Lechuga, Dick Botiller, Harry Bailey, Amora Navarro, Tessie Murray.

*Originally known as Siegfried Rumann, and sometimes as Sig Rumann.

With Jean Arthur, James Millican and Allyn Joslyn, awaiting word on the progress of a disabled plane through a tropical storm.

NOTES:

Only Angels Have Wings was one of the two Columbia blockbusters of 1939 ((the other was *Mr. Smith Goes to Washington)* that was as well received critically as it was financially. By prewar Hollywood standards, it was handsomely produced and its rather ordinary process photography and its none-too-original story-line was strengthened considerably by some first-rate dialogue, vigorous direction, superb aerial stunts and photography, and some fine performances—notably by Cary Grant, Sig Ruman, Noah Beery, Jr., and Rita Hayworth. Jean Arthur, a past mistress at affecting movie moues, was too precisely lacquered in the standard star-status mold and much too psychologically vulnerable an actress to be entirely convincing as a kicked-about nightclub entertainer who's been on her own for too many years. (She seemed more like a recent Bryn Mawr graduate chasing last year's football hero.) Thomas Mitchell won a "Best Supporting Actor" Academy Award for his work in 1939's *Stagecoach,* but this time he gave a carefully-thought-out, professionally expert reading of his lines but an otherwise predictable performance as a loyal, always-on-hand friend to hero Cary Grant, who always had a comforting cliché to spout, no matter what the occasion or the emergency. When you watch his performance today, it seems almost impossible to overlook the fact, that is either by coincidence, accident or deliberate direction and interpretation, there are very decided homosexual undertones in his characterization which did not seem apparent to 1939 audiences and critics.

Richard Barthelmess, as the disgraced pilot seeking one last opportunity to redeem himself by working for a shabby, fly-by-night airline always on the verge of bankruptcy, in what was considered his "comeback" role, eschewed all the youthful vitality and boyish charisma first nurtured by D. W. Griffith, which made him one of the truly great stars of the silent screen who also made a successful transition to sound films merely on the strength of his past record. No longer young, or even attempting to act like a man who ever had a youth, Barthelmess, on his own, or in league with director Hawks, played the wash-up, emotionally burned-out man in a deadpan monotone without ever once letting his eyes betray that somewhere in his soul a small spark of optimism still lingered and obsessed him. The human face, especially the eyes, are a mirror of the mind and heart as well as the soul and consequently Barthelmess's uncompromisingly stoic performance never quite comes off. Audiences wanted to be with him all the way, but they never were.

Because neither the script, the director, nor Barthelmess fully understood the existing human condition of the most important and the really only interesting character in the entire film, *Only Angels Have Wings* leaves the viewer full of empty admiration for what was attempted but deeply disappointed for what was not accomplished.

No one, however, even now, can argue over Rita Hayworth's splendid performance. Her role was relatively minor and rather ambiguously conceived but she still managed to play it with a great deal of style and a perception that seemed to be both beyond years and her previous experience. Her graceful, catlike movements, her sheer animal force and even her sleek clothes, which seemed to be a part of her body rather than adornments to it, made her seem every bit as much a primitive creature of the jungle that was always just out of range of the camera in the steamy tropical setting, and just as unpredictable and dangerous. She never made a false move or gesture during her limited screen time as the bride of the disgraced, aging pilot, the woman who had turned the manager of the airline into a misogynist. Even when she was merely in the background of tense moment, a simple and silent gesture, such as slowly moving her hand to her throat, spoke volumes about a woman whose instincts, rather than her heart, tells her she must react to tragedy. And even in scenes when other players appeared to be disregarding her, everyone felt her presence and her silent gestures vibrated the atmosphere. The effect was much like suddenly hearing a harp string plucked at midnight in a dark and silent graveyard.

So here, for the first time, was a Rita Hayworth with a sudden audience identification whose past performances gave no indication that she was capable of delivering a shaded, fully realized characterization in the company of past and current great screen luminaries. Here indeed was the indisputable proof of her capabilities and the fact that she could indeed be manufactured into a top ranking star.

Not too long ago, Cary Grant, making a rare public appearance at a film retrospective, genially answered audience questions put to him about many of his leading ladies. He had kind things to say of most of them and he lamented the fact that he never got an opportunity to work in a comedy with Claudette Colbert, whom he greatly admired and thought of as the screen's most expert comedienne. His other regret, he said, was never co-starring with Rita Hayworth after she become a top star. When asked what type of film he would like to have made with her, he replied:

"One of those big, splashy Technicolor musicals, of course! The idea isn't as ridiculous as it may sound, you know. After all, I started out on stage singing and dancing and who knows, we might have ended up as the Fred Astaire and Ginger Rogers of Columbia!"

For the first time, in 1939, the Academy of Motion Picture Arts and Sciences realized the special importance to film art of special effects and added that category to others they considered worthy of their citations. Thus Roy Davidson and Edward C. Hahn were nominated by the Academy for their special-effects work. The Awards, however, were won by E. H. Hansen and Fred Sersen for their marvelous achievements with *The Rains Came.*

The *Motion Picture Herald,* in their review of *Only Angels Have Wings* said:

"Seldom if ever have such thrills of aviation been shown on the screen; seldom if ever have such characterizations been blended in a story that have equal spectacle, comedy, feeling."

Frank S. Nugent, in *The New York Times,* said:

"Mr. Hawks has staged his flying sequences brilliantly. He has caught the drama in the meeting of the flier and the brother of the man he killed. He has made proper use of the amiable performing talents. . . . But when you add it all up, *Only Angels Have Wings* comes to an overly familiar total. It's a fairly good melodrama, nothing more."

With Sig Ruman, Cary Grant, Thomas Mitchell, John Carroll and Pedro Regas.

With Tony Martin.

Music in My Heart

A Columbia Picture   1940

Produced by Irving Starr. Directed by Joseph Santley. Assistant Director, Gene Anderson. Screenplay by James Edward Grant, based on his original story, "Passport to Happiness." Photographed by John Stumar. Songs: "I've Got Music in My Heart," "Punchinello," "Oh, What a Lovely Dream," "No Other Love," "Hearts in the Sky," "Prelude to Love" and "It's a Blue World," by Chet Forrest and Bob Wright. Musical Arrangements and Direction by Morris Stoloff. Vocal Arrangements by Charles Henderson. Art Direction by Lionel Banks. Gowns by Kalloch. Dialogue Director, William Castle. Sound Engineer, George Cooper. Edited by Otto Meyer. 70 minutes.

CAST:

Robert Gregory, TONY MARTIN; *Patricia O'Malley,* RITA HAYWORTH; *Mary O'Malley,* EDITH FELLOWS; *Charles Gardner,* ALAN MOWBRAY; *Griggs,* ERIC BLORE; *Sascha,* GEORGE TOBIAS; *Mark G. Gilman,* Joseph Crehan; *Luigi,* George Humbert; *Miller,* Joey Ray; *Taxi Driver,* Don Beddoe; *Leading Lady,* Julieta Novis; *Blake,* Eddie Kane; *Marshall,* Phil Tead; *Barrett,* Marten Lamont; *Themselves,* ANDRE KOSTELANETZ and His Orchestra.

NOTES:

In case you've never seen *Music in My Heart,* the plot is that well-roasted chestnut about boy meeting girl when their taxis collide as each is on the way to an important destination and their detainment, of course, changes their destinies.

The Chet Forrest–Bob Wright song "It's A Blue World" was nominated for an Academy Award (losing to "When You Wish Upon A Star") and has since become a standard of sorts. There is little else of note about *Music in My Heart,* one of those curious films a cut above the average B product which belongs to a genre studios once referred to as "Shaky A's" but which reviewers usually distinguished as programmers. Another trivial note is that André Kostelanetz had his own CBS radio program when the film was released and received a few radio plugs. The picture also plugged the CBS network, an unusual practice in those years since Hollywood considered radio, rather than the stage, its most menacing competitor and the Motion Picture Association Production Code was strongly opposed to actual companies or actual products being shown or otherwise advertised in films.

Columbia's juvenile actress, Edith Fellows, who first attracted attention in Bing Crosby's *Pennies from Heaven,* never achieved the stardom or acclaim that catapulted Universal's Deanna Durbin and MGM's Judy Garland to the topmost height of film stardom. A pleasant, freckle-faced girl with a small but rather infectious singing voice, she was an accomplished actress who lacked that indefinable spark that is so necessary to sustain audience interest whenever the success of a film rested on her small shoulders. After *Pennies from Heaven,* her best film, her chances of genuine stardom became even more remote as the quality of all her subsequent films declined.

Tony Martin, in films a long time before 20th Century-Fox started to promote him in the mid-1930s, was once married to Alice Faye, when she reigned as that studio's top musical star. Just before World War II, Martin became a prominent recording star and nightclub attraction and, after the war, married Cyd Charisse. A veteran of many films, he never achieved screen stardom or even the recognition he seemed to deserve although he has maintained a very high status as a top nightclub attraction over the years. His best screen role, probably, was playing Pepe Le Moko in *Casbah,* the musical remake of *Algiers.*

The first Columbia musical to feature Rita, *Music in My Heart* gave her one dance, none too well staged or photographed.

With Tony Martin.

In *The New York Times,* Bosley Crowther said:

"The only thing which keeps us from remarking that *Music in My Heart* fills a long-felt need is the bare possibility that no one in particular has ever felt any particular need for such a union of musical comedy and conventional, low-budgeted cinema as Columbia's current exhibit presupposes."

And *Weekly Variety* predicted:

"Music in My Heart won't ring a particularly happy tune on the exhibitor's cash register. Plot is trite, threadworn affair which neither the direction nor the performances of the two leads and André Kostelanetz's superb music can overcome."

With Alan Mowbray.

Blondie on a Budget

A Columbia Picture   1940

Produced by Robert Sparks. Directed by Frank R. Strayer. Screenplay by Richard Flournoy, based on an original Charles Molyneaux Brown story and the Chic Young cartoon characters copyrighted by King Features. Photographed by Henry Freulich. Musical Direction by Morris Stoloff. Art Direction by Lionel Banks. Costumes Supervised by Ray Howell. Edited by Gene Havlick. 73 minutes.

CAST:

Blondie Bumstead, PENNY SINGLETON; *Dagwood*, ARTHUR LAKE; *Joan Forrester*, RITA HAYWORTH; *Baby Dumpling*, Larry Simms; *Alvin Fuddle*, Danny Mummert; *Marvin Williams*, Don Beddoe; *Mr. Fuddle*, John Qualen; *Mrs. Fuddle*, Fay Helm; *Mailman*, Irving Bacon; *Brice*, Thurston Hall; *Theatre Manager*, William Brisbane; *Usherettes*, Janet Shaw, Claire James; *Dempsey*, Emory Parnell; *Delivery Boy*, Willie Best; *Bank Teller*, Hal K. Dawson; *Mechanic*, Dick Curtis; *Platt*, George Guhl; *Saleswomen*, Mary Currier, Rita Owin; *Customer*, Gene Morgan; *Bartender*, Ralph Peters.

Penny Singleton feigns delight at meeting husband Arthur Lake's former flame.

Arthur Lake accompanies his former sweetheart on a shopping spree.

NOTES:

Chis Young's cartoon creation *Blondie* was the inspiration for Columbia Pictures's longest-running film series. Beginning with the initial film, simply called *Blondie,* released in 1938, there were twenty-eight entries in the series which concluded in 1950 with Penny Singleton and Arthur Lake featured in all of them. In a few of the early entries Columbia occasionally showcased budding stars (Glenn Ford, Larry Parks, et al.) in guest roles. *It's A Great Life* and *Footlight Glamour,* both released in 1943, are the only two films in the series which did not use the cartoon-strip heroine's name in the title.

Of this, the fifth entry, *Photoplay* said:

"Blondie's yen for a fur jacket and Dagwood's desire to join a trout club he can't afford are hardly important enough problems to make you care. *Blondie* budgets, and Dagwood has his worries because an old girlfriend, of whom his wife is jealous, comes to town, and Baby Dumpling giggles engagingly, and that's all there is. Penny Singleton, Arthur Lake, Rita Hayworth and Larry Simms do what there is to do."

With Arthur Lake, Penny Singleton, Larry Simms, Larry Nunn and Daisy.

Rita, married to an older man, appears to be succumbing to the charms of another weekend guest, John Carroll.

Susan and God

A Metro-Goldwyn-Mayer Picture   1940

Produced by Hunt Stromberg. Directed by George Cukor. Assistant Director, Edward Woehler. Screenplay by Anita Loos, based on Rachel Crothers's play, produced on stage by John Golden. Photographed by Robert Planck. Musical Score by Herbert Stothart. Art Direction by Cedric Gibbons. Set Decorations by Edwin B. Willis. Gowns by Adrian. Hair Styles by Sidney Guilaroff. Sound Recording Engineer, Douglas Shearer. Edited by William H. Terhune. 117 minutes.

CAST:

Susan Trexel, JOAN CRAWFORD; *Barrie Trexel*, FREDRIC MARCH; *Charlotte Marley*, RUTH HUSSEY; *Clyde Rochester*, JOHN CARROLL; *Leonora Stubbs*, RITA HAYWORTH; *Hutchins Stubbs*, NIGEL BRUCE; *Michael O'Hara*, BRUCE CABOT; *Blossom Trexel*, Rita Quigley; *Irene Burroughs*, Rose Hobart; *Lady Wigstaff*, Constance Collier; *Enid*, Gloria DeHaven; *Bob*, Richard Crane; *Paige*, Norma Mitchell; *Mary*, Marjorie Main; *Patrick*, Aldrich Bowker.

NOTES:

Susan and God is a perfect example of how MGM, in the golden prewar movie days, could take a successful stage play designed for the talents of a very specialized star (in this case, Gertrude Lawrence), and turn it into a monumentally miscast, elaborately produced prestige film which, by the sheer vulgarity of its riches, becomes an artificial and blindingly glossy travesty of the original. And whenever you encountered such an MGM screen specter, all you could do was marvel at how gloriously ghastly the whole thing was.

Blessed with such dubious distinctions, *Susan and God* caused most filmgoers, except the Crawford claque (*mental* spinsters of all ages, social status and gender) to look elsewhere in the film for virtues. What few to be had were very good performances by the supporting players—notably Rose Hobart, Ruth Hussey, Rita Hayworth, Bruce Cabot, Nigel Bruce and Marjorie Main—and a set for a Long Island summer estate designed by Cedric Gibbons.

With Nigel Bruce, Joan Crawford and John Carroll.

With Joan Crawford, John Carroll and Nigel Bruce.

Bosley Crowther, in *The New York Times,* said:

"The whole picture drifts away in a cloud of sentiment and melancholy. Nor does Miss Crawford do much to give it the essence of life. Although she obviously imitates the mannerisms and vocal gymnastics of Gertrude Lawrence, who played the original Susan in the Rachel Crothers play, she lacks her predecessor's rich and abundant vitality in creating an eccentric character, and Mr. March is strangely listless in an aggravating role."

And *Time* magazine reported:

"*Susan and God* (MGM) explores the situation that develops when a giddy Long Island matron takes up with something resembling Dr. Frank Buchman's Oxford brand of confessional Christianity, tries hard to talk her husband and friends into it and to death.

"In the latter enterprise Joan Crawford at first comes too close to succeeding."

In her first film with Glenn Ford, when neither of them had any inkling that in subsequent films they would be regarded as one of the screen's great romantic teams.

The Lady in Question

A Columbia Picture   1940

Produced by B. B. Kahane. Directed by Charles Vidor. Assistant Director, Charles C. Coleman, Jr. Screenplay by Lewis Meltzer, based on the H. G. Lustig and Marcel Archard screenplay, *Gribouille,* produced by André Daven for Tri-National Films (France). Photographed by Lucien Androit. Musical Score by Lucien Moraweek. Musical Direction by Morris Stoloff. Chief Sound Engineer, John Livadary. Art Direction by Lionel Banks. Costume Supervision by Ray Howell. Gowns by Kalloch. Makeup Supervision by William Knight. Edited by Al Clark. 77 minutes.

CAST:

André Morestan, BRIAN AHERNE; *Natalie Rouguin,* RITA HAYWORTH; *Pierre,* GLENN FORD; *Michele Morestan,* IRENE RICH; *Defense Attorney,* GEORGE COULOURIS; *Prosecuting Attorney,* Lloyd Corrigan; *Francoise Morestan,* Evelyn Keyes; *Robert LaCoste,* Edward Norris; *Henri Lurette,* Curt Bois; *President,* Frank Reicher; *Fat Boy,* Sumner Getchell; *Nicholas Farkas,* Nicholas Bela; *Marinier,* William Stack; *Antoinette,* Dorothy Burgess; *Guards,* Hamilton Mac Fadden, Allen Marlow; *Second Judge,* Julius Tannen; *Nathalie Roguin,* Fern Emmett; *Wine Salesman,* James B. Carson; *Jurors,* Jack Rice, Harrison Greene, William Castle, Frank Hilliard, Carlton Griffin, Ronald Alexander, Alexander Palasthy, Ted Lorch, Frank Pharr; *Alternate Juror,* Fred Rapport; *Court Clerk,* Louis Aldon; *Miss Morlet,* Mary Bovard; *Flower Woman,* Emma Tansey; *Pedestrian,* Ralph Peters; *Customer,* George Davis; *Barber,* Leon Belasco; *Bit Man,* Eddie Laughton; *Expressman,* Jack Raymond; *Gendarme,* Vernon Dent.

NOTES:

Originally previewed as *It Happened in Paris,* which

Bicycle shop owner Brian Aherne (center) introduces his new shop assistant to his son, Glenn Ford, neglecting to tell him that she has just been acquitted in a murder case on which he served as a juror.

was quickly changed to *The Lady in Question* to dispel any idea that the film might be a war story, this another of those "Shaky A's" which proved stable enough to be offered to theater exhibitors for prime playdates. Critically liked, the public also supported it and *The Lady*

in Question now rates prime time television showings.

There's a good basis for its success as it has a very solid foundation: being a remake of Marc Allegret's excellent French film *Gribouille* (1938), which played U.S. theaters as *Heart of Paris* in 1939.

Brian Aherne and Rita had the roles originated by Raimu and Michele Morgan. (It was the rave reviews for Miss Morgan's performances in *Gribouille* and another excellent French film, *Port of Shadows,* which brought her to the attention of Hollywood and, in 1940, resulted in her being signed to a contract by RKO.) At the time *The Lady in Question* was released, it unquestionably contained Rita's best screen role to date—and her best performance. It's also notable as the first film that paired her romantically with Glenn Ford, the very likable actor she subsequently co-starred with in *Gilda, The Loves of Carmen* and *Affair in Trinidad,* and years later reunited with in *The Money Trap.* Curiously enough, Rita and Ford almost appeared together in an earlier Columbia quickie, *Convicted Woman,* but Rita was replaced in that film by Rochelle Hudson when she was summoned to MGM to make *Susan and God.*

Rita and Ford have remained friends and are actually neighbors in Beverly Hills. As a romantic team they generated the same kind of screen chemistry other well-known cinema duos (such as Powell and Loy, Astaire and Rogers, Gable and Harlow, MacDonald and Eddy, Bogart and Bacall, Ladd and Lake, Tracy and Hepburn, and others also sparked to the delight and well recalled pleasure of old-time filmgoers.

Murder defendant Rita listens intently as her defense attorney, George Coulouris, makes a plea on her behalf to a French court.

Listening as the court returns a "not guilty" verdict.

Brian Aherne, one of the screen's most consistently dependable romantic actors of the 1930s in England and the United States, specifically requested the character role he played in *The Lady in Question* and although the previous year he had been nominated for a "Best Supporting Actor" Academy Award (for *Juarez),* for years he maintained his role as André Morestan as his favorite part and his most self-satisfying screen work. Aherne recently said no subsequent film assignment has ever caused him to change his mind.

"After I got into the swing of creating that bourgeois father," Aherne said in one of "The Role I Liked Best" series that ran in the *Saturday Evening Post* magazine, "living his nature and working it out through the tortuous path of the story, it proved more stimulating than any other role that ever came my way."

A four-minute flashback sequence, narrated by a taxi driver, was in the film when it played first run but it was deleted when the film went into national release, accounting for the four-minute discrepancy which appears in various reference books of the film's correct running time.

In *Motion Picture Daily,* Edward Greif said:

"A domestic comedy of rare charm and graced with performances of unusual understanding . . . the film is distinguished by a fine portrayal of casual habits of ordinary people."

Showman's Trade Review said:

"Distinguished performances are turned in by Brian Aherne and Rita Hayworth. Aherne has never been

seen to better advantage while the lovely Miss Hayworth again proves she is a talented actress."

Photoplay magazine was also enthusiastic:

"Although nothing much seems to happen in this beautifully directed picture, the fine performances of its cast and its purely middle-class background make it well worth your while."

An additional note of interest, especially for cinema buffs, is that in the cast of *The Lady in Question,* in bit roles, were Hamilton MacFadden, who had formerly been a well-known film director, and William Castle, who would eventually become a film director best known for his horror films.

With Evelyn Keyes, Edward Norris, Brian Aherne, Irene Rich and Glenn Ford.

In the first of her really alluring poses.

Angels over Broadway

A Columbia Picture   1940

Produced by Ben Hecht. Associate Producer, Douglas Fairbanks, Jr. Co-directed by Ben Hecht and Lee Garmes. Assistant Director, Cliff Broughton. Original Screenplay by Ben Hecht. Photographed by Lee Garmes. Musical Score Composed and Arranged by George Antheil. Musical Direction by Morris Stoloff. Art Direction by Lionel Banks. Costume Supervision by Ray Howell. Gowns by Kalloch. Makeup Supervision by William Knight. Sound Engineer, John Livadary. Edited by Gene Havlick. 78 minutes.

CAST:

Bill O'Brien, DOUGLAS FAIRBANKS, JR.; *Nina Barona,* RITA HAYWORTH; *Gene Gibbons,* THOMAS MITCHELL; *Charles Engle,* JOHN QUALEN; *Hopper,* George Watts; *Dutch Enright,* Ralph Theodore; *Eddie Burns,* Jack Roper; *Sylvia Marbe,* Constance Worth; *Sylvia's Escort,* Richard Bond; *Joe,* Frank Conlan; *Rennick,* Walter Baldwin; *Tony,* Jack Carr; *Jack,* Al Seymour; *Pawn Shop Proprietor,* Jimmy Conlin; *Cigarette Girl,* Ethelreda Leopold; *Headwaiter,* Edward Earle; *Miss Karpin,* Catherine Courtney; *Gamblers,* Al Rhein, Jerry Jerome, Roger Gray, Harry Strang; *Doorman,* Bill Lally; *Checkroom Boy,* Tommy Dixon; *Hugo,* Fred Sweeney; *Dancer,* Carmen D'Antonio; *Master of Ceremonies,* Stanley Brown; *Waiter,* Carlton Griffin; *Court Clerk,* Henry Antrim; *Police Lieutenant,* Lee Phelps; *Large Woman,* Blanche Payson; *Cab Driver,* John Tyrell; *Street Walker,* Caroline Frasher; *Taxi Driver,* Billy Wayne; *Night Court Judge,* Art Howard; *Lunch Wagon Counterman,* Walter Sande; *Bit Girl,* Patricia Maier.

NOTES:

Angels over Broadway (originally previewed under the title *Before I Die)* is a somber, symbolic drama of extraordinary power, almost lavish in its bare-boned simplicity of plot and settings; job-like in its sincerity of purpose. Because of this, critics who unstintingly raved about it while doubting its box-office appeal also damned it with the praise of being "ahead of its time." And the reviewers most guilty of this were those who continuously denigrated the usual Hollywood formula film with claims that the public could and would support films with thoughtful adult themes above the comprehension of a twelve-year-old mind.

Preceding *Citizen Kane* into theaters by almost a year and a half, *Angels over Broadway* was also a very personal production which Ben Hecht was allowed to create without studio interference. While in production, it caused almost as much talk around Hollywood as the Orson Welles film generated during its closed-door filming. Unlike *Citizen Kane,* however, most people ignored it when they finally had the chance to see it. *(Citizen Kane* was *not* the financial disaster that RKO purported it to be after its original release.) *Angels over Broadway,* however, is still the film that marked Hollywood's prewar "coming of age" so to speak, and deserves recognition for everything it attempted and succeeded in saying and doing and not disparagement for its minor flaws or being a financial failure.

Angels over Broadway was Douglas Fairbanks, Jr.'s first producing effort and cinematographer Lee Garmes's first directorial efforts although neither Ben Hecht nor Columbia studios were prepared to acknowledge his contribution without arbitration. And Thomas Mitchell, an actor who could be as boring as often as he was beguiling, proved himself worthy of being an Academy Award-winning character actor by giving what is surely his best screen performance. As the dipsomaniac playwright with a penchant for playing God, he also delivered some of Ben Hecht's most implacably chilling lines with brilliance: "Dismiss your hearse. Live—little man—live and suffer!" "You have carried the realm of singlemindedness beyond fascination," "Omnipotence often needs a little support," and "Some people must work very hard to avoid redemption."

Instead of giving *Angels over Broadway* the arthouse circuit distribution it rightly deserved, Columbia opted to open it on Broadway at the old Globe Theater, a house that usually screened crime melodramas of predictable plots for a very faithful coterie. Needless to say, Columbia's advertising campaign was designed to appeal to that type of audience and it naturally did very

With Douglas Fairbanks, Jr.

little commercially during its first-run engagement and only slightly better on the neighborhood theater circuits where, reduced to the lower half of a double bill, a word-of-mouth campaign helped a few discerning filmgoers to seek it out. In the middle of 1941, a Greenwich Village theater co-billed it with *The Lady in Question* and it played there ten weeks despite a lurid newspaper and lobby advertising campaign which invited all comers to "See How Rita Hayworth—*The Strawberry Blonde*—Handles Both Sides of the Underworld!" In 1949, when all studios reissued many of their films, just prior to a bulk television sale, Columbia included *Angels over Broadway* in the mistaken belief that perhaps its time had come.

With Douglas Fairbanks, Jr.

Besides the critics, and the smattering of people who did see *Angels over Broadway,* enough Motion Picture Academy members admired it so that it won a "Best Original Screenplay" nomination for Ben Hecht. But after the votes were counted, it turned out that Preston Sturges won that award that year for his delightful screenplay for *The Great McGinty.*

In *The New York Times,* Theodore Strauss said:

"As the writer, director and producer, Mr. Hecht has taken the opportunity to reaffirm the fact that drama is created out of people and not out of a warehouseful of props and sets. From the haphazard conjunction of a small handful of lonely and widely separated characters on a single rainy night in New York, he has wrought a melodramatic fantasy that is mordant, tender and quixotic, shot with ironic humor. If it is not the best work that Mr. Hecht has done for the screen, certainly it is the most satisfying of his work that we have seen. . . . Douglas Fairbanks, Jr. is vigorous and amazingly true as the contradictory young man 'on the make,' and Rita Hayworth and John Qualen both respond sensitively to the demands of the script. And as for the shrewd designer—bravo Mr. Hecht!"

And the *Hollywood Reporter* said:

"A strangely compelling drama of shadowy seams in the background of Broadway's nocturnal glitter, marked for its brilliant interpretation of a brilliant script, *Angels over Broadway* is so far off the beaten track that it fits into none of Hollywood's formulized categories. . . . As the playwright *deus ex machina,* Thomas Mitchell gives a tremendous performance, an unforgettable portrait of Academy Award caliber. Douglas Fairbanks, Jr., offers probably the finest portrayal of his career, while John Qualen is superfine as the would-be suicide. Rita Hayworth is outstanding in the most exacting role she has essayed. . . . It is a distinctive work, worthy of a large audience. Nevertheless, its box-office future is a question. Because of its entire nature, it is a picture which will need distinct exploitation."

In *The New Republic,* Otis Ferguson said:

"The encouraging thing about a picture like this, with its absence of epic and a cast of thousands, is that it is like a carpenter puttering around in his own shop. Men who can learn the ropes and get into Hecht's position can do as much for movies as anybody; there is still the opportunity for opening windows and letting the air in— a vital thing in this magnificent and terrible industry, even if it is only hot air. If you don't need encouragement but only a way to spend an evening, why that's here too. In movies, if stern yearners would someday realize it, that has to be here too. . . .

"Accepting this and not asking for more, you will find the picture pretty good fun, for the talk *is* bright and the various complications well devised—the poker game, in fact, is a first-rate movie sequence all around. Thomas Mitchell as the genial has-been and ham Good Fairy steals the show; the part is juicy, but beyond that he is a character of weight and address and rolling periods with humor and sensitive perception under that."

With Jimmy Conlin and Douglas Fairbanks, Jr.

James Cagney, Billy Newell, Jack Carson, George Tobias, Edward Mc-Namara, and Tim Ryan ogle the neighborhood flirt as she passes the local saloon.

The Strawberry Blonde

A Warner Bros.–First National Picture   1941

Produced by Hal B. Wallis. Associate Producer, William Cagney. Directed by Raoul Walsh. Assistant Director, Russ Sanders. Screenplay by Julius J. and Philip G. Epstein, based on James Hagan's play, *One Sunday Afternoon*. Photographed by James Wong Howe. Special Effects by Willard Van Enger. Original Musical Score by Heinz Roemheld. Musical Arrangements and Direction by Leo F. Forbstein. Orchestral Song Arrangements by Ray Heindorf. Sound Recording by Robert B. Lee. Art Direction by Robert Haas. Makeup Supervision by Perc Westmore. Gowns by Orry-Kelly. Dialogue Director, Hugh Cummings. Executive in Charge of Production, Jack L. Warner. Edited by William Holmes. 98 minutes.

CAST:

Biff Grimes, JAMES CAGNEY; *Amy Lind,* OLIVIA DE HAVILLAND; *Virginia Brush,* RITA HAYWORTH; *Old Man Grimes,* ALAN HALE; *Nick Pappalas,* GEORGE TOBIAS; *Hugo Barnstead,* JACK CARSON; *Mrs. Mulcahey,* Una O'Connor; *Harold,* George Reeves; *Harold's Girl,* Lucille Fairbanks; *Big Joe,* Edward McNamarra; *Toby,* Herbert Heywood; *Josephine,* Helen Lynd; *Young Man,* Peter Ashley; *Woman,* Dorothy Vaughan; *Bank President,* Roy Gordon; *Street Cleaners,* Tim Ryan *(Foreman),* Eddy Chandler, Jack Mower, David Thursby, John Sheehan; *Official,* Addison Richards; *Policemen,* Frank Mayo, Max Hoffman, Jr., Pat Flaherty; *Girls,* Suzanne Carnahan,* Peggy Diggins; *Bartender,* Jack Daly; Sweethearts, Ann Edmonds, Margaret Carthew; *Swains,* Dick Wessel, Billy Newell, Frank Melton, Harry Seymour, Herbert Anderson, Paul Phillips, Richard Clayton; *Baxter,* Frank Orth; *Inspector,* James Flavin; *Sailor,* George Campeau; *Singer,* Abe Dinovitch; *Guiseppi,* George Humbert; *Secretary,* Creighton Hale; *Workman,* Carl Harbaugh; *Nurse,* Lucia Carroll; *Treadway,* Russell Hicks; *Warden,* Wade Boteler; *Hangers-On,* Bob Perry, Harrison Greene.

NOTES:

Replete with period costumes and sets, a half dozen or so nostalgic songs, sung mostly in barbershop quartet style, *The Strawberry Blonde,* a gay, leisurely paced, comedy-drama, found a most welcome reception from critics and the public during the months just preceding the attack on Pearl Harbor.

Rita Hayworth was a last-minute cast addition, replacing Warners's Oomph-Girl, Ann Sheridan, who went on suspension fighting for better and bigger roles, fewer films (in 1941 she simultaneously filmed *Kings Row* during the day and did her role in *The Man Who Came to Dinner* at night plus two other programmers, *Honey-*

*Later known as Susan Peters.

With James Cagney, George Tobias and Jack Carson.

moon for Three and Navy Blues) and a better salary just as *The Strawberry Blonde* was ready to commence filming. Needing a replacement for the justifiably rebellious Miss Sheridan, with comparable box-office appeal and, hopefully, a figure comparable to hers, so the actress who assumed the role could wear the costumes already created, Jack L. Warner happily made Rita his choice, much to the pleasure of Harry Cohn. Instead of creating the expected feud between the stars that gossip

columnists anticipated, the arrangement turned out advantageously for both. Rita got her best role and the best picture of her career to date, and Miss Sheridan got to do *Kings Row* as her next film—the one that contains her all-time best screen performance.

During the filming of *The Strawberry Blonde* there was a feud, however, and it started when James Cagney accused Olivia de Havilland of making attempts to upstage him in their scenes together and do some flagrant scene stealing in the footage she shared with Rita. As a consequence, Cagney saw to it that some of Miss de Havilland's footage was reshot, that her part was slightly trimmed down and Rita given some additional footage. The conflict was of short duration and Cagney later went on record as praising "Livy's" performance, claiming it was one of her best. Miss de Havilland, who was soon to become enmeshed in her own conflict with Warners, has subsequently said only kind things about Cagney and on more than one occasion voiced regret that they never again worked together in a film.

None of these production difficulties showed on the screen when *The Strawberry Blonde* was released and filmgoers were much more pleased with this version of James Hagan's play, *One Sunday Afternoon,* than they had been with the version Paramount released in 1933 with Gary Cooper, or the subsequent musical remake Warners released in 1948 with Dennis Morgan. Beside the excellent public and critical reception of *The Strawberry Blonde,* the Motion Picture Academy added another new category to list of deserving film artists, "Best Musical Scoring," and Heinz Roemheld won a nomination although the Award went to Frank Churchill and Oliver Wallace (for *Dumbo).* Of equal note is the fact

With Jack Carson, James Cagney, Olivia deHavilland and Herbert Heywood after a dinner of spaghetti and meatballs — the current rage of the smart set!

that another of Rita's films, Columbia's *You'll Never Get Rich*, also won a "Best Scoring" nomination for Morris Stoloff.

Another interesting fact is that playwright James Hagan had tried unsuccessfully to sell Paramount his play as a potential movie for a few hundred dollars. After it opened on Broadway and became a hit, Paramount had to pay over $26,000 for the screen rights! Jack L. Warner never divulged how much he paid Paramount for the property but apparently he made a packet on the deal because the *Hollywood Reporter* said:

"*The Strawberry Blonde* comes to the screen as a considerably lighter version of James Hagan's stage play, *One Sunday Afternoon*, than its previous film translation and, on the whole, is pleasing entertainment. Few, if any, pictures ever have aimed for such elaborate emphasis upon the Gay Nineties atmosphere, nor presented it more effectively in pictorial effect, music and dialogue. In this respect, it is a particularly distinctive effort.... James Cagney is at his best as the dentist, excellent in both comedy and serious scenes. As the girl who marries him, Olivia de Havilland gives a brilliant portrayal which will rank as one of the best of her screen career, particularly notable for its subtle shadings. Closely rivaling them, Jack Carson gives a scintillating performance as the egotistic heel in the case. Rita Hayworth is attractive as the self-centered heartbreaker who gives the picture its name."

And *Weekly Variety* raved:

"Rita Hayworth, in the role of the mercenary flirt who plays Cagney and his pal and business associate,

With Olivia deHavilland, James Cagney and Jack Carson.

Jack Carson, off against each other and is generally a heartless wench, blossoms like a rose. Stunning costumes of the period and gorgeously photographed, she gives her role a vivid quality and her personality a showcasing which will enormously increase her importance."

In *The New York Times*, Bosley Crowther chortled:

"Rita Hayworth makes a classic 'flirt' of the one who got away."

With James Cagney.

With Dennis Morgan.

Affectionately Yours

A Warner Bros.–First National Picture   1941

Produced by Hal B. Wallis. Associate Producer, Mark Hellinger. Directed by Lloyd Bacon. Assistant Director, Dick Maybery. Screenplay by Edward Kaufman, based on a story by Fanya Foss and Aleen Leslie. Photographed by Tony Gaudio. Musical Score by Heinz Roemheld. Musical Direction by Leo F. Forbstein. Orchestral Arrangements by Ray Heindorf. Art Direction by Anton Grot. Gowns by Orry-Kelly. Makeup Supervision by Perc Westmore. Executive in Charge of Production, Jack L. Warner. Edited by Owen Marks. 90 minutes.

CAST:

Sue Mayberry, MERLE OBERON; *Richard Mayberry,* DENNIS MORGAN; *Irene Malcolm,* RITA HAYWORTH; *Owen Wright,* RALPH BELLAMY; *Pasha,* GEORGE TOBIAS; *Chester Phillips,* JAMES GLEASON; Queen; *Cullen,* Jerome Cowan; *Mrs. Snell,* Renie Riano; *Tom,* Frank Wilcox; *Miss Anderson,* Grace Stafford; *Harmon,* Pat Flaherty; *Blair,* Murray Alper; *Matthews,* William Haade; *Tomasetti,* James Flavin; *Anita,* Carmen Morales; *Anita's Escort,* George Meeker; *Portuguese,* Antonio Filauri; *Barmaid,* Irene Colman; *Airline Attendant,* De Wolfe Hopper; *Ambulance Driver,* Frank Faylen; *Field Guard,* Garrett Craig; *Airline Officials,* Craig Stevens, Keith Douglas; *Delicatessen Proprietor,* Nat Carr; *Taxi Driver,* Fred Graham; *Copy Boy,* Ed Brian; *Stenographer,* Ann Edmonds; *City Editor,* Charles Marsh; *Bell Captain,* Billy Wayne; *Judge,* Wedgwood Nowell; *Guests,* Peggy Diggins, Alexis Smith; *Traffic Cop,* Edward Gargan; *Hospital Attendant,* Dorothy Adams; *Little Boy,* Henry Blair; *Intern,* Charles Drake; *Nurse,* Faye Emerson; *Mrs. Collins,* Mary Field; *Second Taxi Driver,* Gary Owen.

NOTES:

Because Columbia had no immediate plans for Rita's services she remained on loan-out to Warners to play the secondary feminine lead in this comedy. But whatever luster *The Strawberry Blonde* added to her box-office stature, this silly comedy could well have diminished. Aside from the fact that *Affectionately Yours* once again teamed Hattie McDaniel and Butterfly McQueen (of *Gone With the Wind* fame), as marvelously amusing domestics and that such future luminaries as Faye Emerson, Craig Stevens and Alexis Smith had extra roles, this comedy merely proved what an impossible task it is to make something of a very bad script, with all the assets of a major studio and the resources of a very talented and likable cast.

Rita, taking a decided second place to Merle Oberon with less footage and nothing glamorous in the way of a wardrobe, actually came off better by the simple default of having very little to do. Consequently, Miss Oberon was required to engage in too many slapstick jokes,

take too many pratfalls and try to bring off too many bits of "cute" business, none of which was exactly her forte.

Bosley Crowther, in *The New York Times,* said:

"A good three years after the vogue for screwball comedy has passed its zenith, the Burbank Brothers have very laboriously knocked a couple of empty heads together and struck off this pitiful imitation of frivolity more dull than lead—and heavier . . . To hold the players in any way responsible for the shabbiness imposed by the wretched script and the ponderous direction of Lloyd Bacon would be grossly unfair."

And *Weekly Variety* reported:

"In trying to make the picture light and funny, director Lloyd Bacon lands in a field of corn and boredom . . . Rita Hayworth, as the newspaperwoman in love with Morgan, is by far the best of the cast."

With Ralph Bellamy, Merle Oberon and Dennis Morgan.

With Tyrone Power.

Blood and Sand

A 20th Century-Fox Picture   1941

Produced by Darryl F. Zanuck. Associate Producer, Robert T. Kane. Directed by Rouben Mamoulian. Assistant Director, Sidney Bowen. Screenplay by Jo Swerling, based on the novel by Vicenté Blasco Ebáñez. Photographed in Technicolor by Ernest Palmer and Ray Rennahan. Director for the Technicolor Company, Natalie Kalmus; Associate, Morgan Padelford. Technical Advisor, Budd Boetticher. Musical Score, Direction and Supervision by Alfred Newman. Guitar Solos by Vicenté Gomez. Sound Recording by W. D. Flick and Roger Heman. Art Direction by Richard Day and Joseph C. Wright. Set Decorations by Thomas Little. Costumes by Travis Banton. Jewelry by Flato. Miss Hayworth's Vocal dubbed by Graciela Párranga. Edited by Robert Bischoff. 123 minutes.

CAST:

Juan Gallardo, TYRONE POWER; *Carmen Espinosa,* LINDA DARNELL; *Doña Sol,* RITA HAYWORTH; *Senora Augustias,* NAZIMOVA; *Manola de Palma,* ANTHONY QUINN; *Garabato,* J. CARROL NAISH; *Nacional,* JOHN CARRADINE; *Encarnacion,* LYNN BARI; *Natalio Curro,* LAIRD CREGAR; *Guitarist,* Vicenté Gomez; *Antonio,* William Montague (and Monty Banks); *Captain Pierre Lauren,* George Reeves; *Don José Alvarez,* Pedro de Cordoba; *Pedro Espinosa,* Fortunio Bonanova; *Priest,* Victor Kilian; *La Pulga,* Michael Morris; *Pablo Gomez,* Charles Stevens; *Marquis,* Russell Hicks; *El Milquetoast,* Maurice Cass; *Gachi,* Jacqueline Dalya, Esther Estrella, Cecilia Callejo; *Cafe Singer,* Rosa Granada; *Woman,* Kay Linaker; *Friend,* Francis McDonald; *Ortega,* Paul Ellis; *Attendant,* Albert Morin; *Specialty Dancers,* Elena Verdugo, Mariquita Flores; *The Principals as Children,* Rex Dowing *(Juan);* Ann E. Todd *(Carmen);* Cullen Johnson *(Manolo);* Ted Frye *(La Pulga);* Schuyler Standish *(Nacional);* Cora Sue Collins *(Encarnacion).*

NOTES:

Blood and Sand, one of 1941's most acclaimed films, is also famous as the vehicle which catapulted Rita Hayworth to international stardom. Her unforgettable performance as the luscious but heartless Doña Sol is among her finest screen achievements and to this day many besides film buffs still ponder her failure to be nominated for a "Best Supporting Actress" Academy Award.

Academy members were less remiss with some of the other achievements for *Blood and Sand.* Ernest Palmer and Ray Rennahan won Oscars for their color cinematography, and Richard Day, Joseph C. Wright and Thomas Little were nominated for their masterful interior set decorations but the Oscars went to Cedric Gibbons, Urie McCleary and Edwin B. Willis for their contribution to *Blossoms in the Dust.*

Rouben Mamoulian has said his color consultants on *Blood and Sand* were El Greco, Goya, Velasquez and Murillo, the Spanish masters whose paintings he studied while having sets, costumes and decorations created. Said Mamoulian:

"Instead of just photographing the story, I tried to 'paint' it. I had never been to Spain and although we actually did some filming in Mexico City, I was never really sure I had captured a true Spanish authenticity until I actually went to Spain many years later. I was most pleased to discover it looked exactly the way the Spanish masters had painted it and that it was as I had imagined it would be. People in Spain who had seen and loved the film did not believe I had never visited the country before making the film."

One of Mamoulian's technical consultants on *Blood and Sand* was Budd Boetticher, an Indiana native who had once played football for Ohio State, and was in Mexico City studying bullfighting when the Fox crew arrived for location shooting around the arenas. Boetticher later produced and wrote many films and among those he directed are *Bullfighter and the Lady* and *Magnificent Matador.*

Recalls Boetticher:

"We never actually made a bull mad during the time we shot footage in Mexico. In one closeup we showed the banderillas sticking in the bull's shoulder. In real bullfights you've got to prick the bull to make him angry enough to fight. So we showed the banderillas in the bull. Only they weren't! They were actually sticking in a piece of hide we'd draped across the bull's shoulders.

"One Sunday at the Plaza de Toros we had over 35,000 cheering spectators who never realized they were working as movie extras. Six bulls were killed that afternoon. But we had nothing to do with that. They'd have

Escorted by matador Tyrone Power, Rita encourages the attentions of up-coming matador Anthony Quinn.

been killed whether we were there or not. So we photographed the fights from all angles. When it came time to dispatch the bull, we'd shut off our three cameras, and close our eyes.

"I showed Tyrone Power how to do the capework but he never actually got near a bull! He wanted to but the studio wouldn't let him. They said he was too valuable a property. This was my first film experience. I appreciated the money—but hell, I would have done it for nothing if they had asked me."

It was really Darryl F. Zanuck's idea to purchase and remake *Blood and Sand* when the public began comparing Power to Rudolph Valentino, the star of the silent Paramount film. Strict censorship, however, prevented Fox from using material in the novel utilized in the 1922 film, especially sequences involving Doña Sol, the temptress played by Nita Naldi.

At first Zanuck wanted Carole Landis, whom he was personally grooming for stardom, to be showcased in that role but she refused the part saying that she had spent so much time and effort building herself up as a blonde bombshell that she had no intention of appearing as a redhead in a color film. Miss Landis's rebellion cost her the leading role in a period musical, *My Gal Sal* (which see), that was becoming the most difficult-to-cast property in Fox history. So besides being borrowed by Fox to play Doña Sol, Rita Hayworth also inherited the lead in *My Gal Sal* and Carole Landis found herself reduced to playing a secondary role in that film! Rita, however, was not handed the role on a silver platter. Some sixteen other actresses, including Lynn Bari and Universal's fiery Latin import, Maria Montez, were among those tested.

Recalls Mamoulian:

"The day Miss Montez came into my office is unfor-

A publicity still exploiting the triangle between the beautiful Doña Sol (Hayworth), matador Tyrone Power and his wife (Linda Darnell).

With Tyrone Power.

gettable. She immediately sat on my desk, hiked up her skirt to show me her legs, winked at me suggestively and went into a first-rate vamp act. Unfortunately for her, the test she made wasn't nearly so effective. But the moment I saw Rita Hayworth walk I knew I had my Doña Sol. She was a dancer, so naturally I expected her to be graceful but she had something more than that—a feline sort of movement that was subtle and insinuating—exactly the kind of animation I imagined Doña Sol would possess. I must say she more than fulfilled my expectations. I was not the least surprised when she later became one of the great screen sirens."

The *Hollywood Reporter* said:

"There is a mood about this *Blood and Sand* that will rock any audience to enthusiastic heights; it has

movement and a beauty that few pictures have ever been able to capture; it has sex incidents that cause you to squirm in your chair; it has a story that will keep your eyes and ears glued to the screen and the sound horns every second of its running; it has performances and direction that rank with the best.

"To us there were two standouts—Rita Hayworth and Rouben Mamoulian. In her performance, Miss Hayworth, who has been wildly cheered for her beauty, comes through with a well-defined artistry that must win for her some of the top acting roles. Our impression of Mr. Mamoulian has been attracted more by his artistic successes than for a good sound hand in the making of sock entertainment. But in *Blood and Sand* he moves up into the circle of top entertainment directors and moves in a manner that assures him of holding that position."

And *Daily Variety* said:

"Mamoulian, dramatist and artist in his sense of color, has translated the great Ibañez tale to the level of the general American audience for widest appeal and has capped every entertainment element with brilliant direction . . . Miss Hayworth takes another stride toward her assured position among the stars-in-demand."

Carl Combs, in the *Hollywood Citizen News,* wrote:

"*Blood and Sand* may well be nominated the season's most visually exciting motion picture. Of all the decorative Technicolor films Hollywood has made, this is surely the richest and the splashiest. Rouben Mamoulian, the director, has his players fairly wallowing in the dazzling opulence of costume and sets, while the camera encompasses it all in a sort of lingering indulgence which reflects, no doubt, the pleasure that Mamoulian himself derived from all that mass splendor."

With Tyrone Power.

RITA HAYWORTH
Love Goddess

With Fred Astaire.

Astaire confronts Rita and her bride-groom to be, **John Hubbard**, just before the climactic production number when Astaire marries Hayworth on stage during the performance.

You'll Never Get Rich

A Columbia Picture   1941

Produced by Samuel Bischoff. Directed by Sidney Lanfield. Assistant Director, Gene Anderson. Original Screenplay by Michael Fessier and Ernest Pagano. Photographed by Phil Tannura. Musical Direction by Morris Stoloff. Songs: "Since I Kissed My Baby Goodbye," "Dream Dancing," "The Boogie Barcarolle," "The Wedding Cakewalk," "So Near and Yet So Far" and "Shooting the Works For Uncle Sam"; by Cole Porter. Musical Recording by P. J. Faulkner. Dances Staged by Robert Alton. Art Direction by Lionel Banks and Rudolph Sternad. Gowns by Kalloch. Costume Supervision by Ray Howell. Makeup Supervision by Clay Campbell. Hair Styles by Helen Hunt. Chief Sound Engineer, John Livadary. Edited by Otto Meyer. 88 minutes.

CAST:

Bob Curtis, FRED ASTAIRE; *Sheila Winthrop*, RITA HAYWORTH; *Tom Barton*, JOHN HUBBARD; *Martin Courtland*, ROBERT BENCHLEY; *Sonya*, OSA MASSEN; *Mrs. Cortland*, FRIEDA INESCORT; *Kewpie Blain*, Guinn "Big Boy" Williams; *Top Sergeant*, Donald MacBride; *Swivel Tongue*, Cliff Nazarro; *Aunt Louise*, Mar-

jorie Gateson; *Mrs. Barton*, Ann Shoemaker; *Colonel Shiller*, Boyd Davis; *Costume Designer*, Mary Currier; *Stage Doorman*, Robert Homans; *Marjorie*, Sunnie O'Dea; *Singer*, Martha Tilton; *Justice of the Peace*, Frank Ferguson; *Jenkins*, Emmett Vogan; *Jewelry Clerk*, Jack Rice; *Information Clerk*, Hal K. Dawson; *Foreigner*, Harry Burns; *Young Girl*, Patti McCarty; *Army Doctor*, Edward McWade; *Photographer*, Lester Dorr; *Second Singer*, Gwen Kenyon; *Policeman*, Tim Ryan; *Army Guards*, Frank Sully, Garry Owen; *General Trafscott*, Paul Irving; *Colonel's Orderly*, Harry Strang; *Lieutenant*, Eddie Laughton; *Kewpie's Mother*, Dorothy Vernon; *Draftee*, Stanley Brown; *Sleeper*, Monty Collins; *Captain Nolan*, Paul Phillips; *Captain Williams*, Harold Goodwin; *Sentry*, Jack O'Malley; *Chauffeur*, Eddie Coke; *Privates*, Larry Williams, James Millican; *Soloist*, Forrest Prince; *Prisoners*, Frank Wayne, Tony Hughes; *The Four Tones*, Rudolph Hunter, John Porter, Lucius Brooks, Leon Buck.

NOTES:

After three consecutive loan-out films, Rita returned to

Dancer Fred Astaire singles out the worst dancer in the line-up to be his partner, which has Rita wondering what he's up to.

Columbia as their most important female star. Anxious to remind the public that his new star's forte was dancing, Harry Cohn contracted for her to appear in two films with Fred Astaire.

Although he voiced regret that neither film he made at Columbia with Rita was in Technicolor, Astaire said:

"Rita danced with trained perfection and individuality. She, of course, knew through experience what this dancing business was all about. That was apparent the moment I started working with her. I enjoyed making *You'll Never Get Rich* because of Rita and the fact that it was one of the first films with a World War II service background. It was quite a satisfactory show in its way

Columbia built a series of roadside signs, each lettered with a credit, erected them outdoors and then photographed them as seen from a passing car.

With Fred Astaire.

and we figured to expand with our next one *(You Were Never Lovelier)."*

In his Cole Porter biography, *The Life That Late He Led,* published in 1967 by G. P. Putnam's Sons, author George Eells wrote:

"Cole found writing songs for a plot that utilized military life as the background for the familiar Hollywood triangle was surprisingly difficult. Even his enthusiasm for the cast—Astaire, beautiful Rita Hayworth and humorist Robert Benchley—could not carry him through the assignment with ease. He had been accustomed to the lavish and Olympian rites of production as practiced by MGM, whereas Columbia Pictures was budget-minded and practical. Cole was amused but slightly disconcerted too when studio head Harry Cohn insisted upon submitting the songs to clerical workers to pretest their appeal."

Because the ASCAP radio strike was then in force, the songs for *You'll Never Get Rich* did not get too much prerelease network exposure. Nevertheless, "Since I Kissed My Baby Goodbye" brought Cole Porter a "Best Song" Academy Award nomination (the winner, however, was "The Last Time I Saw Paris," by Jerome Kern and Oscar Hammerstein, II, that was featured in MGM's *Lady Be Good).* And, as previously mentioned, Morris Stoloff's nomination for "Best Musical Score" also went unrewarded by Academy members in the final vote.

The film, nonetheless, received enthusiastic reviews and became a big money-maker.

Daily Variety said:

"Columbia steps into the big-time musical field with *You'll Never Get Rich,* a happy combination of music, dancing and comedy that spells box office. The teaming of Fred Astaire and Rita Hayworth also is another happy combination. Picture ranks easily with Astaire's best, and displays another side of Miss Hayworth's talents—a side that will find much favor. Her work will stand up to any comparisons. In the straight portions she demonstrates an ability to handle a laugh line . . . Sidney Lanfield's direction rates equal praise. His smart development of laughs, the careful introduction of the musical interludes and the speed with which he had guided the picture through its racy eighty-eight minutes makes a standout job."

Theodore Strauss, in *The New York Times,* also enthused:

"With Robert Benchley to strew the script with sheepish gags and with Mr. Astaire and Miss Hayworth out in front most of the time, *You'll Never Get Rich* makes for a gay, lively and fanciful show . . . There is Miss Hayworth, who is something to trouble a night's sleep. Though she doesn't quite make one forget that Mr. Astaire once had Ginger Rogers for a partner, Miss Hayworth does dance with verve and excitement."

Sal Elliott, the Broadway songstress.

With her manager, James Gleason, and her socialite sweetheart, John Sutton, listening to song plugger Phil Silvers sing a new tune.

My Gal Sal

A 20th Century-Fox Picture   1942

Produced by Robert Bassler. Executive Producer, Darryl F. Zanuck. Directed by Irving Cummings. Assistant Director, Henry Weinberger. Screenplay by Seton I. Miller, Darryl Ware and Karl Tunberg, based on the story, "My Brother Paul," by Theodore Dreiser (and Helen Richardson, uncredited). Photographed in Technicolor by Ernest Palmer. Director for the Technicolor Company, Natalie Kalmus. Assistant, Henri Jaffa. Musical Direction by Alfred Newman. Songs: "Me and My Fella," "On the Gay White Way," "Oh, the Pity of It All," "Here You Are" and "Midnight at the Masquerade," by Leo Robin and Ralph Rainger; "Come Tell Me What's Your Answer (Yes or No)," "I'se Your Honey if You Wants Me, Liza Jane," "The Convict and the Bird," "Mr. Volunteer (You Don't Belong to the Regulars, You're Just a Volunteer," "My Gal Sal" and "On the Banks of the Wabash" by Paul Dresser. Dances Staged by Hermes Pan and Val Rasset. Sound Recording by Alfred Bruzlin and Roger Heman. Art Direction by Richard Day and Joseph C. Wright. Set Decorations by Thomas Little. Makeup by Guy Pearce. Costumes by Gwen Wakeling. Edited by Robert Simpson. 103 minutes.

CAST:

Sally Elliott, RITA HAYWORTH; *Paul Dresser,* VICTOR MATURE; *Fred Haviland,* JOHN SUTTON; *Mae Collins,* CAROLE LANDIS; *Pat Hawley,* JAMES GLEASON; *Wiley,* PHIL SILVERS; *Colonel Truckee,* WALTER CATLETT; *Countess Rossini,* MONA MARIS; *McGuiness,* Frank Orth; *Mr. Dreiser,* Stanley Andrews; *Mrs. Dreiser,* Margaret Moffat; *Ida,* Libby Taylor; *John L. Sullivan,* John Kelly; *De Rochemont,* Curt Bois; *Garnier,* Gregory Gaye; *Corbin,* Andrew Tombes; *Henri,* Albert Conti; *Tailor,* Charles Arnt; *Murphy,* Chief Thundercloud; *Specialty Dancer,* Hermes Pan; *Sally's Friends,* Robert Lowery, Dorothy Dearing, Ted North, Roseanne Murray; *Bartender,* Harry Strang; *Bit Men,* Milton Kibbee, Luke Cosgrave, Ernie Adams, Joe Bernard, John "Skins" Miller, Gus Glassmire, Tom O'Grady, Freank Ferguson, Cyril Ring; *Delivery Man,* Billy Wayne; *Policemen,* Edward McNamara, Ed Dearing; *Maid,* Rosina Galli; *Stage Doorman,* Larry Wheat; *Buggy Driver,* Eddie Waller; *Theodore Dreiser,* Barry Downing; *Usher,* Tommy Seidel; *Carrie,* Judy Ford,* *Midget Driver,* Billy Curtis; *Midget Footman,* Tommy Cotton; *Ferris Wheel Operator,* Paul Burns; *Conductor,* George Melford; *Hotel Clerk,* Charles Tannen; *Quartette,* Clarence

With chorus in the title tune production number.

With socialite John Sutton and songwriter Victor Mature.

Badger, Kenneth Rundquist, Delos Jewkes, Gene Ramey.

NOTES:

Paul Dreiser, who Americanized his last name to Dresser, died in 1906 after a successful career as a songwriter and, in spite of his 250 pounds, a stage performer and singer. His brother, Theodore (played as a young boy in the film by Barry Downing), later became one of our greatest novelists *(Sister Carrie, An American Tragedy,* et al.) and wrote the original story, "My Brother Paul," as the basis for a musical film about his life at the direct invitation of Darryl F. Zanuck, who assigned screenwriter Helen Richardson to assist him.

Zanuck had wanted the story tailor-made to the talents of Alice Faye, but after withdrawing from film work because of pregnancy, she declared she would not make any more costume musicals. (She did make one more, *Hello, Frisco, Hello.)* Her announcement caused Zanuck to have the script rewritten and reworked for Irene Dunne, but her busy film schedule would mean holding up production some eighteen months. Zanuck subsequently approached Mae West about playing Sally Elliott, but Miss West didn't cotton to the idea. At this conjuncture, he decided to groom Carole Landis for the role, deciding to showcase her first as Doña Sol in

*Later known as Terry Moore.

Rita and ensemble doing the "Banks of the Wabash" specialty number.

Blood and Sand. When she balked at doing that film, Zanuck retaliated by giving her a secondary role in *My Gal Sal,* as she had already been announced to appear in it anyway. More or less resigned to using an already overworked Betty Grable, then more than amply filling the void caused by Alice Faye's absence, Zanuck changed his mind after Rita's sensational appearance in *Blood and Sand* and her subsequent success in *You'll Never Get Rich.* Knowing Zanuck was up against a wall, Harry Cohn, in bargaining Rita's loan-out finally consented when Fox added the lure of another role, as the unfaithful wife, in the first episode of *Tales of Manhattan,* the first of the all-star films produced and released during World War II.

Rumor had it that while Victor Mature was romancing Rita on screen, they were doing likewise off-screen.

With John Sutton.

The brilliant Fritz Lang was originally to have directed *My Gal Sal* but after a week of preproduction planning he asked to be replaced and Irving Cummings, who had just scored a great success with *Louisiana Purchase* and some Sonja Henie vehicles, took over the film. (Lang was then assigned the direction of *Moontide,* but after four days was replaced by Archie Mayo!)

Alfred Newman was nominated for an Academy Award for his musical scoring of *My Gal Sal* but the award went to Ray Heindorf and Heinz Roemheld (for *Yankee Doodle Dandy)* but Richard Day, Joseph Wright and Thomas Little won Oscars for their color interior decorations. Nan Wynn did the dubbing for Rita's singing.

Daily Variety said:

"*My Gal Sal* is a lively, merry musical treat. Picture is crammed with color, songs and movement, carrying broad appeal for all theatergoers, both young and old . . . Miss Hayworth, garbed in Technicolor and the eye-appealing early-day styles, presents a beautiful picture as the musical comedy star who lifts a young composer from the oblivion of a medicine show to Broadway's bright lights."

In *Script* magazine, Rob Wagner said:

"Those in search of gay diversion should step right up and make the acquaintance of *My Gal Sal.* She is a fetching number, and Darryl F. Zanuck introduces her in a setting that is tops in lavishness, tunes and fun. Spectacularly backgrounded by Day, Wright and Little, handsomely dressed by Gwen Wakeling, the Technicolor photography of Ernie Palmer boldly proclaims that the tint process was invented just to prove how exquisitely lovely is Rita Hayworth."

Life magazine, naming it the "Movie of the Week," said:

"*My Gal Sal* meets a current demand, both in the movies and radio, for the nostalgic delights of the 1890s. Tinted in lush Technicolor, the movie is overloaded with production numbers but scores generally for its gaslight glamour and the saucy dancing of Rita Hayworth."

And *The New York Times* said:

"The most surprising thing about the show is the fact that Victor Mature turns in a rather good performance as Dresser. He still has lots to learn about acting, but he handles a flamboyant biography with considerable skill. Rita Hayworth is fine as the gal of the title, and James Gleason and Walter Catlett help no end. *My Gal Sal* is not noteworthy but it is beguiling. At least Hollywood can still turn out beguiling entertainments. That is a valuable function of an amusement form these days. It explains why the motion picture had thrived this season while the theater had languished."

With Victor Mature in a publicity pose depicting one of the quieter moments in their stormy love affair as songstress and songwriter.

Victor Mature tells songstress Rita that her jealousy is groundless as sultry Mona Maris listens.

Fearing her husband knows of her affair with matinee idol Charles Boyer, Rita enters the trophy room just as her spouse, Thomas Mitchell, is showing a rifle to her lover. (Episode one).

Tales of Manhattan

A 20th Century-Fox Picture   1942

Produced by Boris Morros and S. P. Eagle.* Directed by Julien Duvivier. Assistant Directors, Robert Stillman and Charles Hall. Screenplay and Original Stories by Ben Hecht, Ferenc Molnar, Donald Ogden Stewart, Samuel Hoffenstein, Alan Campbell, Ladislas Fedor, L. Vadnai, L. Gorog, Lamar Trotti and Henry Blankford. Photographed by Joseph Walker. Musical Score by Sol Kaplan. Musical Direction by Edward Paul. Orchestrations by Clarence Wheeler, Charles Bradshaw and Hugo Friedhofer. Vocal Arrangements by Hall Johnson. Songs: "Glory Day," by Leo Robin and Ralph Rainger; "Fare Thee Well to El Dorado," "A Journey to Your Lips" and "A Tale of Manhattan," by Paul Francis Webster and Saul Chaplin. Sound Recording by W. D. Flick and Roger Heman. Art Direction by Richard Day and Boris Leven. Set Decorations by Thomas Little. Costumes by Irene, Dolly Tree, Bernard Newman, Gwen Wakeling and Oleg Cassini. Makeup by Guy Pearce. Unit Manager, J. H. Nadel. Edited by Robert Bischoff. 126 minutes (West Coast Roadshow Version); 119 minutes (General Release Version).

CAST:

Sequence A: *Paul Orman,* CHARLES BOYER; *Ethel*
*Later known as Sam Spiegel.

Halloway, RITA HAYWORTH; *John Halloway,* THOMAS MITCHELL; *Luther,* Eugene Pallette; *Actress,* Helene Reynolds; *Lazar,* Robert Grieg; *Tailor,* Jack Chefe; *Webb,* William Halligan; *Agent,* Charles Williams; *Halloway's Butler,* Eric Wilton.

Sequence B: *Diane,* GINGER ROGERS; *George,* HENRY FONDA; *Harry Wilson,* CESAR ROMERO; *Ellen,* GAIL PATRICK; *Edgar,* ROLAND YOUNG; *Squirrel,* Marion Martin; *Secondhand Dealer,* Frank Orth; *Mary,* Connie Leon.

Sequence C: *Charles Smith,* CHARLES LAUGHTON; *Elsa Smith,* ELSA LANCHESTER; *Arthuro Bandini,* VICTOR FRANCEN; *Wilson,* Christian Rub; *Grandmother,* Adeline deWalt Reynolds; *Piccolo Player,* Sig Arno; *Dignified Man,* Forbes Murray; *Call Boy,* Buster Brodie; *Musician,* Frank Jaquet; *Skeptic,* William Wright; *Elderly Man,* Frank Dae; *Susan,* René Austin; *Grandpa,* Frank Darien; *Proprietor,* Dewey Robinson; *Latecomer,* Tom O'Grady.

Sequence D: *Browne,* EDWARD G. ROBINSON; *William,* GEORGE SANDERS; *Father Joe,* JAMES GLEASON; *Professor,* Harry Davenport; *Hank Bronson,* James Rennie; *Davis,* Harry Hayden; *Judge,* Morris Ankrum; *Henderson,* Don Douglas; *Molly,* Mae Marsh; *Mary,*

With Charles Boyer and Thomas Mitchell. (Episode one).

After "accidentally" shooting his wife's lover, the cockolded husband realizes that his wife is more concerned about them than her mortally wounded paramour. (Episode one).

Barbara Lynn; *Spud,* Paul Renay; *Waiter,* Alex Pollard; *Postman,* Joseph Bernard; *Whistler,* Don Beddoe; *Bit Woman,* Esther Howard; *Chauffeur,* Ted Stanhope.

Sequence E: *Luke,* PAUL ROBESON; *Esther,* ETHEL WATERS; *Lazarus,* EDDIE "Rochester" ANDERSON; *Costello,* J. CARROL NAISH; *Grandpa,* Clarence Muse; *Christopher,* George Reed; *Nicodemus,* Cordell Hickman; *Monk,* John Kelly; *Brad,* Lonnie Nichols; *Rod,* Charles Gray; *Jeff,* Phillip Hurlic; *Bit,* Archie Savage; *Bit Women,* Rita Christiani, Laura Vaughn, Ella Mae Lashley, Olive Ball, Alberta Gary, Maggie Dorsey; *Pilot,* Charles Tannen; *Themselves,* Hall Johnson Choir.

NOTES:

The first of the all-star films to be released during World War II, *Tales of Manhattan* was originally an idea conceived by producer Boris Morros, who then intrigued S. P. Eagle (Sam Spiegel) into joining his project and inducing ten writers to concoct a script of at least six episodes of equal audience appeal which contained roles exciting enough to interest top stars in playing them. At first Morros intended using a different director for each episode, just as Paramount had done in the 1930s with *If I Had A Million.* But when Charles Boyer became interested in the film, he suggested that Morros use just one director, Julien Duvivier, whose famous French film *Un Carnet de Bal* (later remade

very badly by Alexander Korda as *Lydia)* had been an episodic but all-star triumph.

The idea of using a dress tailcoat as the gimmick on which each story is hung and is the connecting link between them is said to have come from Alan Campbell (Dorothy Parker's husband). The first episode filmed starred Charles Laughton and the last one to be written and filmed starred Edward G. Robinson. A sequence filmed which was to immediately precede the finale starred W. C. Fields, but it was deleted after several previews when audience reaction made it apparent that it was not in keeping with the generally dramatic tone of the other sequences. The gambling casino robbery that spins off the last episode was much longer in the version first released on the West Coast, and seven minutes of it was deleted before the film opened in New York at the Radio City Music Hall.

Tales of Manhattan was so commercially successful that Charles Boyer, Edward G. Robinson and Julien Duvivier subsequently got together to produce another all-star feature, *Flesh and Fantasy,* which Universal released a little over a year later and which also had a complete sequence deleted. But Universal, unlike 20th Century-Fox, did not allow their unused footage to re-

Rita and her husband wonder how they can dispose of her lover's remains, a situation which the "corpse" himself soon resolves. (Episode one).

In episode two, Ginger Rogers lets her friend, Gail Patrick, read a love letter she has found in the pocket of her fiancé's dress jacket, apparently written to another woman.

main dormant. Adding footage to it, it was subsequently released as a B feature (Destiny).

In The New York Times, Bosley Crowther said:

"Tales of Manhattan is one of those rare films—a tricky departure from the norm, which, in spite of its five-ring-circus nature, achieves an impressive effect. Neither profound nor very searching, it nevertheless manages to convey a gentle, detached comprehension of the irony and pity of life, and it constantly grapples

In episode three, composer Charles Laughton and his wife, Elsa Lanchester, prepare for the debut of his symphony at Carnegie Hall. After spending years of privation while awaiting his big chance, the evening is almost ruined because of an ill-fitting dress coat.

At a fraternity dinner, society attorney George Sanders exposes the fact that the apparently successful Edward G. Robinson is really a skid row bum, in episode four.

In the fifth episode, deleted after the first previews, W. C. Fields played a magician-con artist who invades the home of society matron Margaret Dumont.

one's interest with its run of assorted incidents. The big surprise is that the actors never dwarf the little fables they play and that the whole film never exposes the rather fragile framework on which it is built."

And *Motion Picture Herald* said:

"Excellent! The excitement about this multi-starred, multi-storied production enterprise is none too much, for the picture not only is a stacking up of personalities and plots but also is a piling-up of entertainment, layer upon layer, prepared, performed and presented with expertness, polish and precision."

The *official* breakdown of writing credits is: *Sequence A:* Ferenc Molnar; *Sequence B:* Donald Ogden Stewart, Alan Campbell and Samuel Hoffenstein; *Sequence C:* Ladislaus Fedor, L. Vadnai and L. Gorog; *Sequence D:* Lamar Trotti; *Sequence E:* Henry Blankford; with overall supervision, revision and coordination by Ben Hecht. The deleted sequence was written by W. C. Fields, Bert Lawrence and Anne Wigton and besides Fields, featured players included Phil Silvers, Margaret Dumont, Maude Eburne, Bess Flowers, Luke Cosgrave, Cyril Ring, Milton Kibbee and Dave Willock.

The epilog sequence depicts the effects that the dress coat, pockets bulging with stolen money, has on a poor Southern community presided over by Eddie (Rochester) Anderson, a preacher who believes in miracles. With him are Ethel Waters and Paul Robeson.

With Fred Astaire.

You Were Never Lovelier

A Columbia Picture   1942

Produced by Louis F. Edelman. Directed by William A. Seiter. Assistant Director, Norman Deming. Screenplay by Michael Fessier, Ernest Pagano and Delmer Daves, based on an original story and screenplay, "The Gay Senorita," by Carlos Olivari and Sixto Pondal Rios. Photographed by Ted Tetzlaff. Musical Score by Jerome Kern. Musical Director, Leigh Harline; Assistant, Paul Mertz. Musical Arrangements by Conrad Salinger. Musical Arrangement of "The Shorty George," by Lyle Murphy. Xavier Cugat's Specialty, "Chiu Chiu," by Nicanor Molinare. Other Songs: "Dearly Beloved," "The Shorty George," "I'm Old-Fashioned," "Wedding in the Spring," "You Were Never Lovelier" and "On the Beam,' by Jerome Kern and Johnny Mercer. Music Recording by P. J. Faulkner. Dance Director, Val Rasset. Art Direction by Lionel Banks and Rudolph Sternad. Set Decoration by Frank Tuttle. Gowns by Irene. Costume Supervision by Ray Howell.

Sound Recording by John Livadary. Edited by William Lyon. 97 minutes.

CAST:

Robert Davis, FRED ASTAIRE; *Maria Acuna,* RITA HAYWORTH; *Eduardo Acuna,* ADOLPHE MENJOU; *Cecy Acuna,* LESLIE BROOKS; *Lita Acuna,* ADELE MARA; *Maria Castro,* Isobel Elsom; *Fernando,* GUS Shilling; *Delfina Acuna,* Barbara Brown; *Juan Castro,* Douglas Leavitt; *Julia Acuna,* Catherine Craig; *Grandmother Acuna,* Kathleen Howard; *Louise,* Mary Field; *Tony,* Larry Parks; *Roddy,* Stanley Brown; *Groom,* Kirk Allyn; *Flower Man,* George Bunny; *Chauffeur,* Ralph Peters; *Themselves,* XAVIER CUGAT and His Orchestra.

NOTES:

The filial custom of progressive marriage among the

With Fred Astaire during one of their
elaborate dance numbers.

daughters of film families of exotic lineage was not exactly unique in December 1942 when *You Were Never
Lovelier* opened. It had been explored four months
earlier that year, via the Dutch in MGM's *Seven Sweethearts* and an Icelandic family in Fox's *Iceland*. But the
precedent had been established much earlier in films,
and all three of these U.S. productions were remakes of
foreign-language films!

Rita's singing was well dubbed by the winsome Nan
Wynn and *You Were Never Lovelier* won Oscar nomi-
nations for "Best Song," "Best Scoring" and "Best
Sound Recording," but, nevertheless went unawarded.

Fred Astaire, who had worked with Eduardo Cansino during their vaudeville days, claimed he had a difficult time finding a suitable location in which to rehearse his dances with Rita and that they finally ended

With Leslie Brooks, Adele Mara, Barbara Brown, Gus Shilling, Fred Astaire, Isobel Elsom, Douglas Leavitt,
and Adolphe Menjou.

With Fred Astaire.

up using a funeral parlor of the nearby Hollywood Cemetery, which Columbia rented. The only problem with that arrangement was that every time a funeral procession came through the cemetery gates rehearsals were halted until the services were over and the mourners had departed.

In his autobiography, "Steps in Time," Astaire wrote:

"Oddly enough, we pulled some good dance ma-terial out of those weird surroundings . . . Rita and I had a good time with 'The Shorty George' number, which, incidentally, did not originate in the funeral par-lor. That was devised on Sundays at the studio when we had the place to ourselves."

Bosley Crowther, in *The New York Times,* said:

"If we all are agreed that a title means absolutely nothing on a film and that plots are of little more con-

Hotel keeper Adolphe Menjou exam-ines wedding gifts with his daughters, Leslie Brooks, Adele Mara, Rita Hay-worth and Barbara Brown, and house-keeper Kathleen Howard.

Rita suddenly suspects that Fred Astaire, a down-on-his-luck dancer, may be her secret admirer.

sequence, especially in musical romance; if we can all be thoroughly contented with the spectacle of Rita Hayworth and Fred Astaire being fluted and fiddled in dancing measures to the lyrical music of Jerome Kern, then little or no exception can be taken to any particular thing in Columbia's new film, *You Were Never Lovelier,* which came to the Music Hall yesterday. For this is that sort of picture—a gay bit of frivolous fluff in which Mr. Astaire and Miss Hayworth dance singly and together quite charmingly, Xavier Cugat's orchestra makes music with plenty of class and Adolphe Menjou whips into tantrums and otherwise behaves in humorous style."

And *Hollywood Reporter* said:

"When two such accomplished dancers as Astaire and Miss Hayworth are brought together, their public has a right to expect a brilliant display of terpsichorean skill. Instead, the accent is on a featherweight romance, its prolonged outcome never for a moment in doubt. Some twenty minutes of small talk concerning the marital futures of the four Acuna daughters precede Astaire's first and only solo stepping, and the picture is more than half over before he and Miss Hayworth join in a dance that is followed by two more routines, all dazzlingly executed but not numerous enough to satisfy fans."

Father of the bride Menjou with his three unmarried daughters, Leslie Brooks, Adele Mara and Rita.

With the Mills Brothers, Fred Mac-Murray, Ginny Simms, Phil Baker and Don Wilson as they appeared on a "Command Performance" broadcast, recorded for servicemen overseas.

Show Business at War

Released by 20th Century-Fox   1943

Volume IX, Issue 10 of *The March of Time*. Produced by the Editors of *Time*. Produced, Directed, Compiled and Edited by Louis de Rochemont and his staff. 17 minutes.

CAST:

Alphabetically Appearing as *Themselves:* Eddie "Rochester" Anderson, Louis Armstrong and His Orchestra, Phil Baker, Ballet Russe de Monte Carlo, Ethel Barrymore, Robert Benchley, Jack Benny, Edgar Bergen, Irving Berlin, Joe E. Brown, James Cagney, Lt. Col. Emanuel Cohen, Bing Crosby, Michael Curtiz, Linda Darnell, Bette Davis, Olivia de Havilland, Marlene Dietrich, Walt Disney, Irene Dunne, Deanna Durbin, W. C. Fields, Errol Flynn, Lt. Cmdr. John Ford, Kay Francis, Clark Gable, John Garfield, Bert Glennon, Rita Hayworth, Alfred Hitchcock, Lou Holtz, Bob Hope, Al Jolson, Brenda Joyce, Kay Kyser and His Band, Hedy Lamarr, Dorothy Lamour, Carole Landis, Gertrude Lawrence, Lt. Col. Anatole Litvak, Mary Livingston, Carole Lombard, Myrna Loy, Alfred Lunt, Fred Mac-Murray, Victor Mature, Mitzi Mayfair, The Mills Brothers, George Murphy, Eugene Ormandy and the Philadelphia Symphony Orchestra, Lily Pons, Tyrone Power, Lt. Col. Robert Presnell, The Ritz Brothers, Ginger Rogers, Mickey Rooney, Ann Rutherford, Anne Shirley, Ginny Simms, Frank Sinatra, Lt. Gregg Toland, Lana Turner, Maj. Anthony Veiler, Hal B. Wallis, Jack L. Warner, Orson Welles, Don Wilson, Loretta Young, Col. Darryl F. Zanuck.

NOTE:

In this issue of the popular series *The March of Time*

stars of radio, theater and screen were shown in some function or another contributing to the war effort. Rita Hayworth, accompanied by Ginny Simms, Don Wilson, Phil Baker, Fred MacMurray and the Mills Brothers were depicted while donating their time, talents and services to a "Command Performance" radio broadcast that was recorded and played on shortwave radio to U.S. troops in all war zones.

Said *Boxoffice:*

"Socko. The manifold tasks that the industry has undertaken to further the war effort is graphically depicted in this latest MOT release. From the standpoint of personalities alone, the featurette packs a wallop that is bound to be reflected at the nation's box offices."

In *Weekly Variety,* Abel Green wrote:

"Unquestionably the all-time tops for cast name-power and, as an institutional ballyhoo in behalf of show biz, it's a gem. In less than twenty minutes, kaleidoscopically, in montage and pithy commentary, is painted a graphic approximation of what show business is doing is its all-out effort for the war.... It's one of de Rochemont's prize packages and, for the exhibitor, a super-duper short that will need a gargantuan marquee just for a handful of the 'cast' names."

And *Showman's Trade Review* said:

"Excellent! Here is a record of what American show business, with emphasis on the motion picture industry, is doing towards the war effort. The public will be interested and amazed at how much is being done."

Cover Girl

A Columbia Picture   1944

Produced by Arthur Schwartz. Directed by Charles Vidor. Assistant Director, Budd (Oscar) Boetticher. Screenplay by Virginia Van Upp, Marion Parsonnet and Paul Gangelin, based on Erwin Gelsey's original screenplay. Photographed in Technicolor by Rudy Maté and Allen M. Davey. Director for the Technicolor Company, Natalie Kalmus; Associate, Morgan Padelford. Musical Score by Jerome Kern. Musical Direction by Morris Stoloff. Orchestrations by Carmen Dragon. Songs: "Long Ago and Far Away," "Cover Girl," "Sure Thing," "The Show Must Go On," "Who's Complaining?," "Put Me To the Test" and "Make Way For Tomorrow, by Jerome Kern and Ira Gershwin; "Poor John," by Fred Leigh and Henry E. Pether. Dances Staged and Directed by Val Rasset and Seymour Felix. "Cover Girl Number," Designed and Staged by John Hoffman and Robert Coburn. Art Direction and Set Decoration by Lionel Banks, Cary Odell and Fay Babcock. Costumes by Travis Banton, Gwen Wakeling and Muriel King. Women's Hats by Kenneth Hopkins. Sound Recording by John Livadary. Assistant to the Producer, Norman Deming. Edited by Viola Lawrence. 107 minutes.

CAST:

Rusty Parker/Maribelle Hicks, RITA HAYWORTH; *Danny McGuire*, GENE KELLY; *Noel Wheaton*, LEE BOWMAN; *Genius*, PHIL SILVERS; *Jinx*, JINX FALKENBURG; *Maurine Martin*, LESLIE BROOKS; *Cornelia (Stonewall) Jackson*, EVE ARDEN; *John Coudair*, OTTO KRUGER; *John Coudair (as a young man)*, JESS BARKER; *Anita*, ANITA COLBY; *Chef*, Curt Bois; *Joe*, Edward Brophy; *Tony Pastor*, Thurston Hall; *Chauffeur*, William Kline; *Bartender*, Victor Travers; *Headwaiter*,

With Gene Kelly and Phil Silvers in the "Make Way for Tomorrow" musical number.

At the altar with uneasy groom Lee Bowman, Rita has a last minute change of mind.

Robert F. Hill; *Electrician,* John Tyrell; *Second Cook,* Frank O'Connor; *Assistant Cook,* Sam Ash; *Busboy,* Eugene Anderson, Jr.; *Waiter,* Vin Moore; *Checker,* Caryl Lincoln; *Harry, the Drunk,* Jack Norton; *Pop, the Doorman,* Robert Homans; *Mac, the Policeman,* Eddie Dunn; *Autograph Hound,* Betty Brewer; *Pianist,* Johnny Mitchell; *Dancer,* Virginia Wilson; *Girl,* Shelley Winters; and *The Cover Girls,* Francine Counihan *(American Home),* Jean Colleran *(American Magazine),* Cecilia Meagher *(Coronet),* Betty Jane Hess *(Cosmopolitan),* Dusty Anderson *(Farm Journal),* Eileen McClory *(Glamour),* Cornelia B. Von Hessert *(Harper's Bazaar),* Karen X. Gaylord *(Liberty),* Cheryl (Archibald) Archer *(Look),* Peggy Lloyd *(Mademoiselle),* Betty Jane Graham *(McCall's),* Martha Outlaw *(Redbook),* Susan Shaw *(Vogue),* Rose May Robson *(Woman's Home Companion).*

NOTES:

Cover Girl came to U.S. screens during the third year of World War II, when everyone needed a bit of glamour, humor and color to brighten the deadly drabness of the times. With an abundance of all three, it also presented "Long Ago and Far Away," one of the most hauntingly beautiful ballads ever written for a film, which won a "Best Song" Academy Award nomination but lost the award to the novelty tune, "Swinging on a Star" from *Going My Way,* which also won Oscars for being the year's "Best Picture" and containing the two best acting performances (by Bing Crosby and Barry Fitzgerald). *Cover Girl* had two other Academy nominations, for "Best Color Cinematography" and "Best Interior Color Decorations" but both those awards went to *Wilson.* Voicing his disappointment that *Cover Girl* failed to win any Oscars for its assorted nominees, Columbia boss Harry Cohn said: "Well, at least it took two priests and a U.S. President to beat us!"

Although Rita's phantom singing voice actually belonged to Martha Mears, her solo dances, and those performed with the innovative and energetic Gene Kelly, were immeasurable facets of her brilliant talents and she was at the peak of her form as the screen's best feminine dancer. Even the late Betty Grable very amiably admitted Rita could dance rings around her.

"She's much more beautiful, too," said Miss Grable and then she winked and added, "but I think blondes have more fun."

Without appearing to contradict Miss Grable, no film released during 1944 was more fun than the glamorous, glib, glittering and gloriously gaudy *Cover Girl.*

In the New York *Daily News,* Kate Cameron said:

"Four Stars! Columbia's elaborate, Technicolor, musical comedy production of *Cover Girl* comes closer to the gay, enchanting musicals made by RKO during the last decade, with Ginger Rogers and Fred Astaire in the leading roles, than any song and dance film made in Hollywood since the beginning of the European war.

A moviehouse lobby display card.

Rita accepts Lee Bowman's marriage proposal as Anita Colby looks on.

A publicity still with Lee Bowman and Gene Kelly feigning a feud for Rita's affections.

With Otto Kruger.

. . . Rita Hayworth takes to Technicolor like a bathing beauty sticks to dry land and her gorgeous auburn hair gives her a perfect right to be called Rusty in the film."

Jim O'Connor, in the New York *Journal-American,* said:

"*Cover Girl,* a page one among elaborate film musical spectacles, is on display today at Radio City Music Hall. And, in Technicolor, she is something to see."

In *The New York Times,* Bosley Crowther said:

"It rainbows the screen with dazzling decor. It has Gene Kelly and Rita Hayworth to sing and dance. And virtually every nook and corner is draped with beautiful girls.

"Further, this gaudy obeisance to divine femininity has some rather nice music in it from the tune-shop of Jerome Kern."

And *Hollywood Reporter* said:

"Big time from the word go, *Cover Girl* deserves to stand among the best filmusicals of all times. The Arthur Schwartz production for Columbia puts to splendid use seven new hit tunes by Jerome Kern and Ira Gershwin; the dancing of Rita Hayworth and Gene Kelly is superb; it is the show for which Phil Silvers has been waiting; the flash of fifteen cover beauties recruited for the entertainment gives just the necessary touch to pay off at the box office; and the whole affair is cleverly put together under the smart direction of Charles Vidor, from a swell script, and photographed for a Technicolor fare-thee-well by Rudolph Mate and Allen M. Davey. All of these statements of facts leaves a reviewer slightly breathless. But that's the way *Cover Girl* leaves an audience."

In *The Nation,* James Agee said:

"There is no reason, after all, why a movie musical should not be as good as any other sort of movie. *Cover Girl* is the first since *Top Hat* which even suggests the possibilities. There is nothing in it that approaches the dance in the jigsawed pavilion in the rain in the old Astaire-Rogers film. Much of *Cover Girl,* for that matter, is not as fresh as it may seem; but its secondhandedness and its occasional failures cannot obliterate the pleasure of seeing the work of a production company which obviously knows, cares about, and enjoys what it is doing."

Entertaining counterman Ed Brophy with Gene Kelly and Phil Silvers at a Brooklyn oyster bar.

Rita and chorus in the sensually thrilling musical number "You Excite Me."

Tonight and Every Night

A Columbia Picture   1945

Produced and Directed by Victor Saville. Assistant Directors, Rex Baily and Louis Germonprez. Screenplay by Lesser Samuels and Abe Finkel, based on Lesley Storm's play, "Heart of a City," produced on the stage by Gilbert Miller. Photographed in Technicolor by Rudy Mate. Consultant for the Technicolor Company, Natalie Kalmus. Camera Operator, Fayte M. Browne. Special Effects by Lawrence W. Butler. Musical Score by Jules Styne. Musical Direction by Morris Stoloff. Orchestral Arrangements by Marlin Skiles. Vocal Arrangements by Saul Chaplin. Songs: "What Does An English Girl Think of a Yank?" "You Excite Me," "The Boy I Left Behind," "Tonight and Every Night," "Cry and You Cry Alone" and "Anywhere," by Jules Styne and Sammy Cahn. Dances Staged by Jack Cole and Val Rasset. Costumes and Gowns by Jean Louis and Marcel Vertes. Art Direction by Stephen Goosson, Rudolph Sternad and Lionel Banks. Set Decoration by Frank Tuttle. Sound Recording by Lambert Day. Assistant to the Producer, Norman Deming. Edited by Viola Lawrence. 92 minutes.

CAST:

Rosalind (Roz) Bruce, RITA HAYWORTH; *Paul Lundy,* LEE BOWMAN; *Judy Kane,* JANET BLAIR; *Tommy Lawson,* MARC PLATT; *Angela,* LESLIE BROOKS; *May Tolliver,* FLORENCE BATES; *The Great Waldo,* Professor Lamberti; *Sam Royce,* Ernest Cossart; *Toni,* Dusty Anderson; *Leslie Wiggins,* Stephen Crane; *Life Photographer,* Jim Bannon; *Reverend Gerald Lundy,* Philip Merivale; *David Long,* Patrick O'Moore; *Group Captain,* Gavin Muir; *Bubbles,* Shelley Winters; *Pamela,* Marilyn Johnson; *Frenchie,* Mildred Law; *Joan,* Elizabeth Inglise; *Mrs. Peabody,* Aminta Dyne; *Mrs. Good,* Joy Harrington; *Annette,* Ann Codee; *Specialty,* Richard Haydn; *Bert,* Cecil Stewart; *Jolly Trio,* Dagmar Oakland, Victor Travers, Charles Meakin; *American Soldiers,* Gary Bruce, Fred Graff; *WAC,* Jeanne Bates; *U.S. CPO,* Robert Williams; *Russian Sailor,* Jon Bleifer; *Showgirl,* Adele Jergens; *English Sailors,* Tom Bryson, Nigel Horton; *Boy,* Donald Dewar; *ARP Man,* P. J. Kelly; *Petty Officer,* Stuart Nedd; *Orderly,* Russell Burroughs; *Father,* George Kirby; *British Servicemen,* John Heath, Dick Woodruff, Richard Deane, Tony Marsh, Nelson Leigh, Keith Hitchcock; *News Vendor,* Wilson Benge; *Air Raid Warden,* Frank Leigh; *Waiter,* William Lawrence; *Old Bobby,* C. Montague Shaw; *Englishman,* Alec Craig; *Police Sergeant,* David Clyde; *Cockney Woman,* Queenie Leonard; *Barmaid,* Sheilah Roberts.

NOTES:

Based on Lesley Storm's rather good but short-lived Broadway play, *Heart of a City,* presented in February 1942, when its theme, based on actual facts, concerning an English hall revue which never missed a performance during the blitz seemed a lot more trenchant, the cast included Gertrude Musgrove, Beverly Roberts, Margot Grahame, Romney Brent, Richard Ainsley, Dennis Hoey and Lloyd Gough, *Tonight and Every Night* had a very solid story foundation into which liberal song and dance routines were easily worked into the dramatic narrative without causing any loss of interest and which, occasionally advanced the story-line.

Told in flashback style by the stage manager of the theater where a London musical had never missed a single performance during the blitz to a writer from *Life* magazine, the film then reverted to an earlier time, a happier period and an early musical montage of Rita, Janet Blair and Marc Platt singing and performing all the latest fads of dancing, with suitable costume changes, established in less than four minutes of screen time the trio's growth as performers and established the romantic triangle in which they became involved. Musical plot clichés such as these usually take thirty to forty-five minutes to establish and are, all too often, the only story-line. But with the war and the sudden appearance of a personable RAF officer to square off the triangle, a new element was added, somewhat unique to musicals and even, at that time, to U.S. films: a man-woman romance based solely on mutual sexual attraction in the beginning and culminating, in the film's final moments, with lovers going their separate ways with

Philip Merivale attempts to interfere in Rita's romance with his son. Janet Blair gives Rita moral support.

only a suggestion that they may eventually get together at some future date, "when the war is over."

The romance between Bowman, as the flying officer, and Rita starts after he first sees her on stage singing and dancing a lush and sensual samba number, "You Excite Me" which, after his first attempt at seduction fails, a group of his buddies reprise the number, with just piano accompaniment, which they sing *off-key,* thereby subtly suggesting that the gorgeous redhead can be conquered, but a more subtle approach and different tactics are called for.

Having gone this far with what in 1945 was a somewhat daring romantic approach, movie censorship

Waiting out a sudden cloud burst with Florence Bates, Marc Platt, Leslie Brooks and Janet Blair, outside the stage door of the London music hall where they perform.

Rita goes on stage as the impromptu assistant of Professor Lamberti after a fire bomb has caused backstage damage and turns his stale comedy act into a sensation by doing a strip-tease.

forced the writers to bring in a new character, who turned out to be the minister-father of the flier and who, in his son's absence, proposes marriage to the showgirl on his son's behalf! This scene is made even more unbelievable since it occurs immediately after Rita has been on stage tormenting a theater full of servicemen by doing a fairly tame striptease act, which the flier's father watches from a box seat. Except for this one device and sequence, *Tonight and Every Night* is really a musical classic since it makes so many departures from what was then standardized screen formula.

All the songs, except the briefly popular ballad "Anywhere," which won an Academy Award nomination for "Best Song," were bright, bouncy and solid tunes which seemed more like the kind of numbers usually composed for a durable theater musical rather than one devised for the screen. Rita's singing was dubbed by Martha Mears—but the bulk of the strictly vocal assignments were well handled by the much underrated Janet Blair. This left Rita the show-type tunes to pretend to sing and expertly interpret with her dancing. "You Excite Me," already noted as a truly lush production number, is probably Rita's all-time best staged and performed song with another number, "Cry and You Cry Alone," running a close second.

Considering that such screen musicals as *Carmen Jones, Porgy and Bess* and *West Side Story* which were all transferred, more or less intact, from the stage to screen years after *Tonight and Every Night* with critics lauding their uncompromising *tragic* endings, it now seems peculiar that this aspect of the film was singled out as *being a fault!*

Besides Jules Styne and Sammy Cahn winning a "Best Song" Oscar nomination (they lost out to Rodgers and Hammerstein for "It Might As Well Be Spring" from *State Fair*), Morris Stoloff and Marlin Skiles were nominated for orchestrating and scoring the music. (But that award, that year, went to Georgie Stoll for *Anchors Aweigh!*)

As a film curiosity, melodic, rewarding and, for its time, somewhat unconventional, *Tonight and Every Night* offered a more-beautiful-than-ever Rita in a tour-de-force performance that allowed her to run the gamut from glamorous gaiety to stark tragedy with an abundance of what is possibly her best on-screen dancing. Now, almost thirty years after its release, it's still eye-appealing with a kind of aura no other musical produced in Hollywood during World War II possessed. But it was still far from being a one-woman vehicle. Marc Platt contributed some expert and unique dance routines and Janet Blair, in an especially strong co-starring role, should have gone on to a much more prominent film career. The whole cast was at the top of their form and director Victor Saville must have inspired a spirit of unity among them which comes through to the audience. And running through the story is a plot syllogism of the three charwomen who clean up the theater and make various comments on the times much like a Greek chorus. So, hinted throughout its footage was this subtle suggestion that what appeared to be an almost-perfect popular Technicolor musical would be something different, a film that would eventually deviate from its genre and end on a note of ironic and uncompromising tragedy.

Lee Bowman, Rita, and Janet Blair get acquainted in a bomb shelter while waiting for the "all clear" whistle.

Weekly Variety said:

"In Rita Hayworth, Columbia has a protagonist of musicals second to none in the industry. Herein she exerts her full charms as a dancer and as a glamorous person, bedecked with whatever costumes and Technicolor photographic bedizenments she might additionally need. Her simulated singing is also done with rare skill. She has also, more than any female star, the power to convince an audience that she is actually in love with the person designated for that enviable spot in the script—a romantic sincerity which gives her scenes genuine passion and emotion. This picture also explores some comparatively new aspects of sex in connection with Miss Hayworth which will not detract from the b.o."

In *The New York Times,* Bosley Crowther said:

"With a blitzed London theater as the locale and the-show-must-go-on as the theme—you know, chin up and face the music while the bombs are coming down—Victor Saville has shaped a very pleasant and sentimentally romantic musical film for Columbia under the title of *Tonight and Every Night.* He has got some melodious songs for it, he has dressed it in lovely pastel shades and he has given it all to Rita Hayworth and a most agreeable cast to play. If your taste is for gaiety touched with pathos, you will find it at the Music Hall. Our ventured guess is that it will be there quite a long time."

And Archer Winsten, in the *New York Post* said:

"If war's gross and grim material can be legitimately translated into the charms and delicious little sorrows of the musical, *Tonight and Every Night* is as good as the next and better than most."

In *New York PM,* John T. McManus said:

"*Tonight and Every Night* is lush and lovely in color and movement, peopled with pleasing folks, punctuated with exciting dance composition and tuneful music . . .

"There is, to start off with, an extremely peppery sailors-and-girls routine that is interrupted by a *Life* photographer sent over to do six pages on hearty May Tolliver's never-failing Music Box. Then there is an inspired rehearsal, apparently blitzed off the regular bill, of personable Marc Platt's impromptu dancing (he makes up steps to anything—Beethoven, Ravel, the whirring of a loom, even Hitler ranting on the radio). Still later there is a breathless samba ensemble, with more swirl than sense but nevertheless wonderful on the eye and ear.

"Also all too brief, for another example, is a severely styled sequence with moods shifting from ballet to hot jazz, danced in a set and costume motif of comic and tragic masks.

"The title sequence is particularly unusual, the characters in it being summoned off a black-and-white newsreel screen to step alive into the colorful on-stage ensemble singing a pretty hep, thumbs-up United Nations number. This is Janet Blair's big moment in the show. Later it is repeated in part as Rita Hayworth steps into Janet's heroic role for the finale, so that the show may go on despite the shattering tragedy rained from the skies on Mrs. Tolliver's stouthearted troupe."

Advance ads and publicity stills such as this suggested much more than the film actually fulfilled, but audiences were still eager to see their "love goddess" begging for the affections of an apparently disinterested Glenn Ford.

Gilda

A Columbia Picture   1946

Produced by Virginia Van Upp. Directed by Charles Vidor. Assistant Director, Art Black. Screenplay by Marion Parsonnet, based on Jo Eisinger's adaptation of E. A. Ellington's original story. Photographed by Rudy Mate. Musical Direction by Morris Stoloff; Arrangements and Orchestrations by Marlin Skiles. Songs: "Put the Blame on Mame" and "Amado Mio," by Doris Fisher and Allan Roberts. Art Direction by Stephen Goosson and Van Nest Polglase. Set Decorations by Robert Priestley. Sound Recording by Lambert Day. Makeup by Clay Campbell. Hair Styles by Helen Hunt. Gowns by Jean Louis. Assistant to the Producer, Norman Deming. Edited by Charles Nelson. 110 minutes.

CAST:

Gilda, RITA HAYWORTH; *Johnny Farrell*, GLENN FORD; *Ballin Mundson*, GEORGE MACREADY; *Obregon*, Joseph Calleia; *Uncle Pio*, Steven Geray; *Casey*, Joseph Sawyer; *Captain Delgado*, Gerald Mohr; *Gabe Evans*, Robert Scott; *German*, Ludwig Donath; *Thomas Langford*, Don Douglas; *Second German*, Lionel Royce; *Little Man*, S. Z. Martel; *Huerta*, George Lewis; *Maria*, Rosa Rey; *Girl*, Ruth Roman; *Socialite*, Ted Hecht; *Woman*, Argentina Brunetti; *Doorman*, Jerry DeCastro; *Man at Masquerade*, Robert Stevens (Kellard); *Bendolin's Wife*, Fernando Eliscu; *Argentine*, Frank Leyva; *Americans*, Forbes Murray, Sam Flint, Bob Board; *Frenchmen*, Jean DeBriac, Oscar Lorraine; *Italian*, George Humbert; *Bendolin*, Eduardo Ciannelli; *Escort*, Russ Vincent; *Englishman*, Herbert Evans; *Clerk*, Robert Tafur; *Peasant Man*, Rodolfo Hoyos.

For every publicity still which showed Rita at the feet of Glenn Ford, there was one with the situation reversed.

Of the slightly more than 300 Hollywood-made feature films released during 1946, only one, Warner Bros.'s *The Big Sleep,* had a script as complicated and as unfathomable as *Gilda.* The film count of that year, which includes the features of major, minor and independent companies, was the lowest annual total since 1928. Columbia Pictures led all others with fifty-three feature films released. No other major company came any closer than releasing half that amount of product (20th Century-Fox) and the prolific runners-up were, respectively, Republic, Monogram and PRC (Producer's Releasing Corporation).

Undisputably, Samuel Goldwyn's *The Best Years of Our Lives,* released by RKO, was the year's most popular and critically acclaimed U.S. film. Two of the next most commercially successful features were *The Jolson Story* and *Gilda,* a pair of gilt-edged blockbusters produced by Columbia, the studio generally referred to as the minor of the majors.

The Jolson Story was the year's happiest surprise since no one, least of all Harry Cohn, or columnist-turned-producer Sid Skolsky, expected it to have such audience appeal or box-office returns of such phenomenal proportions. But the unexpected commercial success of *Gilda* seemed even more startling. Most critics, including Kate Cameron (Dorothy King) of the New

The carnival masquerade sequence in which lovers Rita and Glenn Ford unmask their faces and feelings was given many different interpretations by critics and audiences.

York *Daily News,* who actually called it "high-class trash," many years before Pauline Kael was credited with coining that descriptive phrase, dismissed it. And in spite of a generally poor press reception, *Gilda* inspired the esteemed Bosley Crowther, of *The New York Times,* to refer to Rita Hayworth as Columbia's "Superstar," some twenty years before underground film maker Andy Warhol ostensibly invented that adjective. (Warhol has never taken credit for doing it, but his partisans attribute it to him anyway.)

While the critics, at best, remained lukewarm about *Gilda* and its dubious virtues, the public had no such reservations. It was *the* film to which the returned GIs took their wives and sweethearts to see. (Most of whom returned to see it again and again to find out what part of Miss Hayworth's image attracted their particular male to see if they could attempt to emulate it to advantage in their own romantic lives.) For *Gilda* was a screen heroine of ambiguous morality, breathtaking beauty and oscillating romantic affections who inhabited a luxurious world in which her own expensive tranpings were backgrounded by exotic surroundings and international intrigue. Probably her closest screen counterpart was the "heroine" Jean Harlow had played so delightfully years earlier in *Red Dust.* And if *Gilda* lacked anything at all that such a woman of the world needed, it was probably a sense of humor. (Indeed, not a few of

Contrary to every published reference work and every film student who claims Rita Hayworth never sang on screen with her own voice, this climactic reprise of "Put the Blame On Mame" did indeed use her voice and her own guitar accompaniment.

After her torrid rendition of "Put the Blame On Mame," Rita needed the strong-arm tactics of Joseph Sawyer to ward off the advances of admiring males.

With husband George Macready, Rita was involved in a unique domestic relationship in which one was the vixen and the other the villain. French film critics questioned which was which.

the film's detractors thought she had a certain hilarity, albeit unintentional.)

And whether she was pretending to sing a suggestively bawdy ditty like "Put the Blame on Mame," or pretending to hate her leading man, Glenn Ford, as much as she loved him, Rita Hayworth was always in complete control of the situation and whether on screen or merely being alluded to in dialogue, she was always the main attraction. She kept her audiences in suspense just by having them wonder whether or not she was sufficiently endowed to keep her strapless gown suspended above the censor's wrath and occasionally relieved such tensions and speculation generated with a suitable line of dialogue—"If I'd have been a ranch they would have called me the Bar *Nothing*"—delivered in a tradition equal to some of Mae West's most scintillatingly sexual salvos. Rita's *Gilda* was sensual, tempestuous, beautiful, amoral and vengeful. In the hands of any

Buenos Aires detective Joseph Calleia is among the spectators who watch Rita foolishly gamble away her husband's fortune.

Casino owner George Macready has just saved the life of down-on-his-luck vagabond Glenn Ford. The battle for Gilda's affections is yet to come.

Rita also danced and sang (dubbed), the seductively alluring ballad "Amato Mio."

other actress, she would probably have been called the world's most ludicrous female impersonator! But her *Gilda* was always a creature of constant fascination for all men to contemplate and for all interested women to try to imitate. (In some circles the genders switched, but not the fascination.)

But *Gilda's* hit record had a flip side!

Some French film critics declared, in all sincerity, that the film was really Hollywood's first attempt to dare to exploit a homosexual theme which they insisted was explicitly established between the hero (Glenn Ford) and the heroine's husband (George Macready) and that Gilda herself was merely a pawn in their romance and the script device which permitted the film's writers to get away with it. If *Gilda* really deserves this consideration, which the French seem to believe it does, it's hardly the first Hollywood film to tread such forbidden ground in the days of censorship. By applying the "French" appraisal of *Gilda* to earlier Hollywood films, what does one say about a film like *Casablanca,* which climaxes by having the swishy police prefect walk off into the fog of a North African airport with the hero (who has just sent his lady love flying away in the arms of another man) and say, as he tenderly takes his arm,

The affair between Rita and Glenn Ford was interpreted by foreign critics, especially the French, as being a unique *ménage à trois* in actuality, with Rita as the catalyst in a love-hate relationship between George Macready and Glenn Ford.

"I have the feeling this is going to be the beginning of a long and beautiful friendship?" Or the sequence in *Test Pilot* between Clark Gable and Spencer Tracy when Tracy, dying in Gable's arms after an airplane smash-up, looks longing into his tear-stained eyes and says, "If I could come back, you'd be the only reason I'd want to?" Even the earlier Rita Hayworth film, *Only Angels Have Wings,* can also be included as having a homosexual connotation by recalling the way the script called for Thomas Mitchell to lavish wounded-dog devotion on Cary Grant!

When director Charles Vidor heard about the French critic's appraisal of his *Gilda,* his reaction was

Publicity poses such as this convinced a war-weary public that the Hayworth-Ford chemistry was real enough, at least on screen, making this lurid melodrama a box-office bonanza.

by the simple expedient of having the testing crew at Bikini Atoll name the first atomic bomb detonated in peacetime named after the film and adorned with a photographic likeness of Rita!

In recording the event for posterity, *Time* magazine recorded:

"In christening the deadly missile *Gilda,* in honor of the russet-haired Columbia star's latest film, a smitten ground crew and technicians had lovingly pasted her pinup on its side. This spontaneous tribute earned Miss Hayworth nearly as much publicity as the fearsome Gilda got for itself by exploding on schedule. To Miss Hayworth's studio, it amounted to the most literally earth-shaking free plug in the history of the world."

Gilda reunited Rita with Glenn Ford, the likable, handsomely baby-faced actor with the sheepish grin, an implacably grim jaw line and appreciatively twinkling eyes, who had exactly the right male chemistry to merge with her flamboyantly feminine personality. Their love scenes emanated the kind of magical rapport which had everyone aware that they were the most sexually compatible co-stars currently teaming on-screen. And those of us old enough to remember, recalled their encounters as being as sexually stimulating as those in which Garbo and Gilbert accelerated each other's body pressures and the occasions when Gable and Harlow meshed gears with perfect clutching.

Although *Gilda* used singer Anita Ellis to dub most of Rita's singing, it's a film in which Hayworth's own singing voice can be heard in the sequence near the climax when seated by the gambling casino's bar she idly strums a guitar and reprises a chorus of "Put the Blame on Mame." Granted Rita does not have a large

the same as that of all innocent, formerly unaware and now-enlightened filmgoers. "Really?" he said in a condescending way, "I never had any idea those boys were supposed to be like *that!*"

In addition to critical dissertations of its assets and liabilities, *Gilda* is also the film which made Rita Hayworth the world's best-known film star. This occurred

Doing "Put the Blame On Mame" and her famous glove striptease.

Casino owner George Macready introducing his new wife to his new employee (Glenn Ford) for what he thinks is the first time.

In line with her theory that "If I had been a ranch they would have called me the bar nothing," Rita blatantly encourages the attentions of Latin-looking Gerald Mohr during a torrid tango.

voice or an especially trained tone, it is melodious, on-key and quite pleasant. And to further dispel stories that she cannot sing at all, it's a matter of record that she sang in public for servicemen during World War II and on stage in *Charlot's Revue,* which was presented at the El Capitan Theatre in Hollywood in 1940.

Gilda turned out to be durably profitable for Columbia and was reissued twice with international success before being made available for television. And whenever it is telecast, its fascination remains as omnipotent as ever, even with commercial interruptions! If nothing else, *Gilda* is *the* classic example of just how enjoyable a really good bad movie can be.

Howard Barnes, in the New York *Herald Tribune,* said:

"Miss Hayworth does all that one might expect in the title role of the tramp. But she never makes the character stand up with perilous and dynamic quality that it demanded. Glenn Ford is excellent as the stumblebum who runs a casino in Buenos Aires without any notion of the score. George Macready is altogether sinister as the villain of the piece and Joseph Calleia and Joe Sawyer add the melodramatic accents which are obviously demanded. *Gilda* has employed plenty of talent. It is still a boring and slightly confusing production."

John Maynard, in the New York *Journal-American,* said:

"*Gilda* is one of those dramas in which no one is willing to dilly-dally with a remark not endowed with covert menace, or covert something, and in which, as a

Glenn Ford and Rita Hayworth in the tradition of the sound-era's "Great Screen Teams."

result, the most casual observation seems likely to precipitate an explosion of one sort or another.

"The effect, of course, is to achieve a running rather than a mounting suspense, which in general makes for more excitement, if likewise a certain amount of superfluous wear and tear on the nervous system.

"This sort of exhibit, dutifully referred to as 'taut' without the reviewer's even having to look up from his knitting, can be done very badly. Therefore it is my special pleasure to be able to tell you that in *Gilda* it is done very well, written with skill a nice feeling for restraint, and constructed with enough urbanity to make you clean forget for minutes at a time that the proceeding are largely nonsense."

Archer Winsten, in the *New York Post,* said:

"Gilda is exceedingly evanescent entertainment. Its seductive and elegant promises, further weighed with production values, good performances, and flashy action, carry you rapidly forward from scene to scene. Afterwards, toying with the picture's stale morsels of wisdom (Hatred is akin to love, and Marriage on the rebound is no good), you may be willing to pass the picture all right for most of the time it lasts, but not worth a second thought or a first enthusiasm."

Kate Cameron, in the New York *Daily News,* said:

"★ ★ ★ ½ ★ (Three and a half stars) The characters of the drama are interesting and well enough played and although the story has all the elements of high-class trash, director Charles Vidor and his experienced players have given it considerable holding power, by keeping the audience in suspense from one dramatic shift to another."

Ruth Waterbury, in the *Los Angeles Examiner,* said:

"When Judy Garland and Alice Faye got the urge for drama, they went the whole way and in their pictures *The Clock* and *Fallen Angel,* respectively, they handed out the acting straight, without so much as a jazz note or a single twinkle of a toe, to highlight it.

"Rita Hayworth, going heavily dramatic for the first time in *Gilda,* proves herself a smarter show woman. For how this glorious pinup does emote in this one! What a glittering gamut of drama she reveals, plus much of her beautiful self while also singing and dancing! The result is an exciting, glamorous, rich, ruddy melodrama—and if the plot is most incredible at times, you will be more than willing to ignore it while concentrating on its star."

Louise Levitas, in *New York PM,* said:

"With all the possibilities for excitement the movie travels slowly from one near-climax to another, always on the verge of exploding, but never coming out with an honest thrill—except when Miss Hayworth is on the screen.

"In strapless evening gowns which just barely contain her, Miss Hayworth wiggles through some violent emotions.... Opulent is the one special word for *Gilda.*"

As Terpsichore, Greek goddess of the dance.

Down to Earth

A Columbia Picture   1947

Produced by Don Hartman. Directed by Alexander Hall. Assistant Director, Wilbur McGaugh. Screenplay by Edward Blum and Don Hartman, based on characters created by Harry Segall in his play, *Heaven Can Wait*. Photographed in Technicolor by Rudy Mate. Consultant for the Technicolor Company, Natalie Kalmus; Assistant, Francis Cugat. Musical Score by George Duning and Heinz Roemheld. Musical Direction by Morris Stoloff. Orchestral Arrangements by Earl Hagen. Songs: "This Can't Be Legal," "Let's Stay Young Forever," "People Have More Fun Than Anyone" and "They Can't Convince Me," by Doris Fisher and Allan Roberts. Vocal Arrangements by Saul Chaplin. Music Recording by P. J. Faulkner. Dances Staged by Jack Cole. Art Direction by Stephen Goosson and Rudolph Sternad. Set Decoration by William Kiernan. Makeup by Clay Campbell. Hair Styles by Helen Hunt. Gowns and Costumes by Jean Louis. Sound Recording by George Cooper. Assistant to the Producer, Norman Deming. Edited by Viola Lawrence. 101 minutes.

CAST:

Terpsichore/Kitty Pendleton, RITA HAYWORTH; *Danny Miller,* LARRY PARKS; *Eddie Marin,* MARC PLATT; *Mr. Jordan,* ROLAND CULVER; *Max Corkle,* JAMES GLEASON; *Messenger 7013,* EDWARD EVERETT HORTON; *Georgia Evans,* ADELE JERGENS; *Joe Mannion,* GEORGE MACREADY; *Police Lieutenant,* WILLIAM FRAWLEY; *Betty,* Jean Donahue; *Dolly,* Kathleen O'Malley; *Spike,* William Haade; *Kelly,* James Burke; *Orchestra Leader,* Fred Sears; *Muses,* Virginia Hunter, Lynne Merrick, Dusty Anderson, Doris Houck, Shirley Molohon, Peggy Maley, Dorothy Brady (Hart), Jo Hattigan, Lucille Casey; *Escort 3082,* Lucien Littlefield;

Terpsichore and producer Danny Miller (Larry Parks) listen to Broadway agent Max Corkle (James Gleason).

Sloan, Myron Healey; *Dancer,* Harriette Ann Gray; *Stage Manager,* Rudy Cameron; *Mr. Somerset,* Arthur Blake; *Unnumbered Messenger,* Wilbur Mack; *Coupier,* Jean Del Val; *Conductor,* Billy Bletcher; *Porter,* Nicodemus Stewart; *Policemen,* Raoul Freeman, Bob Ryan; *Henchman,* Matty Fain; *Janitor,* Frank Darien; *Sleeping Man,* Jack Norton; *Announcer,* Tom Hanlon; *Dow-ager,* Mary Forbes; *Frenchman,* Count Stefenelli; *Stage Hand,* Eddie Acuff; *Police Sergeant,* Al Bridge; *Reporter,* Tom Daly; *Chorine,* Francine Kennedy; *Bit Women,* Winifred Harris, Grace Hampton, Cora Witherspoon, Mary Newton, Ottola Nesmith; *Rosebud,* Kay Vallon; *Bit Men,* Ernest Hilliard, Fred Howard, Forbes Murray, Boyd Irwin, Cecil Weston, Edward Harvey.

NOTES:

Because all of the ingredients that went into concocting *Down to Earth* had been successfully pretested in other films, Columbia rightly felt they had a musical comedy that came with a built-in box-office guarantee.

Two of its fictional characters, Mr. Jordan and Messenger 7013, had been an integral part of the fantasy of their 1941 comedy *Here Comes Mr. Jordan* and a third character from that film, Broadway agent Max Corkle, had been one of its comedy highlights. The actors who originated the roles of Max and the messenger, James Gleason and Edward Everett Horton were successfully recruited to repeat their parts and the stars of the previous year's most outstandingly successful films *(Gilda* and *The Jolson Story),* Rita Hayworth and Larry Parks, were handed the co-starring assignments.

The advertisements for *Down to Earth* declared that "Larry Parks Sings It His Way!" and that Rita Hayworth was "The Screen's Most Gloriously Gorgeous Goddess." Parks, sans the benison of Al Jolson's singing emanating from his lips, turned out to have a pleasant enough singing voice of his own, but it lacked the "Folks, you ain't heard nothin' yet!" force of Jolson which audiences wanted and had expected. On the other

Terpsichore holds conference on Mount Parnassus with some of the Muses.

hand, Rita, seemingly more earthy than ever, was never more breathtakingly beautiful on screen or more magnificently photographed. Nobody appeared to be the least bit dismayed to discover she was not an especially adroit ballet dancer, since her other charms were otherwise amply exploited. And as Terpischore, Goddess of the Dance disguised as an earthly socialite showgirl, who came to earth to prevent producer Parks from producing a musical about swinging the muses, she had an opportunity to play what amounted to a dual role.

The songs were more than serviceable and they were lyrically witty and lavishly staged. Except for "People Have More Fun Than Anyone," most of them remained in the memory musically about as long as last week's shopping list. The color photography was eye-arresting with accents on gold, silver, vivid greens and aquamarine shades rather than the usual gaudy reds and oranges which made many Technicolor musicals eye-assaulting. And since the average filmgoer couldn't discern much difference between esthetically adroit ballet and the awkwardly awful kind, they concentrated on ogling and appreciating the physical assets of the show and ignoring the dubiously artistic ones. Nobody gave a passing thought to the fact that Rita's singing was dubbed (by Anita Ellis) since her lip synchronization was perfect. All of which meant that Columbia's prediction of a resounding box-office triumph was fulfilled and their efforts in giving *Down to Earth* their most expensive sales campaign paid off. The fact that most critics rather liked the show was just so much more icing on an already delectable cake.

If anything at all can be deduced from all this it's

Terpsichore poses as a chorus girl who inherits the leading role in a show "Swinging the Muses" which, she insists, must be authentic. Here she stops rehearsal to correct a historical point.

With Marc Platt.

Terpsichore convinces heavenly host Roland Culver that she is needed on earth to prevent her legend from being defamed.

simply the fact that Columbia proved twice that fantasy can be successful on the screen even though film wiseacres always maintained otherwise.

Howard Barnes, in the New York *Herald Tribune,* said:

"A few intrepid producers have wisely disregarded the theater, the concert hall and variety to establish a new and exciting song and dance pattern, peculiarly suited to the screen. Curiously enough, the earliest efforts in the field were the happiest. *42nd Street* or René Clair's delightful *Sous les Toits de Paris* have not been surpassed for a couple of decades. The great dance team of Fred Astaire and Ginger Rogers, with the aid of fine songs and superb direction, appeared to advantage in several musicals that had the definite filmic character. Unfortunately, most screen musicals have failed to concentrate on qualities indigenous to the screen.

"It is pleasant, then, to report that *Down to Earth,* which has come to the Music Hall, makes a brave try to capture the nice blend of music, dancing and drama which has characterized the best of its predecessors. Instead of making over a Broadway show, it has ornamented a motion picture fantasy with fret notes, faststepping and fancy backgrounds . . .

"The fluency is mostly contrived by Rita Hayworth, who has what is possibly the fattest role of any song and dance actress's career. Not only does she play Terpsichore in a two-way version of a big Broadway musical, but she actually is Terpsichore, coming down to earth to defend the honor of the muses. She dances all

Being escorted to Earth by heavenly messenger Edward Everett Horton.

With Marc Platt and Larry Parks doing "People Have More Fun Than Anyone."

over the place, sings pleasantly and makes the fantasy beguiling. She might have had better songs, but she rarely fails to enliven the production."

And *Newsweek* said:

"According to *Down to Earth,* Columbia's lavish musical, one should still beware of Greeks bearing gifts. This time the Greek is the goddess Terpsichore (Rita Hayworth), and her ostensible gift, as the Muse of the Dance, is to help Larry Parks rehearse a musical comedy about the nine muses. What happens isn't exactly up to *The Jolson Story* standard, but it's entertaining fare . . . the music, dancing and sets are lively and imaginative."

Motion Picture Herald said:

"*Down to Earth* has all the indications of being one of the year's best musicals. It glows with excellent Technicolor, is based on an imaginative and amusing story involving the by now quite famous Mr. Jordan of Columbia's 1941 release *Here Comes Mr. Jordan* and, in addition to a marquee combination that will fill any exhibitor's heart with joy, offers a number of eye-and-ear-filling production numbers of high quality . . . The film blends humor, drama, dance and music into a most enjoyable whole."

Here Comes Mr. Jordan (Columbia; 1941) was also directed by Alexander Hall and the stars were Robert Montgomery, Evelyn Keyes and Rita Johnson. But James Gleason (as *Max Corkle*), Edward Everett Horton (as *Messenger 7013*) and Claude Rains (as *Mr. Jordan),* are all equally well remembered for their adroit comedy performances in what was one of that year's best films.

With Larry Parks.

With James Gleason, James Burke and Roland Culver.

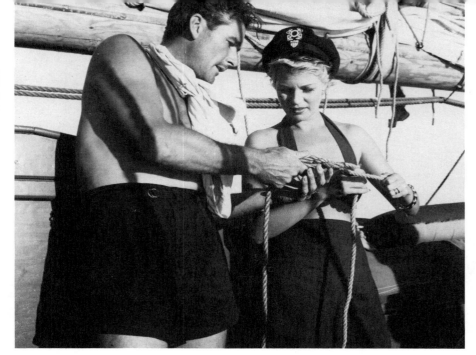

Between scenes with Errol Flynn, owner of the yacht "Zaca." Flynn did a gag guest appearance (unbilled) in the film as one of the yacht's crew members.

The Lady from Shanghai

A Columbia Picture   1948

Produced, Directed and Written for the Screen by Orson Welles. Associate Producers, Richard Wilson and William Castle. Assistant Director, Sam Nelson. Welles's Screenplay based on Sherwood King's novel, *If I Should Die Before I Wake*. Photographed by Charles Lawton, Jr. Musical Score by Heinz Roemheld. Musical Direction by Morris Stoloff. Song: "Please Don't Kiss Me," by Doris Fisher and Allan Roberts (singing dubbed by Anita Ellis). Art Direction by Stephen Goosson and Sturges Crane. Set Decoration by Wilbur Menefee and Herman Schoenbrun. Makeup by Robert Schiffer and Clay Campbell. Hair Styles by Helen Hunt. Gowns by Jean Louis. Sound Recording by Lodge Cunningham. Edited by Viola Lawrence. 81 minutes.

CAST:

Elsa Bannister, RITA HAYWORTH; *Michael O'Hara,* ORSON WELLES; *Arthur Bannister,* EVERETT SLOANE; *George Grisby,* GLENN ANDERS; *Sidney Broome,* Ted De Corsia; *Judge,* Erskine Sanford; *Goldie,* Gus Schilling; *District Attorney,* Carl Frank; *Jake,* Louis Merrill; *Bessie,* Evelyn Ellis; *Cab Driver,* Harry Shannon; *Li,* Wong Show Chong; *Yacht Captain,* Sam Nelson; *Old Lady,* Edythe Elliott; *Police Lieutenant,* Joseph Granby; *Policemen,* Al Eben, Norman Thomson, Edward Coke, Harry Strang, Phillip Morris, Steve Benton, Milton Kibbee, Philip Van Zandt; *Reporters,* William Alland, Alvin Hammer, Mary Newton, Robert Gray; *Waiter,* Gerald Pierce; *Truck Driver,* Maynard Holmes; *Guards,* Jack Baxley, Edward Peil, Heenan Elliott; *Schoolteacher,* Jessie Arnold; *Court Clerk,* John Elliott; *Court Reporter,* Byron Kane; *Old Woman,* Dorothy Vaughn; *Jury Foreman,* Charles Meakin; *Chinese Girls,* Doris Chan, Billy Louie; *Bit Women,* Tiny Jones, Mabel Smaney; *Garage Attendant,* Joe Recht; *Ticket Seller,* Jean Wong; *Ticket Taker,* Artane Wong; *Bit Men,* George "Shorty" Charello, Vernon Cansino; *Chinese Couple,* Grace Lem, Preston Lee; *Second Cab Driver,* Joseph Palma.

NOTES:

The Lady From Shanghai is the last film Rita made for Columbia under the terms of her old contract. In accepting the role, she took over an assignment originally promised to Ida Lupino. Reluctant at first to accept the part, because she was in the process of divorcing Orson Welles, she changed her mind when a temporary reconciliation was effected and she believed their daughter, Rebecca, might financially benefit from the project since Welles's salary as an actor would be a percentage of the film's gross. Welles was already in debt to Columbia President Harry Cohn and his function as writer,

A publicity still with Orson Welles.

In a dark amusement park concession, Rita takes deadly and accurate aim at her husband.

A publicity still in the Hall of Mirrors.

producer and director would expunge that obligation.

Cohn, none too keen about the film from the time Welles first proposed it, was even less enthusiastic about having Miss Hayworth involved in it since this would be the last chance Columbia would have to reap a large profit from her. (She had already formed her own production company, Beckworth, and her new deal called for Columbia to assume all production costs of her subsequent films but for her to share equally in the profits in lieu of a salary.) And before production got underway, Cohn's mild reservations turned to wild outbursts of damnation against his producer-writer-director-star. Seeing Rita for the first time after Welles ordered her russet hair cut to a short feather bob and bleached a metallic blonde, called "champagne blonde," the Columbia prexy screamed, "Oh, my God! What has that bastard done?"

Miss Hayworth's loyal legion of fans were equally adamant about her transformation although somewhat more contained. Not so, however, with some of Welles's film-colony enemies.

Louella Parsons, who had remained a loyal Hayworth partisan, made no bones about her dislike of "awesome Orson, the self-styled genius," and told her readers he was washed up in Hollywood and, being "washed up" as Rita's husband, his intent was to destroy his ex-wife's screen image in an attempt to revenge himself on the entire Hollywood film colony and industry because no one in it either understood, appreciated or accepted him.

Welles, whose rightful place in motion picture history is a lot more certain and assured than that of the late Miss Parsons, conceded, however, that *The Lady from Shanghai* was "an experiment in what not to do."

Whether he meant that statement to mean his attempts to change Rita's image or not to again work under the pressures of being writer, producer, director and actor for a major studio honestly attempting to fulfill a financial obligation with success and work in professional harmony with a leading lady he had already discovered he could not live with, or trying his best to complete a project in which he had obviously lost all interest, or a combination of all these circumstances, is something only Welles himself can clarify. One thing, however, is certain: *The Lady from Shanghai,* albeit a financial fiasco, is far from being the artistic disaster he let everyone—Harry Cohn, the critics and the public—convince him it was.

First of all, it's imaginative, well directed, though often consciously so, and occasionally innovative. The

As she lies dying on the floor of an amusement park concession after a gun battle with her husband, Rita fails to gain the sympathy of her lover, Orson Welles.

script, however, was not well coordinated and the film lacks an overall continuity flow because important cover shots, necessary to maintain the suspense, and hence the audience interest, are missing. Whether these flaws are the result of Cohn's decision to edit it down to the shortest possible running time after being convinced it was a bomb (or ordered it down to assure its being a disaster), or Welles's own oversight, can conjure up all sorts of interesting speculation. The longest running time ever established, after the first rough-cut screening, was only ninety-one minutes and parts of the known missing footage, including an airplane sequence

Rita seeks out sailor Orson Welles in a Chinese theater in San Francisco, for a previously arranged rendezvous.

With Orson Welles.

and a montage, could not account for its uneven tempo. It's difficult to think, or even believe, Welles would sabotage his own film and even more improbable to believe that Cohn, "the tightest-fisted bastard in the business" (his own appraisal), would jeopardize an opportunity to make a buck.

The Lady from Shanghai seems to get better and better with subsequent viewings whenever it is included in an Orson Welles retrospective but, unfortunately, it seems to be even more confusing and unsatisfying than it originally was whenever it's shown on television and further obfuscated by eight or ten commercial interruptions.

Filmed partly at Columbia studios and on locations in San Francisco (the Sausalito waterfront and the in-terior of the Mandarin Theatre in the Chinatown district), Welles and his cast and crew also spent twenty-eight days filming in Acapulco, including that Mexican resort's harbor and its picturesque native quarters. The luxurious yacht that figures so prominently in the story was the *Zaca,* chartered from its owner, Errol Flynn, who served as skipper (off-camera) during its filming and who can actually be glimpsed, very briefly, in the background of one scene outside a cantina. Principal photography on *The Lady from Shanghai* was completed on the last day of February in 1947 but its release was held up over fifteen months.

Said *Time* magazine:

"*The Lady from Shanghai* is a piece of sleight of hand by Orson Welles. The big trick in this picture was to divert a head-on collison of at least six plots, and make of it a smooth-flowing, six-lane whodunit. Orson brings the trick off . . . But not all his magic works. He makes a blonde out of his onetime wife, redhead Rita Hayworth, but not an actress."

Bosley Crowther, in *The New York Times,* said:

"For a fellow who has as much talent with a camera as Orson Welles and whose powers of pictorial invention are as fluid and as forcible as his, this gentleman certainly has a strange way of marring his films with sloppiness which he seems to assume that his dazzling exhibitions of skill will camouflage. . . . Indeed his performance in the picture—and his exhibitionistic coverups of the story's general untidiness—give ironic point to his first line: "When I start out to make a fool of myself, there's very little can stop me!""

With Orson Welles in the Hall of Mirrors.

Rita as the gypsy enchantress who has induced Glenn Ford to desert his duties, kill her husband in a fight for her affections, and take over the leadership of a gang of mountain-dwelling marauders.

The Loves of Carmen

A Beckworth Corporation Production,
Released by Columbia Pictures   1948

Produced and Directed by Charles Vidor. Assistant Director, Earl Bellamy. Screenplay by Helen Deutsch, based on Prosper Mérimée's story of Carmen. Photographed in Technicolor by William Snyder. Operating Cameraman, Fayte Brown. Consultant for the Technicolor Company, Natalie Kalmus; Associate, Francis Cugat. Musical Score by Mario Castelnuovo-Tedesco. Musical Direction by Morris Stoloff. Song: "The Love of A Gypsy," by Morris Stoloff and Fred Karger. Director of Swordplay, Ralph Faulkner. Choreography by Robert Sidney and Eduardo Cansino. Art Direction by Stephen Goosson and Cary Odell. Set Decoration by Wilbur Menefee and William Kiernan. Makeup by Clay Campbell. Hair Styles by Helen Hunt. Gowns and Costumes by Jean Louis. Sound Recording by Frank Goodwin. Script Supervisor, F. McDowell. Grip, Walter Meins. Edited by Charles Nelson. 99 minutes.

CAST:

Carmen, RITA HAYWORTH; *Don José,* GLENN FORD; *Andres,* RON RANDELL; *Garcia,* VICTOR JORY; *Dancairé,* LUTHER ADLER; *Colonel,* ARNOLD MOSS; *Remendado,* JOSEPH BULOFF; *Old Gypsy Crone,* MAR-GARET WYCHERLY; *Pablo,* Bernard Nedell; *Lucas,* John Baragrey; *Sergeant,* Philip Van Zandt; *Groom,* Anthony Dante; *Bride,* Veronika Pataky; *Bride's Mother,* Rosa Turich; *Ancient Gypsy Woman,* Leona Roberts; *Shopkeeper,* Helen Freeman; *Soldiers,* Vernon Cansino, Peter Virgo; *Gypsy Dancers,* Fernando Ramos, Roy Fitzell, José Cansino; *Stagecoach Passengers,* Joaquin Elizonda, Paul Bradley, Lala DeTolly, Maria Scheue, Barbara Hayden; *Dragoon,* Wally Cassell; *Dragoon's Sergeants,* Paul Marion, Paul Fierro, John T. Verros; *Footman,* Trevor Bardette; *Orderly,* Joseph Malouf; *Toreador,* Juan Duval; *Beggar,* Francis Pierlot; *Carmen's Dancing Partner,* Robert Sidney; *Bit Women,* Tessie Murray, Angella Gomez, Roselyn Strangis, Lulu Mae Bohrman, Virginia Vann, Rosita Delva, Lucille Charles, Delores Corral, Frances Rey, Claire DuBrey, Kate Drain Lawson, Inez Palange, Nanette Vallon, Eula Morgan, Celeste Savoi, Florence Auer, Lupe Gonzalez, Alma Beltram, Nina Campana; *Bit Men,* George Bell, Thomas Malinari, Julio Rojas, Peter Cusanelli, David Ortega, Roque Ybarra, Dimas Sotello, Cosmo Sardo, Alfred Paix, Jerry De Castro, Andrew Roud, Al Caruso.

With fugitive soldier Glenn Ford in their mountain hideout.

NOTES:

Advertisements for *The Loves of Carmen* stressed the fact that the film was "not an opera—but a dramatic version of the Prosper Mérimée Story!" While there can be no argument with the film's box-office success, it seemed a rather unusual way to exploit it since all previous U.S. versions of *Carmen* had all been filmed sans songs and music by Bizet. In fact all prior U.S. versions had been silent films—the earliest was made by the Edison Company (1904), three versions appeared during 1913 with Marion Leonard (Monopol), Marguerite Snow (Tannhauser) and Pearl Sindelar (Pathé) and in 1915 Cecil B. DeMille's version starred the diva of the Metropolitan Opera, Geraldine Farrar and William Fox's version starred Theda Bara. In the 1916 burlesque of *Carmen,* Charlie Chaplin played *Don José* and Edna Purviance was the fiery cigarette factory girl of the title. The Mérimée heroine apparently kicked the cinema habit until 1921 when Ernst Lubitsch directed Pola Negri in a version called *Gypsy Blood,* and in 1927 Fox made a new version, *The Loves of Carmen* with Dolores Del Rio. The following year Raquel Meller made a French silent version which had limited U.S. distribution. The first talkie version was made in England in 1931 with Marguerite Namara and was called *Gypsy Love.* In 1933 Lotte Reiniger made an animated burlesque of it in Germany and Imperio Argentiña starred in a 1940 version filmed in Mexico. The 1947 Italian version, which did very well on the U.S. art-house circuits, starred Vivian Romance and, it has been bruited about, inspired Rita to roll her own interpretation.

The Bizet Opera had premiered on the stage in

Paris, at the Opéra Comique, in March of 1875, just a few months before the composer died. It was first performed in the United States at New York's Academy of Music in 1878 and made its Metropolitan Opera debut in 1884, sung in Italian. Later Metropolitan versions were performed in German and French.

Some of the most famous divas to sing the title role on stage were Calvé, Hauk, Brema, Breval, Farrar, Chenal, Delna, Destinn, Fremstad, Galli-Marie, Garden, Gay, de l'Isle, Lunn, Leblanc, Lehmann, Lucca, Royce, Schumann-Heink and Vix. Some of the most glamorous divas to sing the title role, Swarthout, Stevens, Pons and Callas, although physically suited to it, were the least musically successful!

The 1948 film version of *The Loves of Carmen* turned out to be a financially shrewd, if not artistically well-realized, production with which to launch Rita's producing company, Beckworth. And, as an employer, she had the opportunity to indulge in the Hollywood nepotism tradition by having her father assist in the choreography, her uncle José, appear as one of the dancers, and her brother Vernon doing an extra bit as a soldier. She availed herself of the best technicians on the Columbia lot, including her favorite director, Charles Vidor. It was, however, as an actress that she functioned best. Making lavish use of her considerable charms, physical assets and whatever acting ability was necessary, she made her *Carmen* the most colorful, heartless and hot-blooded screen heroine of the year.

But Rita's one lapse of filmmaking acumen seemed to be in having her favorite co-star, Glenn Ford, play Don José. The possessor of one of the great American screen faces, and an actor whose mere presence emanated a strength of character, Ford was never able to make audiences believe in him as the Spaniard with the blighted love life since his acting forte usually followed a much different romantic approach. (Offer the heroine yourself, the prospects of a happy future and a direct,

With Glenn Ford.

nonneurotic, sexual approach, open and above-board. And if that fails, a few fast slaps across the chops would usually bring any reluctant heroine to her senses.)

The Loves of Carmen was in production eighty-one days and budgeted in the neighborhood of around two and a half million dollars. Every cent spent showed on the screen. Most of the exteriors were filmed at Lone Pine, California, on and around Mount Whitney. When

Don José (Glenn Ford) and another soldier (Ron Randell) come to arrest Carmen after a hair-pulling street brawl.

[175]

someone casually mentioned to director Vidor that the local terrain was quite a contrast to Seville and the surrounding countryside, he replied in typical Hungarian obduracy:

"So what? After seeing these beautiful mountains and all this natural scenery, people aren't going to quibble about the scenery not matching the story locale."

Vidor had a rather valid point but most filmgoers believed the film's physical attraction was named Rita Hayworth and not Mount Whitney.

Said *Weekly Variety:*

"There has never been a gypsy so fascinating or so tempting as Rita Hayworth makes her character here, and the entertainment it offers is the exploitable sort which should have long lines outside the theatres."

Said *Hollywood Reporter:*

"The saga of the Spanish beauty has never been played against such a lavish backdrop before. The studio and the producer do themselves proud in the artistry of the settings, the exquisite details of the costumes, and the breathtaking grandeur of the Technicolor. These elements breathe considerable vitality into the ancient Carmen melodrama and give it an unexpected fillip . . . Rita Hayworth's Carmen is just as the character should be played—strutting, posturing, fiendishly clever, and, as beautiful as the dawn. Glenn Ford's attempts at Don José are less successful, through no fault of his own. For all the makeup and the costumes, his appearance remains that of a schoolboy on his first visit to a peep show."

Rita's flamboyant Carmen.

Champagne Safari

A Jackson Leighter Associates Production,
   Released by Defense Films   1952

Produced, Directed and Photographed in Pathé Color by Jackson Leighter. Compiled and Edited by Herbert Bregstein. Narration Written by Larry Klingman. 60 minutes.

NOTES:

Champagne Safari (sometimes called *Safari So Good*) is a documentary film that motion picture agent and executive Jackson Leighter photographed in 1950 and 1951 when, accompanied by wife, he was invited by Rita Hayworth and Prince Aly Khan to share their honeymoon trip through the jungles and palaces of Africa, prologued by a trip to the Near, Middle and Far East.

   Footage showed Rita accompanying her husband, Prince Aly Khan, on visits to the African nations under Moslem rule and also depicted them as visitors to the fabulous gambling casinos of the East. Additional footage depicted Rita, without her husband, inspecting the Acropolis in Greece and the Pyramids and Sphinx in Egypt. From Cairo, the safari traveled to Luxor and then up the Nile to the African domains of the Aga Khan. Transportation for the party was supplied by riverboat, airplane, Jaguar, Rolls-Royce, rickshaw and Jeep.

   In Uganda and Tanganyika, the royal honeymooners were entertained, worshipped and lavishly gifted by the Moslem natives.

In *American Weekly,* Larry Klingman, who wrote the narration, reported:

   "While Rita's romance with crooner Dick Haymes

had been making the headlines—with the help of U.S. Immigration authorities, who want him deported to his native Argentina—the public is being invited to see her in an unusual movie called *Champagne Safari*.

"This picture turns the clock back to the days when she was married to Aly Khan, who, oddly enough, was visiting this country at the height of the romantic Mr. Haymes' troubles with Uncle Sam. It is the pictorial record of the trip, which Rita and her Moslem prince made together in 1950 and 1951, through the jungles and palaces of Africa and the Middle East plus 'side trips.'"

Public interest in Rita had been at fever pitch since the first time she met Prince Aly Khan at a party hostessed by Elsa Maxwell a few years earlier, and ultimately, after her parting with the prince and seeking a divorce, she agreed to allowing this documentary to be released when promised a percentage of the gross it would ostensibly amass.

The documentary actually premiered at New York's Rialto Theatre on the last day of 1951 but reviews were neither good nor bad, they are simply nonexistent! *Champagne Safari* ultimately played the Midwest—one Chicago theater coupled it with *Affair in Trinidad* and did fabulous business. That indicated very little, since all theaters did well with *Affair in Trinidad* without additional program inducements. In 1952 exhibitor-theater owner Norman Elson booked it into his five theaters, four in the Greater New York area and one in Jersey City, which usually showed newsreels. During this run it had the distinction of playing New York City in different theaters simultaneously under different titles!

In 1954, with a lurid and revamped publicity campaign, it played the grind houses of the larger cities. After that *Champagne Safari* went into a sort of limbo from which it apparently emerged only once when a Los Angeles television station scheduled it for exhibition but on the night of its telecast only twenty-five minutes of it was shown before it was preempted for a baseball game. Viewers were told it would be telecast again at a later date. That was sometime in the summer of 1955. As of the end of 1973, it has never, to my knowledge, been shown again on television in the Los Angeles area. Whether it ever was is debatable.

It's doubtful that *Champagne Safari* ever earned back its negative cost of prints, advertising, publicity and transportation.

In 1973 Miss Hayworth said:

"As far as I know it bombed. I never made a cent out of it but at one time I did have a print of it which I thought might interest Yasmin when she was old enough to understand it. I suppose I still have it around . . . somewhere . . ."

With photographer Jackson Leighter.

Thumbing her nose at cameramen during a walking tour while on her honeymoon.

With Glenn Ford and George Voscovek.

Affair in Trinidad

A Beckworth Corporation Production,
Released by Columbia Pictures   1952

Produced and Directed by Vincent Sherman. Associate Producer, Virginia Van Upp (uncredited). Assistant Director, Earl Bellamy. Screenplay by Oscar Saul and James Gunn, based on Virginia Van Upp and Berne Giller's original story. Photographed by Joseph Walker. Musical Score by George Duning. Musical Direction by Morris Stoloff. Songs: "I've Been Kissed Before" and "Trinidad Lady," by Lester Lee and Bob Russell (singing for Miss Hayworth dubbed by Jo Ann Greer). Vocal Arrangements by Saul Chaplin. Choreography by Valerie Bettis. Art Direction by Walter Holscher. Set Decoration by William Kiernan. Makeup by Clay Campbell. Hair Styles by Helen Hunt. Gowns by Jean Louis. Executive Consultant for the Beckworth Corporation, Jackson Leighter. Edited by Viola Lawrence. 98 minutes.

CAST:

Chris Emery, RITA HAYWORTH; *Steve Emery,* GLENN FORD; *Max Fabian,* ALEXANDER SCOURBY; *Veronica,* VALERIE BETTIS; *Inspector Smythe,* TORIN THATCHER; *Anderson,* Howard Wendell; *Walters,* Karel Stepanek; *Dr. Franz Huebling,* George Voskovec; *Wittol,* Steven Geray; *Peter Bronec,* Walter Kohler; *Dominique,* Juanita Moore; *Olaf,* Gregg Martell; *Martin,* Mort Mills; *Pilot,* Robert Boon; *Coroner,* Ralph Moody; *Neal Emery,* Ross Elliott; *Refugee,* Franz Roehn; *Mr. Peters,* Don Kohler; *Stewardess,* Kathleen O'Malley; *Airport Clerk,* Fred Baker; *Bobby,* Don Blackman; *Passenger,* Leonidas Ossetynski; *Fishermen,* Joel Fluellen, Roy Glenn, Ivan Browning; *Englishman,* John Sherman.

NOTES:

At the time of its release. *Affair in Trinidad* had one valid virtue: an inside joke involving Valerie Bettis, a dancer who had recently made quite a name for herself on Broadway with her *Tiger Lily* ballet and who choreographed the film as well as playing the inebriated and flashy wife of a nervous saboteur. During the film,

Rita, caught snooping, is strong-armed by Gregg Martell.

after Rita finishes her second flamboyant dance, Miss Bettis, who had been one of the spectators to it, says with a completely straight face:

"Gee, I wish I could dance like that!"

Everyone familiar with Miss Bettis's brilliance found this to be a cinema moment delightful enough to cherish and suggested the film that might have been: a sober spoof of *Gilda,* instead of an imitation, and of other outrageous screen heroines who were involved in international intrigue right up to their naval bases.

Instead, *Affair in Trinidad,* merely rehashed the doings of such damsels who dabble in spying with a plot that any ten-year-old could sing off-key with more originality. As Miss Hayworth so aptly put it some years later:

"It wasn't really a movie. It was a culmination of compromises made by everyone from the gateman at Columbia right up to Harry Cohn himself."

Although the public has always been led to believe that nobody ever deliberately starts out to make a bad film, and this particular one was apparently conceived in sincerity and good intentions, the circumstances in-

In an effort to save Glenn Ford's life by forcing him to leave the dinner party in disgust, Rita performs a lurid song and dance number in front of guests.

The "Trinidad Lady" number.

Dining with Alexander Scourby and Glenn Ford.

volving its production, and preproduction, would probably make a good movie.

Affair in Trinidad was Rita's first feature film released in four years, and the public was therefore anticipating her return with great pleasure. Much of this pleasure could be derived from the fact that shortly after her marriage to Prince Aly Khan, Miss Hayworth announced that she would probably never again make a film. Her divorce changed all that and was in actual arbitration during the time the film was in production.

And just four days prior to beginning principal photography, Rita announced her dissatisfaction with the script and advised Harry Cohn, through her Beckworth Corporation, that she would vacation until a script was revised to her complete approval.

Well aware that the public and the exhibitors and the Columbia stockholders, of whom he was one, wanted Hayworth back on screen, Harry Cohn put writers James Gunn and Oscar Saul to work revising the script and sweet-talked Rita into beginning on schedule and shooting only those scenes which met with her approval. But everything was far from resolved and *Affair in Trinidad* was becoming known around Hollywood as *Compromise at Columbia*. After several weeks, when the script still wasn't satisfactory, Rita walked off the film, maintaining that returning to the screen in an inferior vehicle might jeopardize whatever box-office power she still possessed. Her action caused Harry Cohn to suspend her, prepare a lawsuit against her and sue for damages of all costs involved while she held up

Testifying at the inquest.

production. Mulling that over, Rita elected to return and finish the film.

And when the trade-paper reviews appeared after the first sneak preview, nobody at Columbia suspected that *Affair in Trinidad* would outgross *Gilda* by more than a million dollars! Resigned to the fact that Hayworth apparently could do no wrong, Cohn reissued *Gilda* and announced that all subsequent films with the Love Goddess would be Technicolor specials.

Here are some excerpts from the reviews of one of 1952's top-grossing films.

Hollywood Reporter:

"*Affair in Trinidad* is lengthy and the shots are called, telegraphed, radioed. Four writers, seemingly at odds with each other, hacked away at fashioning this cloak-and-dagger plot against the Port of Spain and Trinidad background . . . When Rita dances the Valerie Bettis choreography the pictorial atmosphere warms up considerably, but somehow the graceful, subtly sexy element of *Gilda* and other pictures is absent."

Hollis Alpert in *The Saturday Review:*

"There are no compliments owing to anyone who has had anything to do with *Affair in Trinidad* (Columbia), which brings Rita Hayworth back to the American screen. It is a mess of inept writing, directing and acting from beginning to end, and I see no point in mentioning any of the preposterous details of the story."

Bosley Crowther in *The New York Times:*

"The demurely returning Miss Hayworth proves no bargain after an absence of four years. In that time, we had probably forgotten what a mediocre actress she is, and now the bald fact—politely winked at in the past—hits one right between the eyes.

"Tawny she is and sometimes handsome in a highly shellacked and tailored way, but her acting is vastly unimpressive of anything but the postures of a doll. And the dancing she does in this picture makes her look both vulgar and grotesque. Miss Hayworth is getting her comeuppance for being a harum-scarum girl."

Cue magazine:

"Before carrot-topped Rita Hayworth became royalty, she played (in *Gilda*) a tough, sexy songbird stranded in South America and sought after by every man within a thousand miles. Tempus fugits, and actress becomes princess and *vice-versa* and lo, and behold!—Rita is back again in Hollywood. And know what she's playing? A tough, sexy songbird stranded in South America and sought after etc., etc.

"For students of cinematic *curiosa,* it is worth knowing that it was Glenn Ford who slapped her then and

With Howard Wendell and Torin Thatcher.

slaps her now, who saved her from an international cartel then and from a Russian espionage ring now. If this scratchy sound track seems to be repeating itself, it's no accident. The plot is hemstitched a little differently, but not enough to disturb the fact that if you think you've seen and heard all this before, it's simply because you have. . . . All this is unwittingly comic rather than melodramatic, since Rita is supported (if that's the word), in addition to Mr. Ford, by a large cast that includes sneering villain Alexander Scourby, dancer Valerie Bettis (who never gets a chance to dance, with Rita in the picture), and Torin Thatcher."

Howard McClay in the *Los Angeles Daily News:*

"Rita Hayworth and Glenn Ford are pitted against a villainous ring of international spies in *Affair in Trinidad* and not the least among their adversaries is a tricky, cloak-and-dagger script which, despite occasional flairs of completely literate dialogue, becomes so knotty it would take an Eagle Scout to unravel it."

The *Los Angeles Examiner:*

"Rather than resembling *Gilda,* this new Columbia film seems like a 1930s poverty-row predecessor that was refined, rewritten and remade into that film. This simply means that the dedicated and sincere attempt that *Affair in Trinidad* has made to set the industry back a good 20 years looks as if it could accomplish that goal single-handed."

With Glenn Ford.

For his black-and-white costume design for *Affair in Trinidad,* designer Jean Louis was nominated for an Academy Award (won by Helen Rose for her costuming for *The Bad and the Beautiful).*

At the risk of provoking the wrath of many of Miss Hayworth's partisans and film critics in general, *Affair in Trinidad* is another of those curious Hayworth films, like *The Lady from Shanghai,* which appears much better now than it did when first released. It's handsomely mounted and a physically expensive production and Rita's simulated song and sensual dance number, "Trinidad Lady," is actually much better than "Put the Blame on Mame," if for no other reason than the fact that it hasn't been as overused, imitated or lampooned. And women's styles immediately following World War II, when *Gilda* came out, have dated badly, while the Jean Louis creations Rita wears in *Affair in Trinidad* have a much more contemporary look.

There is still another perverse reason *Affair in Trinidad* manages, more than *Gilda* did, to hold an audience: the script is so predictable you are more or less hypnotized into watching it merely to confirm the fact that you know exactly what will happen next and can, therefore, feel quite superior to it. With *Gilda,* audiences always had the uneasy feeling that the projectionist had forgotten to screen one reel of it somewhere and the film concludes long before all the loose story ends have been explained.

With Alexander Scourby and Glenn Ford.

Stewart Granger, as Claudius, confesses his conversion to Christianity and begs Salome to become a follower.

Salome

A Beckworth Corporation Production,
Released by Columbia Pictures   1953

Produced by Buddy Adler. Directed by William Dieterle. Assistant Director, Earl Bellamy. Screenplay by Harry Kleiner, based on an original screen story by Kleiner and Jesse L. Lasky, Jr. Photographed in Technicolor by Charles Lang. Consultant for the Technicolor Company, Francis Cugat. Technical Consultant, Millard Sheets. Musical Score by George Duning. Music for the Dances by Daniele Amfitheatrof. Musical Direction by Morris Stoloff. Orchestrations by Arthur Morton. Chorales by the Robert Wagner Chorale. Choreography by Valerie Bettis. Art Direction by John Meehan. Set Decorations by William Kiernan. Men's Costumes by Emile Santiago. Gowns by Jean Louis. Makeup by Clay Campbell. Hair Styles by Helen Hunt. Sound Engineer, Lodge Cunningham. Edited by Viola Lawrence. 105 minutes.

CAST:

Princess Salome, RITA HAYWORTH; *Commander*

As the lecherous King Herod, Charles Laughton makes no attempt to conceal his interest in his step-daughter, Salome.

Claudius, STEWART GRANGER; *King Herod,* CHARLES LAUGHTON; *Queen Herodias,* JUDITH ANDERSON; *Caesar Tiberius,* SIR CEDRIC HARDWICKE; *John the Baptist,* ALAN BADEL; *Pontius Pilate,* BASIL SYDNEY; *Ezra,* MAURICE SCHWARTZ; *Marcellus Fabius,* REX REASON; *Micha,* ARNOLD MOSS; *Courier,* Robert Warwick; *Salome's Servant,* Carmen D'Antonio; *Captain Quintas,* Michael Granger; *Slave Master,* Karl (Killer) Davis; *Oriental Dancers,* Sujata and Asoka; *Advisors,* Joe Shilling, David Wold, Ray Beltram, Joe Sawaya, Anton Northpole, Franz Roehn, William McCormick; *Roman Guard,* Eduardo Cansino; *Herod's Guard Captain,* Mickey Simpson; *Guards,* Barry Brooks, Bruce Cameron, John Crawford, Tristram Coffin; *Executioner,* Lou Nova; *Sword Dancers,* Fred Letuli, John Woodd; *Fire Eater,* William Spaeth; *Juggler,* Duke Johnson; *Acrobats,* Alel Pina, Jerry Pina, Henry Pina, Henry Escalante, Gilbert Maques, Richard Rivas, Miguel Gutierez, Ramiro Rivas, Ruben T. Rivas, Hector Urtiaga; *Galilean Soldiers,* Earl Brown, Bud Cokes; *Assassins,* George Khoury, Leonard George; *Herodias's Servant,* Eva Hyde; *Simon,* Charles Wagenheim; *Court Attendant,* Leslie Denison; *Politicians,* Henry dar Boggia, Michael Couzzi, Bobker Ben Ali, Don De Leo, John Parrish, Eddy Fields, Robert Garabedion, Sam Scar; *Old Farmer,* Michael Mark; *Old Scholars,* David Leonard, Maurice Samuels, Ralph Moody; *Officers,* Guy Kingsford, Carleton Young; *Sailmaster,* Paul Hoffman; *Patrician,* Stanley Waxman; *Dissenting Scholar,* Saul Martell; *Townsmen,* Jack Low, Bert Rose, Tom Hernandez; *Blind Man,* Trevor Ward; *Sailors,* Fred Berest, Rick Vallin, George Keymas; *Slave,* Roque Barry; *Converts,* Italia De Nublia, David Ahdar, Charles Soldani, Dimas Sotello, William Wilkerson, Mario Lamm, Tina Menard.

NOTES:

Salome, the world's first famous ecdysiast, has chal-

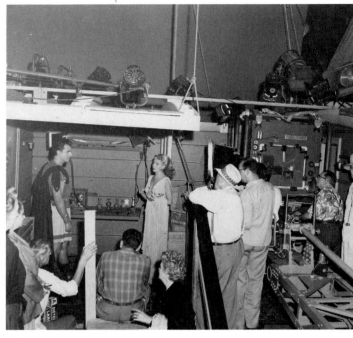

With crew members and technicians waiting for a take.

lenged the resources and abilities of many actresses of the stage and a few of the more prominent ones of the screen. Whatever Theda Bara's impersonation of the vamp of the veils lacked in terpsichorean aptitude, she more than made up for with an abundance of pulchritude. Alla Nazimova's version, designed after the erotic drawings of Aubrey Beardsley, was a stylized production that confounded more critics than it captivated. Neither of these silent films, however, seemed to offend and outrage as many reviewers, of all faiths (including believers in the art of motion pictures who were indeed put to the test), as this Technicoloraturing of the Bible according to Buddy Adler.

The presentation of Princess Salome to King Herod. Left to right: Maurice Schwartz, Arnold Moss, Charles Laughton, Basil Sydney, Stewart Granger, Judith Anderson and Rita.

Planning to doublecross her husband and daughter, Judith Anderson evolves a plot of intrigue and tricks Rita into participation.

Quite possibly, because she is, at best, a Scripture figure of only vague allusion, and never really described by deed as the deceptive dancer, *Salome* remains a personality for whom writers can conjure up almost any kind of characterization without really being accused of tampering with the Testament. The same, however, does not apply to her contemporaries effected by John the Baptist and the coming of Christianity. Consequently, the screenplay for this particular *Salome* was not only historically dubious, it was dramatically boring and completely void of the special kind of vulgarity which always made Cecil B. DeMille's biblical spectacles engrossing films, if not enlightening experiences.

This *Salome* was a physically handsome production and Rita was an eye-filling spectacle by herself. Her heroine, however, written and performed in a sort of *Gilda Goes to Galilee* style, had her vacillating through a story which changed points of view as often as she changed clothes. More as a tribute to DeMille's religious opuses than an imitation, the inclusion of a bath sequence for the heroine seemed almost de rigueur. But apparently Rita never really got close to being in hot water and she never seemed to be able to work Stewart Granger into much of a lather. In fact, Granger looked, at time, as if he was having trouble staying wide awake.

Apparently aware of just how dull things really were, and cognizant of just how much the scenery must have cost, Charles Laughton and Judith Anderson attacked the script and sets with theatrical appetites of such gusty proportions they appeared to be chewing up about a million histrionic calories a minute whenever the opportunity to bite off a line or nibble on a prop presented itself. Their contribution of a large portion of well-seasoned theatrical ham was, however, insufficient nutrition for what was otherwise a spiritually barren banquet.

The one fascinating facet of the film is the fact that the biblical scholar listed in the credits as technical advisor of this account of the siren of the seven veils was named Millard Sheets. But, as one trade paper aptly put it, this film script needed a lot more than even six more Sheets could supply.

Milton Schulman, in the London *Evening Standard,* said:

"A ponderous and clumsy attempt to eke sex out of religion."

And the London *Daily Sketch* said:

"This shameful film should be scrapped because it's

With Judith Anderson, Basil Sydney, Charles Laughton and Stewart Granger.

Rita and Stewart Granger behold the
head of John the Baptist.

As a sort of warm-up for things to
come (which never did), Rita dances
to entertain her Roman friends.

As the Bible's most tempting siren.

nothing more than a shameless perversion of the Bible and a blot on Hollywood's record."

John McCarten, in *The New Yorker* magazine, said:

"The only version of *Salome* on the screen that has ever appealed to me was one that employed the talents of Ben Turpin and some of the Mack Sennett boys many years ago. . . . Now there's another *Salome* around, in which Rita Hayworth, Stewart Granger, Charles Laughton, Judith Anderson and Sir Cedric Hardwicke participate. Although this one cost a billion dollars or so, and introduces the highly original notion that Salome's striptease was actually intended to coax Herod into giving John the Baptist a break, rather than induce the king to make *tête-de-Jean nature* the palace blue-plate, I still think the Turpin* method of handling the subject is best."

*Mr. McCarten was referring to Paramount's 1919 two-reeler, produced by Mack Sennett and directed by Erle C. Kenton called *Salome vs. Shenandoah.*

Anyone who happened to walk or drive down Gower near Sunset, past Columbia Studios had little doubt about which film they considered to be their blockbuster of the year.

Confronted by Marine Sergeant Aldo Ray.

Miss Sadie Thompson

A Beckworth Corporation Production,
Released by Columbia Pictures   1953

Produced by Jerry Wald. Directed by Curtis Bernhardt. Assistant Director, Sam Nelson. Screenplay by Harry Kleiner, based on W. Somerset Maugham's story, "Miss Thompson" and the dramatization by John Colton and Clemence Randolph, as produced on the New York stage as *Rain* by Sam H. Harris. Photographed in Technicolor and 3-D by Charles Lawton, Jr. Consultant for the Technicolor Company, Francis Cugat. Musical Score by George Duning. Musical Direction by Morris Stoloff. Songs: "The Heat Is On," "Hear No Evil, See No Evil" and "Blue Pacific Blues" ("Sadie Thompson's Song"), by Lester Lee and Ned Washington; "A Marine, A Marine, A Marine" by Lester Lee and Allan Roberts. Vocals for Miss Hayworth Sung by Jo Ann Greer. Choreography by Lee Scott. Art Direction by Carl Anderson. Set Decoration by Louis Diage. Gowns by Jean Louis. Makeup by Clay Campbell. Hair Styles by Helen Hunt. Sound Engineer, George Cooper. Assistant to the Producer, Lewis J. Rachmil. Edited by Viola Lawrence. 91 minutes (2-D Version); 90 minutes (3-D Version).

CAST:

Sadie Thompson, RITA HAYWORTH; *Alfred David-son*, JOSE FERRER; *Sergeant Phil O'Hara*, ALDO RAY; *Dr. Robert MacPhail*, RUSSELL COLLINS; *Ameena Horn*, DIOSA COSTELLO; *Joe Horn*, HARRY BELLAVER; *Governor*, Wilton Graff; *Margaret Davidson*, Peggy Converse; *Griggs*, Henry Slate; *Hodges*, Rudy Bond; *Edwards*, Charles Buchinsky (Bronson); *Mrs. MacPhail*, Frances Morris; *Chung*, Peter Chong; *Reverend*, John Grossett; *Marines*, Billy Varga, Teddy Pavelec, Frank Stanlow, Harold T. Hart, Ben Harris, Ted Jordan, Eduardo Cansino, Jr., John Duncan; *Native Children*, Clifford Botelho, Erlynn Botelho, Elizabeth Bartilet, Dennis Medieros; *Dispatcher*, Robert G. Anderson; *Native*, Joe McCabe; *Secretary*, Al Kikume; *Messenger*, Fred Letuli.

NOTES:

The first stage actress to play Somerset Maugham's tropical tramp was the late Jeanne Eagels. It was a performance so brilliant that its memory has become a theatrical legend. Miss Eagels opened in *Rain*, the title given to the John Colton-Clemence Randolph dramatization, at New York's Maxine Elliott Theatre on November 7, 1922 and she subsequently played *Sadie* for a record 648 performances!

With missionary director Jose Ferrer, pleading not to deport her back to San Francisco where the police are looking for her in connection with a gambler's murder.

Since that time, *Sadie Thompson* has been impersonated by budding, aspiring, inspiring, exasperating, popular, has-been, unheard-of, good and merely adequate actresses in stage revivals on Broadway, in summer stock, with touring road companies, with theatrical workshop groups and by amateurs in semiprofessional productions. She has further been explored in a stage musical by June Havoc and lampooned in a musical revue by Bette Davis. Feather-boa-ed shady ladies have appeared in a plethora of imitations, complete with portable phonographs, parasols, parakeets and patent leather pumps in plays and films which have more than bordered on out and out plagiarism.

On the screen, *Sadie* has been essayed successfully by Gloria Swanson (her performance won her an Academy Award nomination) and unsuccessfully by Joan Crawford and imitated endlessly by such luminaries as Marlene Dietrich *(Seven Sinners)*, Kay Francis *(Mandalay)*, Brenda Marshall *(Singapore Woman)*, Shelley Winter*s (South Sea Sinner)* and Mae West, who transferred her variation to the Frozen North (in *Klondike Annie)*. A young Diana Barrymore played her in a play-within-a-movie sequence of *Between Us Girls* and further approximations of her have been featured in musicals by Dorothy Lamour, Betty Hutton and Betty Grable during various song and dance production numbers. Even Tondelayo, the steamy baggage of *White Cargo,* is merely a darker-skinned sister of Sadie's

But Rita Hayworth, continuing her quest to breathe new life in old cinema heroines (Doña Sol, Virginia Brush, Carmen, Salome, et al.) gave Sadie just that, *new life,* with her own unique variation which gave the

Surrounded by a platoon of woman-hungry U.S. Marines on a remote tropical atoll, Rita offers to entertain them with a song.

Attempting to cool off on the tropical island where she has been stranded during a quarantine.

Rita struggles in vain to repulse Jose Ferrer's fervent attack.

Dispensing beer to thirsty Marines.

old slut a new slant in a somewhat censored but otherwise unshellacked version. Weighing a good ten pounds more than she usually did on screen, her shady lady was slightly sloppy, outwardly easygoing and ready to dance, sing a well-dubbed tune, or go along with any suggestion that carried the promise of a good time unencumbered with emotional hang-ups which allowed her to wake up with nothing more than a slight hangover to confuse her otherwise clear conscience. More of a promiscuously plump playgirl trying to keep up the appearance and pace of her frenzied popularity of the recently ended World War II, instead of the profit-seeking prostitute, who was usually a between-wars professional, Rita's Sadie paused to catch her breath after a strenuous dance, glistened with perspiration and sat down and soaked her feet after a night on the town. There was an uncompromising naturalness about her performance and it considerably altered the image of both the character and the performer. For once neither Rita nor Sadie was the lacquered, precisely-turned-out damsel but a very

As hotel owner Harry Bellaver (standing) listens, Rita apologizes to guests Russell Collins, Frances Morris, Peggy Converse and Jose Ferrer for a noisy night of revelry in her room.

[195]

With Aldo Ray and Rudy Bond.

real and slightly wilted broad whose dress had an uneven hemline and whose aroma was faintly reminiscent of a day-old hothouse corsage not quite faded enough to be tossed away.

Unfortunately, censorship problems, which resulted in a less-than-satisfactory delineation of the Davidson

After being sexually attacked by a missionary, Rita denounces him and his hypocrisy.

character, now reduced to being a missionary board member instead of an ordained cleric, was inadequately performed by Academy Award-winning actor José Ferrer. But even this liability could not obscure the plain truth: *Miss Sadie Thompson* was Rita's best screen performance to date. And most critics unquestionably considered her the ideal actress for the role. Edwin Schallert, in the *Los Angeles Times,* said:

"Rita Hayworth does her flashiest portrayal, bar none, in *Miss Sadie Thompson*. Some of it is very good acting too, outshining the star's prior efforts along more serious lines."

The *Hollywood Reporter* opined:

"A strikingly good performance by Rita Hayworth . . . who plays with fire and conviction, making a thoroughly believable Sadie."

Daily Variety said:

"The dramatic pacing of Curtis Bernhardt's direction

With Henry Slate.

Miss Sadie Thompson.

achieve a frenzied jazzlike tempo, quite in keeping with the modernization, and most of the performances respond in kind, especially that of Rita Hayworth. She catches the feel of the title character well, even to braving a completely deglamourizing makeup, costuming and photography to fit her physical appearance to that of the bawdy, shady lady that was Sadie Thompson."

Jesse Zunser, in *Cue* magazine, said:

"I never thought I'd live to see the day when Rita Hayworth would steal acting honors from José Ferrer. But that's exactly what she does in this sanitary version of Somerset Maugham's classic short story about a bad woman and a clergyman-bigot in the South Seas—the story famed on stage and screen as *Rain*.

"Miss Hayworth as the stranded tramp persecuted without reason by this sanctimonious hypocrite, gives what is probably her best performance. . . . Its Technicolor is dazzling and Miss Hayworth sizzles."

"Blue Pacific Blues" ("Sadie Thompson's Song"), by Lester Lee and Ned Washington, was nominated for an Academy Award but lost out to Paul Francis Webster and Sammy Fain for their song, "Secret Love" (featured in *Calamity Jane.)*

Miss Sadie Thompson was released in 3-D for its premiere engagement at New York's Capitol Theatre (on December 23, 1953) but the version ultimately put into general release throughout the country was in 2-D. Columbia Picture and most theater exhibitors felt that movies made with the optical illusion of the third dimension, whose exhibition meant supplying patrons with Polaroid glasses, had passed its popularity peak and its novelty was no longer an inducement to bring people into a theater. And since *Miss Sadie Thompson* was a critical and commercial success, albeit less so than some of her previous films, Miss Hayworth still had enough drawing power on her own without additional gimmicks.

Fire Down Below

A Warwick-Columbia Picture   1957

Produced by Irving Allen and Albert R. Broccoli. Directed by Robert Parrish. Assistant Directors, Gus Agosti and Bluey Hill. Screenplay by Irwin Shaw, based on Max Catto's novel. Photographed in CinemaScope and Technicolor by Desmond Dickinson. Second Unit Photography by Cyril Knowles. Camera Operators, Ernest Day and Gerald Turpin. Special Effects by Cliff Richardson. Musical Score by Arthur Benjamin, Kenneth V. Jones and Douglas Gamley. Dance Music by Vivian Comma. Harmonica Theme by Jack Lemmon. Music Conducted by Muir Mathieson and the Sinfonia London. Song: "Fire Down Below," by Lester Lee and Ned Washington; Vocal by Jeri Southern (courtesy of Decca Records). Dance Arrangements by Ken Jones. Production Supervisor, William Kirby. Assistant Art Director, Syd Cain. Sets Designed by John Box. Unit Manager, John Merriman. Miss Hayworth's Costumes by Balmain (of Paris) and Bermans (of London). Sound Recordists, Peter Davies and J. B. Smith. Sound Editor, David Elliott. Continuity by Angela Martinelli and Kay Rawlings. Associate Producer, Ronald Kinnoch. Edited by Jack Slade. 110 minutes.

CAST:

Irena, RITA HAYWORTH; *Felix Bowers,* ROBERT MITCHUM; *Tony,* JACK LEMMON; *Harbor Master,* HERBERT LOM; *Lieutenant Sellers,* BONAR COLLEANO; *Doctor Sam,* BERNARD LEE; *Jimmy-Jean,* Edric Connor; *Captain of* Ulysses, Peter Illing; *Mrs. Canady,* Joan Miller; *Miguel,* Anthony Newley; *Hotel Owner,* Eric Pohlmann; *The American,* Lionel Murton; *U.S. Sailors,* Vivian Matalon, Gordon Tanner, Maurice Kaufman; *Young Man,* Phillip Baird; *Drunk,* Keith Banks; *Limbo Dancers,* "Stretch" Cox, Shirley Rus, Anatole Smirnoff, Sean Mostyn, Terry Skelton, Greta Remin, Robert Nelson, Lorna Wood, Brian Blades, Barbara Lane, Ken Tillson, Gina Chare, Roy Evans.

The carnival dance sequence (disapproving lover, Robert Mitchum, watching from balcony).

With Jack Lemmon.

With Robert Mitchum and Jack Lemmon; the romantic trio in this drama of intrigue among small-time smugglers.

NOTES:

A co-production of Great Britain's Warwick Films and Columbia Pictures, made on location in Trinidad, *Fire Down Below* was Rita Hayworth's return-to-the-screen film after a four-year absence. No longer married to crooner Dick Haymes and her Beckworth Film Corporation dissolved, her return ended years of speculation over whether she would ever return to films. During her absence, her stormy private life kept her newsworthy and *Fire Down Below* was a box-office attraction although hardly the commercial blockbuster most of her top Columbia films had been.

One thing which helped make Miss Hayworth a conversation topic was that during her screen absence Joseph L. Mankiewicz's *The Barefoot Contessa,* which starred Ava Gardner as a Spanish dancing-girl who becomes first an international film star and then a contessa, was released with great success. Although Mankiewicz had always denied there were fictional similarities between his film and Miss Hayworth's own private life, most filmgoers and film gossips felt otherwise. In fact they regarded *The Barefoot Contessa* as a blatant imitation or approximation of Rita's life, just as they

With Robert Mitchum.

had found similarities between her husband Orson
Welles's film *Citizen Kane* and the life of newspaper
tycoon William Randolph Hearst.

Therefore *Fire Down Below* had a sort of "built-in"
curiosity about it and critics who for years had ignored
Rita's acting abilities or were even willing to admit
their possibilities, were now beginning to regard her as
an actress instead of just a sex symbol. Considerably
older-looking, and playing a woman used and abused
by many men, Rita had a few lines that contained cruel
accuracies about her own life.

With Jack Lemmon and Robert Mitchum.

With Jack Lemmon.

[201]

With Erich Pohlmann.

Said *Time* magazine:

"*Fire Down Below* rises high and could have soared higher but for a curious fact: its proper beginning seems uncomfortably wedged in its middle. Two of the three principals disappear in the midst of the story for half an hour. . . . The curious result is a fast-paced adventure yarn laced around an interlude of high drama.

"The great bond between Robert Mitchum, small-boat captain and Caribbean smuggler, and Rita Hayworth, a stateless tramp ill-used by a long succession of lechers, is mutual worthlessness. They've both had it;

all that's left for them is each other. Mitchum utters life-weary lines and Rita wears her under her eyes. But scripter Irwin Shaw has imbued the two with so much vitality that the characters emerge intact, and a movie whose eye sometimes strays from subtle human values to trite box-office appeal (*e.g.,* a superfluous chromium-plated Mardi Gras festival) survives as a sharp study of three lost souls in a crisis. . . . Rita, whose role is in the nature of a comeback after four years of sporadic squabbling with Columbia, and Jack Lemmon are both wide-awake, turn in solidly realistic performances."

Newsweek said:

"It is very nearly an unsympathetic role Miss Hayworth plays here, though not quite. She is forced to look—and does—hard to the core and leathery on the surface, throughout the picture. Sympathy swells up, though, as she characteristically explains to Mitchum: 'Armies have marched over me.' "

And *Weekly Variety* said:

"Miss Hayworth is excellent as the comely femme who is always just one step ahead of the law. . . . Cast in a rather disreputable role, Miss Hayworth is shown in an eye-filling closeup garbed in a bathing suit and later doing a dance hardly to be found in any ballroom. She furnishes the exciting love interest, and motivation for much of the yarn . . . a fitting vehicle for her reappearance in films.

With Robert Mitchum, Bernard Lee and Jack Lemmon.

Frank Sinatra, a down-on-his-luck nightclub heel, toasts his new patroness, Rita, a wealthy San Francisco widow he once romanced when she was burlesque star Vanessa, the Undresser.

Pal Joey

An Essex-George Sidney Production,
Released by Columbia Pictures   1957

Produced by Fred Kohlmar. Directed by George Sidney. Assistant Director, Art Black. Screenplay by Dorothy Kingsley, based on the musical play by John O'Hara, produced on the stage by George Abbott. Photographed in Technicolor by Harold Lipstein. Color Consultant, Henri Jaffe. Music Supervised and Conducted by Morris Stoloff. Musical Arrangements by Nelson Riddle. Musical Adaptations by George Duning and Nelson Riddle. Orchestrations by Arthur Morton. Songs: "Bewitched, Bothered and Bewildered," "I Could Write A Book," "Zip," "What Is A Man?" "What Do I Care for A Dame?" "That Terrific Rainbow," (excerpts of "In Our Little Den of Inquity," "Happy Hunting Horn," "Plant You Now, Dig You Later," "Do It the Hard Way" and "Take Him"), from the original score; Additional Songs, "My Funny Valentine," "The Lady Is a Tramp," "I Didn't Know What Time It Was" and "There's A Small Hotel"; all written by Richard Rodgers and Lorenz Hart. Vocal Arrangements by Fred Karger. (Songs for Rita Hayworth dubbed by Jo Ann Greer; Songs for Kim Novak dubbed by Trudi Erwin.) Choreography by Hermes Pan. Art Direction by Walter Holscher. Set Decoration by William Kiernan and Louis Diage. Gowns by Jean Louis. Makeup by Ben Lane. Hair Styles by Helen Hunt. Sound Recording by John Livadary and Franklin Hansen. Edited by Viola Lawrence. 112 minutes.

CAST:

Vera Simpson, RITA HAYWORTH; *Joey Evans,* FRANK SINATRA; *Linda English,* KIM NOVAK; *Ned Galvin,* BOBBY SHERWOOD; *Mike Miggins,* HANK HENRY; *Gladys,* BARBARA NICHOLS; *Mrs. Casey,* Elizabeth Patterson; *Bartender,* Robin Morse; *Colonel Langley,* Frank Wilcox; *Forsythe,* Pierre Watkin; *Anderson,* Barry Bernard; *Carol,* Ellie Kent; *Sabrina,* Mara McAfee; *Patsy,* Betty Utey; *Lola,* Bek Nelson; *Specialty Dance Double,* Jean Corbett; *Boyfriend,* Robert Rietz; *Red-Faced Man,* Jules Davis; *Hatcheck Girl,* Judy Dan; *Fat Woman,* Gail Bonney; *Girlfriend,* Cheryl Kubert; *Detective,* Tol Avery; *Policeman,* Robert Anderson; *Girl,* Genie Stone; *Army Captain,* Raymond McWalters; *Sailor,* Bob Glenn; *Secretary,* Sue Bonner; *Traveler's Aid Counterwoman,* Helen Eliot; *Club Owner,* Hermie

At the prodding of nightclub owner Sinatra, Rita offers a packed house audience her rendition of "Zip," a reminder of her former days in burlesque.

Deliberately staged to remind audiences of Rita's famous "Life" magazine pin-up of World War II, the musical number "Bewitched, Bothered and Bewildered" has her reclining on a bed, dancing in the bathroom and washing her doubts away in a shower.

Rose; *Hot Dog Vendor,* Jack Railey; *Waiter,* Roberto Piperio; *Chef Tony,* Ernesto Molinari; *Headwaiters,* George Nardelli, Ramon Martinez; *Stanley,* John Hubbard; *Livingstone,* James Seay; *Barkers,* Frank Sully, Maurice Argent, Eddie Bartell, Albert Nalbandian, Joseph Miksak, Sydney Chatton; *Sidewalk Photographer,* Howard Sigrist; *Pet Shop Owners,* Paul Cesari, Everett Glass; *Chinese Club Owner,* Andrew Wong; *Chinese Pianist,* George Chan; *Chinese Drummer,* Allen Gin; *Chinese Dancers,* Barbara Yung, Pat Lynn, Jean Nakaba, Lessie Lynne Wong, Nellie Gee Ching; *Electricians,* George Ford, Steve Benton; *Flower Lady,* Jane Chung; *Choreographer,* Hermes Pan; *Tailor,* Michael Ferris; *Printer Salesman,* Leon Alton; *Vera's Maid,* Giselle D'Arc; *Bit Woman,* Bess Flowers; *Bit Men,* Oliver Cross, Franklyn Farnum; *Sidewalk Artist,* Frank Wilimarth; *Strippers,* Bobbie Lee, Connie Graham, Bobbie Jean Henson, Edith Powell, Jo Ann Smith, Ilsa Ostroffsky, Rita Barrett.

NOTES:

Pal Joey first enchanted the public in the late 1930s in a series of *New Yorker* magazine stories, written in the form of letters signed "Your Pal Joey," and which recounted the ups and downs of a lovable heel, probably the first of our modern antiheroes. Author John O'Hara was induced to help get *Joey* before an audience when producer George Abbott urged him to return his magazine gems into the book of a musical. The eventual show, a critical success, was something of a phenomenon: a bawdy musical, loaded with sophisticated songs full of double entendre and equally scintillating dialogue—but completely barren of a single character with even a nodding acquaintance with any virtue or, for that matter, any redeeming qualities whatever!

The Broadway musical opened at the Ethel Barrymore Theatre on Christmas night 1940 and lasted a respectable 198 performances. During that time, audiences were divided into two camps—those who hated it

and those who loathed it. The original *Joey* was Gene Kelly and one of the chorus boys was Van Johnson. For their efforts, both won Hollywood contracts. The original Vera Simpson, the matron of the kept-boy arts, was Vivienne Segal, who had already been to Hollywood and, like the public, wanted to forget about it. Lovely Leila Ernst played Linda, the mouse among the mice, and an inside Broadway joke seemed to be that Gladys the stripper was played by June Havoc, the sister of stripper Gypsy Rose Lee, who is immortalized in one of the show-stopping songs, "Zip."

If the public was adamant about their dislike of *Pal Joey,* it can justly be asked why it ran so long. The answer is really simple: people actually adored the play and the characters but were too hypocritical to admit it, and they also loved the Rodgers and Hart score. It was chic to see *Pal Joey,* but crass to admit liking it.

Columbia Pictures bought the screen rights in 1941 and while a dozen or more screenwriters tried to rework the book into a property that would satisfy the censors without destroying the acerbity of the plot and characters, the studio announced once that they would seek James Cagney to play *Joey* and then changed their mind and offered the role to Cary Grant! More than half a dozen different actresses had all but signed to play Vera: Bebe Daniels, Gloria Swanson, Gladys Swarthout, Grace Moore, Ethel Merman and Irene Dunne! But a satisfactory script never evolved and, within a year, *Pal Joey* went into limbo for the duration of World War II and then some.

Its successful Broadway revival in the early 1950s, with Vivienne Segal again playing Vera and Harold Lang as Joey, Columbia's interest in their prewar acquisition was revived. By 1956 Hedda Hopper and Louella Parsons reported the studio now had what they considered a satisfactory script and readers of the columnists were bug-eyed to learn that the spectacular casting problem had been solved. Marlon Brando, who had proved he could handle himself in a musical *(Guys and Dolls)* would play *Pal Joey* and none other than Mae West would play Vera.

But Frank Sinatra, still smarting because Brando had gotten to do *On the Waterfront,* which Harry Cohn had promised him, determined Brando would not play *Joey,* a part Sinatra himself had long coveted. By "buying into the action" via his Essex Productions association, Sinatra got the role and when Rita buried the hatchet with Harry Cohn, she was given the plum role of Vera. Before which-star-will-be-top-billed? became a Hollywood pastime Sinatra announced that top billing rightfully belonged to Rita because, as he put it, "She *is* Columbia Pictures."

Miss Hayworth, well past the apex of her glamour days, was delighted, and even being juxtaposed against

Columbia's new sex symbol, Kim Novak, did not dismay her. Miss Novak, with youth and beauty on her side, found herself pitted against a pair of professional powerhouses who each instinctively knew what the magic of the movies was all about.

The plot was transferred from Chicago to San Francisco, the dialogue and lyrics were laundered and *Pal Joey* underwent a general overhauling in which over half the original songs were dropped in favor of other Rodgers and Hart standards. The finished film was far removed from the Broadway original but, nonetheless, *Pal Joey* on screen was a smash hit that still ranks as one of the better musicals. The reason is simple: it's melodious, it moves and it's delightfully entertaining.

Philip K. Scheur, in the *Los Angeles Times,* said:

"The innuendoes are broader than ever and the repartee—some of it obviously ad-libbed on the spot by Sinatra—is so racy that it had even blasé reviewers doing double-takes . . . the new *Pal Joey* is not the old *Pal Joey,* but, just the same, as Frankie would say, it's a 'gasser' for audiences . . .

"Miss Hayworth, older now, is almost too well-cast as the ex-stripper and matron who subsidizes Joey. Her attractiveness is as world-weary as Miss Novak's is eye-battlingly naive and fresh."

Dick Williams, in the *Los Angeles Mirror,* said:

"Enough spice and ribald realism remains in this account of a night club lady-killer and the rich widow he mesmerizes to make *Pal Joey* one of Hollywood's raciest movies of the season. Also, I suspect, one of its most popular . . .

"Rita Hayworth, no longer the dewy young belle, is brittle, sharp and sexy as the blasé matron who realizes that Sinatra is taking her for a ride, but goes along just for the kicks, anyway. The big screen is merciless in exposing Rita's aging face, but in many ways she is a more fascinating-looking beauty than ever before."

And *Hollywood Reporter* said:

"Because the original stage presentation had a book by John O'Hara, from his own *New Yorker* sketches, it is common to assume it was a particularly good one. A rereading of the published version today is likely to dismay anyone with that idea. Aside from the character of Joey and aside from Lorenz Hart's incomparable lyrics, there is not much there. Dorothy Kingsley has done the screenplay and any wit and charm there is in the current presentation is almost entirely Miss Kingsley's contribution. Certain characters have been combined, songs have been reassigned and the ending is altered, but basically Miss Kingsley has done a marvelous job of preserving and enhancing the original intent. . . .

Rita as Vera Simpson.

"Sinatra does not cheat at all in his characterization. His Joey is as glittery and vulgar as a three-carat little finger ring and still—and here is O'Hara's contribution—you are utterly fascinated with his nasty little heel. You pull for his comeuppance but still when he gets that kick in the teeth you hope it does not disarrange them too much. Sinatra is great, and he was born to play Joey. Miss Hayworth is very lovely and does a fine job."

Pal Joey was nominated for four Academy Awards for Art Direction and Set Decoration, for Sound Recording, for Film Editing and for Costume Design. *Sayonara* won the first two awards mentioned, *The Bridge on the River Kwai* won for film editing, and the costume for *Les Girls* won an Oscar for Orry-Kelly.

The "Chez Joey" dream sequence with Frank Sinatra and Kim Novak.

RITA HAYWORTH
Superstar

With Burt Lancaster.

David Niven, Gladys Cooper, Deborah Kerr, Rita Hayworth, Cathleen Nesbitt and Burt Lancaster.

Separate Tables

A Clifton/Joanna Production,
 Presented by Hecht, Hill and Lancaster
 and Released by United Artists   1958

Produced by Harold Hecht, James Hill and Burt Lancaster. Directed by Delbert Mann. Assistant Director, Thomas F. Shaw. Screenplay by Terence Rattigan and John Gay, based on Mr. Rattigan's play. Photographed by Charles Lang, Jr. Musical Score by David Raksin. Song: "Separate Tables," by Harry Warren and Harold Adamson. Associate Producer and Production Designer, Harry Horner. Art Direction by Edward Carrere. Set Decoration by Edward G. Boyle. Executive Production Manager, Gilbert Kurland. Miss Hayworth's Gowns by Edith Head. Costume Designer, Mary Grant. Makeup by Harry Maret and Frank Prehoda. Hair Stylists, Joan St. Oegger and Helen Parrish. Sound Recording by Fred Lau. Edited by Marjorie Fowler and Charles Ennis. 98 minutes.

CAST:

Ann Shankland, RITA HAYWORTH; *Sybil Railton-Bell,* DEBORAH KERR; *Major Pollock,* DAVID NIVEN; *John Malcolm,* BURT LANCASTER; *Miss Cooper,* WENDY HILLER; *Mrs. Railton-Bell,* GLADYS COOPER; *Lady Matheson,* CATHLEEN NESBITT; *Mr.*

Fowler, FELIX AYLMER; *Charles,* Rod Taylor; *Jean,* Audrey Dalton; *Doreen,* Priscilla Morgan; *Miss Meacham,* May Hallatt; *Mabel,* Hilda Plowright.

NOTES:

Terence Rattigan's *Separate Tables* was originally presented on the London stage with great success and repeated, with equal acclaim, on Broadway. In each instance it was performed as two one-act plays within a single setting with Eric Portman and Margaret Leighton each performing two distinctly different roles. Quite justly, the event was celebrated more as an occasion to witness an acting tour de force by its notable stage stars than it was as a dramatic triumph for its author.

No one, however, was more aware of this condition than Rattigan, who stated that for *Separate Tables* to be a successful, or even feasible, motion picture it would be necessary to reconstruct the entire dramatic continuity within the same framework into a unified narrative so that the events of each play would become contrapuntal to the other. Consequently, with the sale of the film rights to Hecht, Hill and Lancaster, Rattigan

With Wendy Hiller.

included a stipulation that he would assist in the screen-play. In a brilliant collaboration with John Gay, the stage curiosity became a much more meaningful (albeit somewhat overburdened) screenplay that was surprisingly fluid on screen despite its somewhat stagebound limitations.

What helped make *Separate Tables* such a notable film was a uniformly superb cast which en masse overcame the obvious shortcomings of director Delbert Mann and seemingly on its own made each character an individual and wholly believable human being. The ensemble acting was so skillful that it almost completely obscured the fact that each character was really a psy-chological case history composite engaging in a rather unorganized group-therapy session at the English seaside.

In addition to winning David Niven a "Best Actor" Academy Award and a "Best Supporting Actress" Award for Wendy Hiller, *Separate Tables* had five additional Oscar nominations for "Best Picture" (won by *Gigi*); "Best Actress" Deborah Kerr (won by Susan Hayward); "Best Screenplay" (based on material from another medium) that was awarded the scenarists of *The Defiant Ones,* which also won out over *Separate Tables* for "Best Black-and-White Cinematography." David Raksin lost the Oscar for "Best Score" to Dimitri Tiomkin (for *The Old Man and the Sea).*

With Deborah Kerr and Gladys Cooper.

The New York Film Critics also named David Niven the year's Best Actor and *Film Daily* placed *Separate Tables* in seventh place as one of 1958s ten best films. In awarding it second spot on their annual ten-best-of-the-year list, the National Board of Review said:

"Separate Tables is flawlessly acted by an all-star cast. As a matter of fact, Deborah Kerr's performance in it almost won the Board's accolade of best actress of the year, and David Niven's as the major who is afraid of people, life and sex, is the best performance of his career. Wendy Hiller, Gladys Cooper, Felix Aylmer, Cathleen Nesbitt, Rod Taylor, Audrey Dalton, May Hallatt, and even Rita Hayworth and Burt Lancaster, proved that the play is not always the thing."

Redbook magazine said:

"Separate Tables will long be remembered for its excellent characterizations and magnificent acting. David Niven gives a performance far above anything he's ever done before. All the portrayals, even to the smallest part, are memorable and each character is so convincing and so fascinating that interest in the film never drops."

Cue magazine said:

"Terence Rattigan's duet of dramas which had so successful a run on Broadway two years ago, has been skillfully, tastefully and effectively joined by the playwright and his collaborator, John Gay, into a single and quite superlative motion picture—to be rated among the best of the year . . . a splendid cast contributes outstanding performances: Rita Hayworth and Burt Lancaster as long-separated, vain, selfish wife and disillusioned husband who decide, finally, to make another go of it; Wendy Hiller as the lonely hotel landlady whose backstairs romance with the husband is shattered when the ex-wife returns to haunt; David Niven who poses as a World War II hero and is cruelly exposed as a pathetic fake with a psychological quirk; Deborah Kerr

With Burt Lancaster.

as a shy, homely spinster dominated by an iron-handed mother; Gladys Cooper as that tight-lipped matron; with Cathleen Nesbitt, Felix Aylmer, Audrey Dalton and many others in excellent support."

Peter John Dyer, writing in *Sight and Sound,* was the one dissenting voice and it came all the way from England, where *Separate Tables* was set, but not made. Said Dyer:

"The director is Delbert Mann, whose part in the proceedings is ambiguous, to say the least. It seems just possible, judging by the intensity he brings to the better scenes, that he sees his material potentially as Bournemouth's *Marty*. But this is hard to reconcile with Vic Damone's voice over the credits throbbing out a theme song, or with a score encouraged to explode at times of crisis. Finally there is the casting. It ranges from serviceable Shaftsbury Avenue (Cathleen Nesbitt's Lady Matheson, the quiet feeling of Wendy Hiller as the proprietress) to *Now, Voyager* pyrotechnics (Deborah Kerr's cringing Sybil, the superb playing of Mrs. Railton-Bell by Gladys Cooper's right eyebrow) and the hopeless misplacement of the Hollywood couple, Burt Lancaster and Rita Hayworth. Left unclassifiably to the last is David Niven—by no means the likeliest choice for an inhibited and unattractive old blusterer, but acting with such intelligence, feeling and uncanny intuition that at least something remains to glow, with the warmth of real life, long after the lights have fused."

With Burt Lancaster.

With Richard Conte, Van Heflin, Dick York, Gary Cooper and Tab Hunter.

They Came to Cordura

A Goetz-Baroda Production,
    Released by Columbia Pictures   1959

Produced by William Goetz. Directed by Robert Rossen. Assistant Director, Milton Feldman. Second Unit Director, James Havens; Assistant Second Unit Director, Carter DeHaven, Jr. Screenplay by Ivan Moffat and Robert Rossen, based on Glendon Swarthout's novel. Photographed in CinemaScope and Eastman Color by Pathé by Burnett Guffey. Second Unit Photographer, Frank G. Carson. Color Consultant, Henri Jaffe. Photographic Lenses by Panavision. Musical Score by Elie Siegmeister. Musical Direction by Morris Stoloff. Orchestrations by Arthur Morton. Song: "They Came to Cordura," by James Van Heusen and Sammy Cahn. Art Direction by Cary Odell. Set Decoration by Frank A. Tuttle. Technical Consultant, Col. Paul Davidson, U.S.A. (Ret.). Men's Costumes Supervised by Tom Dawson. Miss Hayworth's Costumes by Jean Louis. Makeup Supervision by Clay Campbell. Hair Styles by Helen Hunt. Sound Recording by John Livadary. Edited by William A. Lyons. 123 minutes.

CAST:

Major Thomas Thorn, GARY COOPER; *Adelaide Geary,* RITA HAYWORTH; *Sergeant John Chawk,* VAN HEFLIN; *Lieutenant William Fowler,* TAB HUNTER; *Corporal Milo Trubee,* RICHARD CONTE; *Private Andrew Hetherington,* MICHAEL CALLAN; *Private Renziehausen,* DICK YORK; *Colonel Rogers,* ROBERT KEITH; *Captain Paltz,* James (Jim) Bannon; *Colonel DeRose,* Edward Platt; *Mexican Federale,* Maurice Jara; *Correspondents,* Sam Buffington, Arthur Hanson; *Cavalry Soldier,* Wendell Hoyt; *Arreaga,* Carlos Romero.

NOTES:

Glendon Swarthout, a professor of English at Michigan State University at the time he wrote the novel on which *They Came to Cordura* is based, had been an awards writer for the U.S. government during World War II, whose function was to put military citations into proper prose. This background later helped him to develop the

Preparing to face bandits with Van Heflin, Tab Hunter, Dick York, Gary Cooper, Michael Callan and Richard Conte.

unique theme of his novel, the 1916 punitive expedition by the U.S. Army against Pancho Villa, that impressed producer William Goetz so much he paid $250,000 for the screen rights to it.

The script that Ivan Moffat and director Robert Rossen, a heavy financial investor in the production, derived took almost a year to complete. When casting was completed, the production unit went on location to St. George, Utah, in the summer of 1958, where for nine weeks filming proceeded with over four hundred local citizens participating as extras, stand-ins and commissary employees. But due to some unseasonal cold weather, the company was forced to move its location to the Moapa Valley, outside of Las Vegas, Nevada.

There the footage was completed and much of what had been filmed in Utah was refilmed there. None of the people in the company complained when the film ran way over schedule since they were all quartered at the posh Sands Hotel in Las Vegas.

Everything about the production, including the musical score by Elie Siegmeister, then a professor of music at Hofstra College in New York, was first-class. Siegmeister's score, known as the "Cordura Symphonic Suite," was premiered in Indianapolis by Isler Solomon and his Symphony Orchestra to help promote interest in the film there. Similar publicity gimmicks were arranged in other large cities to promote public interest in *They Came to Cordura* but the public at large was com-

Captain Gary Cooper reprimanding his men, Tab Hunter, Dick York, Richard Conte, Van Heflin and Michael Callan after their attempted rape of prisoner Rita.

Rita plays a U.S. citizen who has been arrested by the army for giving aid to the enemy during the 1916 "border skirmish" with Pancho Villa.

Captain Gary Cooper suddenly discovers he has respect and affection for his prisoner.

pletely indifferent to the film and it laid a box-office egg which cost its producers, director and Columbia Pictures something in the neighborhood of a $5,000,000 loss!

Everything, as I said before, was first-class except the script and its curious viewpoints into what makes a soldier a hero and what brands him a coward.

Logan MacDonald, in *Films in Review,* said:

"*They Came to Cordura* is unsuccessful not only cinematically. Ideationally it is absurd. Its main plot is that four U.S. soldiers cited for the Order of Merit for bravery beyond the call of duty—in the course of our 'punitive expedition' into Mexico after Pancho Villa's raid upon Columbus, New Mexico, on March 8, 1916—were basically cheats, thieves, rapists and murderers. A second point is that an officer assigned to promote such low-life into heroes—so the United States could exploit them for recruiting purposes when it got into World War I—was a coward in combat *but otherwise heroic.*

A posed publicity still depicting Gary Cooper and Rita (in an off-the-shoulder blouse she did not wear in the film) as a romantic duo.

With Gary Cooper at the commencement of their long trek to Cordura.

And third, that the semialcoholic daughter of a U.S. crook self-exiled in Mexico, who had helped the Villistas against her own country, was really a good Joe at heart.

"The churning of moral values and patriotic loyalties into such relativistic hash may not be too hazardous for book publishers, whose financial loss is small when the public decides not to buy. But Goetz's cost figures aren't hay. What went on in his mind? He is too experienced a showman not to have debated whether the U.S. public would pay to see itself besmirched and its army denigrated. Could he have banked on the foreign market's shelling out to see the U.S. army demeaned and the American people ridiculed, if not worse?

"I doubt that the foreign market *will* shell out, for *They Came to Cordura* has too many cinematic faults. Gary Cooper is much too old for the part of the cowardly officer assigned to make heroes out of riffraff. And the riff is portrayed—by Van Heflin, Richard Conte, Michael Callan and Dick York—with only one performance at all credible (Heflin's). Rita Hayworth *did* endeavor to substitute acting for sex and glamour, but her part was too inadequately written. And Robert Rossen's direction was downright incompetent (he also shares the blame for the synthetic script on which he collaborated with Ivan Moffat)."

Daily Variety said:

"Gary Cooper is very good as the central figure, although he is somewhat too old for the role. It is a little hard to believe that a man of his maturity would only then be finding out the things about himself which Cooper explores as part of his character. Miss Hayworth, looking haggard, gives the best performance of her career. If she shows only half the beauty she usually does, she displays twice the ability."

And *Hollywood Reporter* said:

"Rita Hayworth gives one of the finest performances of her career as the tough-luck dame who sacrifices herself to the sergeant's lusts so that the exhausted major can get some much needed sleep. Her characterization gets some powerful assists by the makeup of Clay Campbell and the hair styling of Helen Hunt."

At night, in her cell, Rita writes a letter to her young daughter.

The Story on Page One

Produced by The Company of Artists, Inc.,
    Released by 20th Century-Fox Pictures   1960

Produced by Jerry Wald. Written for the Screen and Directed by Clifford Odets. Assistant Director, Jack Gertsman. Photographed in CinemaScope by James Wong Howe. CinemaScope Lenses by Bausch and Lomb. Musical Score by Elmer Bernstein. Orchestrations by Edward B. Powell. Art Direction by Lyle Wheeler and Howard Richmond. Set Decoration by Walter M. Scott and G. W. Bernstein. Makeup by Ben Nye. Hair Styles by Myrl Stoltz. Sound Recording by Alfred Bruzlin and Harry M. Leonard. Edited by Hugh S. Fowler. 123 minutes.

CAST:

Jo Morris, RITA HAYWORTH; *Victor Santini,* ANTHONY FRANCIOSA; *Larry Ellis,* GIG YOUNG; *Mrs. Ellis,* MILDRED DUNNOCK; *Judge Nielson,* HUGH GRIFFITH; *Phil Stanley,* Sanford Meisner; *Nordau,* Robert Burton; *Lieutenant Mike Morris,* Alfred Ryder; *Mrs. Brown,* Katherine Squire; *Judge Carey,* Raymond Greenleaf; *Alice,* Myrna Fahey; *Morrie Goetz,* Leo Penn; *Francis Morris,* Sheridan Comerate; *Detective Kelly,* Tom Greenway; *Eddie Ritter,* Biff Elliott; *Lau-ber,* Jay Adler; *Avis,* Carol Seflinger; *Dr. Kemper,* Theodore Newton; *Hauser,* James O'Rear; *Calvin Lewis,* Richard Le Pore; *Court Clerk,* Dan Riss; *Lieutenant Morris,* Joseph McGuinn; *Gallagher,* Joe Besser; *Jury Foreman,* Leonard George; *Court Stenographer,* George Turley; *Miss Monroe,* Miranda Jones; *Bartender,* Art Salter; *Man at Bar,* Jerry Sheldon; *Cook,* Bru Danger; *Waitress,* Valerie French; *Lemke,* William Challee; *Police Matron,* Virginia Carroll.

NOTES:

Clifford Odets, actor, stage director and one of the founders of the Group Theatre is also the author of such plays as *Waiting for Lefty, Awake and Sing, Paradise Lost, Golden Boy, Clash by Night, The Big Knife, Rocket to the Moon, Night Music, The Country Girl* and *The Flowering Peach* and such screenplays as *The General Died at Dawn* (originally written for his one-time wife, Luise Rainer), *Humoresque* (one of Joan Crawford's most absurd films), *None But the Lonely Heart* (one of Cary Grant's all-time best films), *Deadline at Dawn* and *The Sweet Smell of Success.* Prior to

Anthony Franciosa is the attorney who defends clients Rita and Gig Young who have been charged with murdering her husband.

writing and directing *The Story on Page One,* Odets directed one other film, *None But the Lonely Heart,* for which he also did the screenplay, adapted from Richard Llewellyn's novel.

Said Odets (in 1959):

"I started *The Story on Page One* as an eight-scene play, twelve years ago. The title for it was *The Murder Story.* I'd go back to it between other jobs. I'd talk about it. I told Jerry Wald and Bill Goetz about it. Then one night Wald said to me 'How would you like to write and direct your own *Murder Story* as a movie?' To be able to direct a movie was the fat bait. The most interesting and stimulating job in movies is to direct. This way the story is not out of my hands. And that is an advantage. There are other advantages though.

"The other afternoon Rita Hayworth and Gig Young are playing a scene when I stopped them. They wanted to know what was wrong. I told them maybe the author liked the screen but the director doesn't. It had to be

The story finds housewife Rita married to a policeman and in love with another man.

cut in half. Too long. The writer wouldn't ordinarily know that unless the actors had played it right by his desk. But I'm not a library writer like S. N. Behrman, Maxwell Anderson and many other fine playwrights. I've got the stage under my feet. I was an actor. So that's another advantage of directing your own work."

Unfortunately, director Odets did not realize that some advantages in directing author Odets' *The Story on Page One* could also be liabilities.

In tightening his screenplay directorially, Odets left loose story ends dangling which, as a writer, he should have resolved. And from the version of his work seen on the screen, he also apparently changed his script drastically during filming and failed to shoot important cover shots to match those changes. For how else can the fact that the attorney played by Anthony Franciosa is first established as a down-on-his-luck shyster, who has taken to the bottle and arguing against taking clients instead of accepting them, and then appear, without any cursory explanation, in court as a sartorially splendid defense attorney with a courtroom flair equal to that of Jerry Geisler and proceed, without a single dramatic setback, to present a brilliantly executed defense that results in the never-for-a-moment-doubted acquittal of his seedy clients be otherwise explained?

As a director, Odets should have realized that Franciosa was a casting mistake, and Gig Young an even greater mistake. Instead of attempting to play a weak, mother-dominated man of romantic indecision, Young would have been a better choice as the attorney. And

On the witness stand, with defense attorney Anthony Franciosa.

producer Wald should have taken the time to screen the dailies of Odets's work and realize something was amiss. Because the version put into general release contained some "cinema magic" which must have confused even casual filmgoers considerably. During the testimony sequences in the courtroom, witness Joseph McGuinn can be observed on the witness stand, in civilian clothes, offering testimony as the camera pans the spectators and picks up McGuinn, dressed as a police officer, listening to himself! The same thing occurs with Mildred Dunnock. While on the stand giving testimony, the

Katherine Squire seeks legal assistance for her daughter (Rita) from Anthony Franciosa and his assistant, Biff Elliott.

[221]

Rita is harassed by her husband, Alfred Ryder.

Anthony Franciosa's one acting device—an ocular and bronchial tension—merely emphasized the banality of Odets's lines for the defense attorney; Hugh Griffith had to fight for a few seconds' screen time with lines a lesser actor would have refused to speak above a whisper; Sanford Meisner, allowed far too much screen time and given carte blanche, rewarded Odets with a performance as subtle as that of a Coney Island barker; and Gig Young was so totally miscast as the incomprehensible mamma's boy he should have withdrawn when he discovered how incompetently the role had been conceived and written. However, despite Writer-Director Odets

camera pans to the courtroom spectators, and she is one of them!

And yet in spite of its casting flaws, script inconsistencies, directorial incompetence and the sloppiest editing job ever done on a major film, *The Story on Page One* still has a gnashing vitality, a compelling sort of fascination and a few expert performances, by Katherine Squire and Rita Hayworth, which remain in the viewer's memory. The performance of Alfred Ryder, as the cruel, unfeeling husband who inadvertently becomes the victim of what appears to be a murder plot but is, in reality, a case of self-defense, is equally memorable.

Said *Films in Review:*

"Judging from the Group Theaterites in the cast, I assume director Odets had cast approval on this picture. If so, he must share with producer Jerry Wald responsibility for some egoistic gyrations that could be called acting only by people more charitable than I.

Under cross examination of district attorney Sanford Meisner.

there *was* some good acting. Rita Hayworth, now that she is no longer a sexpot, gave a good trouper's performance; Mildred Dunnock, whose inanition is usually such a bore, showed unexpected spirit in depicting a domineering middle-class woman with pretensions to breeding, even though Odets obviously wanted the part to be wholly unsympathetic; Katherine Squire was more than a routine mother of the wife; and Bill Challee was creative in a bit as an unwittingly baffled hotel clerk."

In the visiting room of the county jail, Franciosa implores his client to take the witness stand and testify in her own behalf.

With her daughter, Carol Seflinger.

Paul V. Beckley, in the New York *Herald Tribune,* said:

"The general sponginess of the film is the result not only of factual muddiness, but also the strong effort to shift audience sympathy toward the lovers, an effort unnecessarily frantic in view of the circumstances. . . . Miss Hayworth takes a long stride forward here from mere glamour toward serious and individual performance."

And *Time* magazine said:

"Actress Hayworth, the onetime pinup girl, has now mastered the role of the beat-down broad, and when she is on-camera, she holds the show in shape. When she is not, the suspense dissolves into a mess of sentimental pablum—hardly the dish a customer expects from playwright Odets. Scriptwriter Odets here takes his first crack in fifteen years at directing a picture, and perhaps should be forgiven some errors of inexperience. But seasoned producer Jerry Wald might have done something about actor Franciosa, an almost comically intense young man who reads every line as though it were his last. No such luck."

Daily Variety added:

"Being a courtroom melodrama, *The Story on Page One* should be as tidily constructed as a coroner's report, but it shows more loose ends than the back view of a burlesque chorus line. . . . The whole cast is lit by the performance of Katherine Squire as Miss Hayworth's mother. Miss Squire achieves an intensity and credibility that is a thrill to watch."

In court with Katherine Squire, Biff Elliott, Anthony Franciosa, Gig Young, Raymond Greenleaf and courtroom spectators.

In order to make Rita his accomplice and prevent her from ever testifying against him, Rex Harrison induces her to marry him. They celebrate their nuptials with a bottle of champagne.

The Happy Thieves

A Hillworth Production,
    Released by United Artists   1962

Produced by James Hill and Rita Hayworth. Directed by George Marshall. Screenplay by John Gay, based on Richard Condon's novel, *The Oldest Confession*. Photography by Paul Beeson. Musical Score by Mario Nascimbene. Art Direction by Ramiro Gomes. Miss Hayworth's Wardrobe by Pedro Rodrigues (Madrid) and Pierre Balmain (Paris). Sound Recording by Sash Fisher. Edited by Oswald Hafenrichter. 88 minutes.

CAST:

Eve Lewis, RITA HAYWORTH; *Jim Bourne,* REX HARRISON; *Jean Marie Calbert,* JOSEPH WISEMAN; *Dr. Munoz,* GREGOIRE ASLAN; *Duchess Blanca,* ALIDA VALLI; *Cayetano,* Virgilio Texera; *Mr. Pickett,* Peter Illing; *Mrs. Pickett,* Brita Ekman (Britt Ekland); *Señor Elek,* Julio Peña; *Antonio,* Gerard Tichy; *Museum Guards,* Lou Weber, Antonio Fuentes; *Inspector,* George Rigaud; *Chern,* Barta Barri; *Police Official,* Karl-Heinz Schwerdtfeger; *Little Girl,* Yasmin Khan.

NOTES:

Filmed entirely in Spain in black and white and on a somewhat modest budget, *The Happy Thieves* had a curious script which vacillated from light comedy to stark drama without ever achieving much success at either. It was financed by Miss Hayworth and her fifth husband, James Hill, formerly of the Hecht-Hill-Lancaster Company, and it lost considerable money at the box office. Miss Hayworth's daughter by Prince Aly Khan, Yasmin, also appeared in the film in a bit part.

It was a little painful to watch two such former screen beauties as Miss Hayworth and Alida Valli, neither of whom was especially well made up, lighted or photographed, attempting to act whimsically romantic in a vehicle which gave them no help whatever. Rex Harrison, who usually exuded charm from every pore,

and who had been the Professor Higgins of *My Fair Lady* for hundreds of stage performances prior to making this film, simply looked and acted tired.

Said *Motion Picture Exhibitor:*

"This confused comedy drama never really gets off the ground, and that is a shame because the fine cast could have been used for an effort far more worthwhile than this one. Audiences are more likely to be mystified by the goings-on than entertained. The story seems to have trouble making up its mind whether or not to be serious, and the actors are more or less left to flounder in this indecision. Editing is uneven, and production and direction are pedestrian."

Daily Variety said:

"Regrettably, this latest cinematic toast to the comic facets of larceny does not measure up to the standards and requirements of imaginative inspiration that must be realized by such a film in order for it to spur the enthusiastic word-of-mouth that attracts the more selective picturegoer."

With Rex Harrison.

With bullfighter Virgilio Texera, Alida Valli, the duchess who loves him, and Rex Harrison.

Dick Williams, in the *Los Angeles Times,* said:

"Regrettably, *The Happy Thieves* cannot be considered a success in the zany thieves and bold robberies department. Italy's *Big Deal on Madonna Street,* for example, was a far superior comedy.

"But the fault is not that of the cast. Harrison, eyes twinkling in his patented, special style, is quite right as the debonair, unruffled leader. Joseph Wiseman, as the nervous painter who copies the masters in flawless style, is amusing. Even Rita Hayworth, who has never reached the heights as a comedienne, does reasonably well. . . . No, the shortcomings may be laid to screenplay problems, first, and direction second."

By the time *The Happy Thieves* was put into gen-

Joseph Wiseman and Rita listen intently as Rex Harrison explains his plan to steal a painting by Goya from the Prado Museum and replace it with an expert fake.

Rita, an innocent dupe who loves an art thief, learns about his capers from his adversary, Gregoire Aslan.

eral release, Miss Hayworth had dissolved the Hillworth Company and divorced her co-producer fifth husband, James Hill. But before it was released, and before Hill and Rita parted, they intended filming a script called *I Want My Mother!* in Hollywood on which they completed all production details, right down to final casting and wardrobe and sets, before canceling the project on a single day's notice. Neither Hill nor Rita have ever offered an explanation for the cancellation which came after an extensive and very expensive trade-paper publicity campaign.

Watching a pre-bullfight fiesta celebration with Virgilio Texera and Rex Harrison.

With John Wayne.

Circus World

A Samuel Bronston-Midway-Cinerama Production,
Released by Paramount Pictures   1964

Produced by Samuel Bronston. Directed by Henry Hathaway. Assistant Director, José Lopez Rodero. Second Unit Director, Richard Talmadge; Assistant, Terry Yorke. Circus Coordinator, Frank Capra, Jr. Screenplay by Ben Hecht, Julian Halevy and James Edward Grant, based on Philip Yordan and Nicholas Ray's original story. Photographed in Super Technirama 70 and Technicolor by Jack Hildyard. Second Unit Photographer, Claude Renoir. Musical Score Composed and Conducted by Dmitri Tiomkin. Special Effects by Alex Weldon; Supervising Technician, Carl Gibson. Technical Advisor for Circus Sequences, Alfredo Marquerie. Art Direction and Production Design by John DeCuir. Executive Production Manager, C. O. Erickson. Master of Properties, Stanley Detlie. Director of Sound Recording, David Hildyard. Supervising Electrician, Bruno Pasqualini. Continuity by Elaine Schreyeck. Second Unit Continuity by Kay Rawlings. Title Drawings and Design by Dong Kingman. Casting, Maude Spector. Dialogue Coach, George Tyne. Costumes by Renie. Wardrobe Supervision by Ana Maria Fea. Hairdressing by Grazia De Rossi. Executive Associate Producer, Michael Wasznynicki. Edited by Dorothy Spencer. Production Copyrighted in 1964 by Bronston-Roma Productions. Roadshow Engagement, 138 minutes (plus intermission).

CAST:

Matt Masters, JOHN WAYNE; *Toni Alfredo,* CLAUDIA CARDINALE; *Lili Alfredo,* RITA HAYWORTH; *Cap Carson,* LLOYD NOLAN; *Aldo Alfredo,* RICHARD CONTE; *Steve McCabe,* JOHN SMITH; *Emile Schumann (Lion Tamer),* Henri Dantes; *Mrs. Schumann,* Wanda Rotha; *Giovanna,* Katharyna; *Flo Hunt,* Kay Walsh; *Anna Hunt,* Margaret MacGrath; *Molly Hunt,* Kathrine Ellison; *Billy Rogers,* Miles Malleson; *Hilda,* Katharine Kath; *Bartender,* Moustache; *Themselves,* Acts and Individual Members of the Franz Althoff Circus.

With John Wayne.

NOTES:

Circus World was originally intended as a small-scale, European-made film venture, based on a story by Philip Yordan and Nicholas Ray which interested producer Joseph Sistrom enough to buy it for Paramount Pictures. But when Cecil B. DeMille's *The Greatest Show on Earth* was reissued by Paramount with such tremendous success, Sistrom saw his small circus property in a new light. Ultimately he interested director Frank Capra in the project.

Capra, who really belonged to another Hollywood era and had not made a worthwhile film since *It's A Wonderful Life,* envisioned the property as a superspectacle that could reestablish his name. Consequently he worked on the script and preproduction plans over six months. In Europe he auditioned circus acts and contracted David Niven, Claudia Cardinale and Lilli Palmer for important roles. John Wayne, the star Joseph Sistrom provided, became impatient with Capra's way of working and sent his favorite screenwriter, James Edward Grant, to Europe to assist him. Capra and Grant did not get along and found working together an impossibility.

Wayne, none too happy with the script Capra had concocted, insisted that Grant rewrite it completely.

In his autobiography, *The Name Above the Title,* Capra wrote:

"Jimmy Grant was something new to me—a writer who attached himself to a male star and functioned as that star's confidant, adviser, bosom playpal, baby sitter, flatterer, string-puller and personal Iago to incite

mistrust between his meal ticket and film directors, especially name directors. . . . Grant bragged about how he had convinced the Duke that he had gotten too big to be directed by 'decrepit old bastards like John Ford' and all that Grant and Wayne needed was a young TV director they could handle. . . . I could have kicked Jimmy Grant out of the country—just as Hathaway did after he took over. I could have cowed the big Duke into giving his best performance. I could have made a hit out of *Circus.* . . . But I didn't."

Instead Capra walked off the film and before John Wayne also abandoned it, Henry Hathaway was called in as a replacement. Hathaway later said it was a big mistake for him to have taken it over. He accused Rita Hayworth, who had now replaced Lilli Palmer, of holding up production by her heavy drinking, and he fired James Edward Grant. He then closed production down for two weeks while he had Ben Hecht rewrite a script which could incorporate footage already filmed.

With John Wayne and Lloyd Nolan.

By now Samuel Bronston had taken over as producer. Interiors were filmed at his Madrid studios and exteriors on location in Paris, Hamburg, Vienna and Barcelona where, at the famous Price Circus Theater, the spectacular footage involving the Frank Althoff Circus of Austria, was filmed.

When *Circus World* was completed and ready for release, Cinerama, faced with a product shortage for their newly acquired and equipped theaters, made a deal with Paramount to release it. Consequently, they converted onto single-strip Cinerama film stock and using a single-camera projection, released it as a roadshow attraction on a two-performances-a-day policy at advanced prices into Cinerama Theaters.

But in spite of the expensive trappings, the all-star cast, and the prestigious road show treatment, the critics called it exactly what Philip Yordan and Nicholas Ray had first envisioned it—a minor, European-made programmer.

Said *Sound Stage* magazine:

"Lacks the spectacle that most of Cinerama's travelogues—and *How the West Was Won*—contained. Without any audience participation scenes (no roller-coaster thrills), *Circus World* must depend on the power of its stars and its story to keep the ticket wickets active.

"John Wayne, the big man at the box office, will attract a lot of people to *Circus World* just on his name. A completely different audience will be interested in seeing Claudia Cardinale and Rita Hayworth as a mother-daughter circus act. Miss Hayworth, incidentally, has the film's best role and she gives the best performance. . . .

"As entertainment, *Circus World* is a natural. Naturally the wild animals get loose. Naturally, Claudia Cardinale discovers her father committed suicide because her mother (Miss Hayworth) was in love with Wayne. Naturally, Wayne—who raised Miss Cardinale—will have his father image temporarily shattered. Naturally, this will have an adverse effect on Claudia's romance (with John Smith). Naturally, the young lovers will be reconciled after Smith saves Claudia from a fate worse than a high-wire fall (Richard Conte). Naturally, Miss Hayworth will pay for her transgressions. Naturally, there are first-rate circus acts.

"Take the kids! Take popcorn! Take a bankroll too. You'll need more than peanuts to pay the reserve-seat ticket prices. Then, when you're comfortably seated, take a snooze. Have the kids tell you about the picture after you get back home. They may be able to do it from a new angle."

In *Films in Review,* Henry Hart said:

"It seems incredible that anyone could make a dull picture out of circus acts, John Wayne and Claudia Cardinale. But producer Samuel Bronston has succeeded in doing so.

"The flaws of this film are so many it is pointless to particularize. . . . The cast also includes Rita Hayworth in a middle-aged role. Believe it or not, her performance is good, and the only good thing in *Circus World*."

In *The New York Times,* Bosley Crowther said:

"Out of regard from Cecil B. DeMille's great circus

With John Wayne.

picture, *The Greatest Show on Earth,* it should be said that this one bears no comparison to it. This one might be labeled the worst."

And *Time* magazine said:

"Still doggedly reproducing the collected epics of Cecil B. DeMille, Producer Samuel Bronston has launched a three-ring *Circus*. Though likeable enough, this least pretentious of Bronston spectacles cannot compart with *The Greatest Show on Earth*. It is just a minor romantic tearjerker, a *Stella Dallas* with sawdust. . . . To sit through the film is something like holding an elephant on your lap for two hours and fifteen minutes."

With Claudia Cardinale.

Startled detectives Glenn Ford and Ricardo Montalban encounter the result of a family quarrel after the husband has discovered his wife supplementing their income by part-time prostitution.

The Money Trap

A Max E. Youngstein Production,
    Released by Metro-Goldwyn-Mayer, Inc.   1966

Produced by Max E. Youngstein and David Karr. Directed by Burt Kennedy. Assistant Director, Hank Moonjean. Screenplay by Walter Bernstein, based on Lionel White's novel. Photographed in Panavision by Paul C. Vogel. Photographic Lenses by Panavision. Musical Score by Hal Schaefer. Art Direction by George W. Davis and Carl Anderson. Set Decoration by Henry Grace and Robert R. Benton. Sound Recording by Franklin Milton. Edited by John McSweeney. 91 minutes.

CAST:

Joe Baron, GLENN FORD; *Lisa Baron,* ELKE SOMMER; *Rosalie Kenny,* RITA HAYWORTH; *Dr. Horace Van Tilden,* JOSEPH COTTEN; *Pete Delanos,* RICARDO MONTALBAN; *Matthews,* Tom Reese; *Detective Wolski,* James Mitchum; *Aunt,* Argentina Brunetti; *Mr. Klein,* Fred Essler; *Father,* Eugene Iglesias; *Daughter,* Teri Lynn Sandoval; *Delivery Man,* Bill McLean; *Banker,* Parley Baer; *Police Inspector,* Robert S. Anderson; *Phil Kenny,* Than Wyenn; *Police Captain,* Ted De Corsia; *Madam,* Helena Nash; *Women in Bar,* Marya Stevens, Charlita, Stacey King; *Bartender,* Fred Scheweiller; *Man in Bar,* Ward Wood; *Jack Archer,* William Campbell; *Detective,* Walter Reed; *Intern,* Paul Todd; *Parking Attendant,* Herman Boden; *Angelo,* George Sawaya; *Drunk,* Stacey Harris; *Dead Mother,* Joe Summers; *Nurses,* Cleo Tibbs, Sallie H. Dornan; Detective, Budd Landreth.

NOTES:

Although crooked cops and corrupt police officials have figured prominently in films, almost since their incep-

tion, the genre of the honest, hard-working cop who suddenly succumbs to the lure of illegally amassing a fortune when routine police work and an otherwise insurmountable personal dilemma gives him the opportunity and the motivation to become dishonest, was never really explored in films until the 1950s. True, there had been prior instances in which such crooked cops figured in films, but usually they were only minor characters. The 1950s, however, was the decade in which Hollywood really explored and exploited these doubly despicable antiheroes and more or less exhausted the subject with such films as *Shield for Murder, Between Midnight and Dawn, Private Hell 36, Rogue Cop, The Killing, The Big Heat* and *Pushover.*

In all of these films, and others not cited, the motivation which caused an otherwise respected policeman to become a criminal was sound, thoughtfully detailed and plausible enough for audiences to accept. And because audiences had to either identify and pull for the cop turned crook (e.g.: Robert Taylor in *Rogue Cop)* or involve themselves in rooting for the good-guy cop (Phil Carey in *Pushover),* whose buddy (in that film, Fred MacMurray) has become the bad guy, the script more or less worked.

The Money Trap, which more or less curiously revived this film genre, was foredoomed to fail as a film since not only were *both* cops of the standard police team turned into criminals, the script failed to provide either with a sufficient motive for doing so. Consequently, audiences were left without a single character on whom they could focus attention and work up an interest in their dilemma. Even film villains, who often possess evil connotations of unspeakable proportion (such as the Tommy Udo character Richard Widmark played in *Kiss of Death*), can be fascinating to watch, but the principals in *The Money Trap* were so routine and so lacking in cunning they were something of a bore. Therefore, except for one script device, *The Money Trap* is hardly worthy of discussion. But because such a device was used, the film should be discussed and damned.

Ricardo Montalban, a Mexican-American actor of some social, as well as cinema, stature plays a Mexican-American policeman who turns sour. That such a situation could happen is certainly not beyond the realm of possibility but the script of *The Money Trap* deliberately denigrated a person from a minority group without ever establishing a bona fide motivation. And having Ricardo Montalban, a sincere and wholly dedicated activist who has worked very hard fighting oppression and prejudice against Chicanos, play the role, is just about the cheapest kind of showmanship existing.

By accepting such a role, Montalban, a performer of surprisingly small talent, who manages to obscure his almost total lack of acting ability with variations of a single device—overreading lines and overexuding Latin charm with a myopic intensity that attempts to convey the idea that every line he utters was written by someone with at least the stature of Cervantes—apparently abandons his social conscience. But after one studies the film, a close examination makes it obvious that the product released was not the project conceived.

In *The Money Trap,* a subplot which appears to serve no purpose whatever other than to pad out the running time, deals with a Mexican-American housewife who is murdered by her husband when he learns she turned part-time hooker to help support their children because his unskilled labor could not provide an adequate family income. These now-otherwise extraneous scenes confirm the fact that the film had once intended having a lofty and honorable purpose: being a modern parable of an oppressed people struggling to survive in a society policed by underpaid guardians equally passionate in their struggle to rise but who find themselves trapped by the very establishment they are dedicated to upholding.

It's almost a certainty that it was that unrealized film, and not the cheap, clichéd melodrama made instead, that induced Montalban, as well as Glenn Ford, Joseph Cotten and Miss Hayworth to accept the assignment.

On the set with her daughter, Yasmin.

Crooked cop Glenn Ford brings his equally crooked partner, Ricardo Montalban, home to be tended by his wife, Elke Sommer.

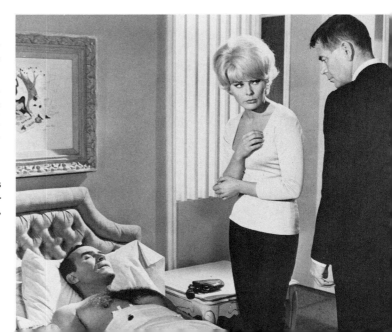

The Money Trap reunited Rita and Glenn Ford on the screen for the first time since *Affair in Trinidad* in 1952.

And the presence of this extraneous subplot footage make it apparent that the changes in the script were made after filming had commenced. A few likely possibilities of why the script was rewritten are: (1) MGM, which agreed to partially finance and distribute it, insisted on such changes because message films are seldom money-making films; (2) the film intended was made and didn't jell and the least expensive way out was an attempt to make it marketable solely as a thriller; or, (3) the money ran out and a fast rewrite made it possible to finish a film in which all participants rightly lost interest in what they were doing.

Said *Film Daily:*

"It's movie-you've-seen-before time again. This isn't a remake, but it might well have been, for the idea has been used in various guises. Doing a new film about a cop who turns dishonest and tries for the big financial grab would be a good idea only if it was turned into something special that made us lose our allegiance to the old ones. But *The Money Trap* is unconvincing and drab, even with Glenn Ford, Rita Hayworth, Joseph Cotten, Ricardo Montalban, and Elke Sommer on hand. One might think it would be nice to have Miss Hayworth back again after a long absence. But the role is a thankless one and Rita would have been better advised to wait for a part that did something for her. Here she appears as washed out as the picture."

Newsweek magazine said:

"Everyone in *The Money Trap* is contemptible but Rita Hayworth, and she gets pushed off a building. Glenn Ford is a contemptibly crooked $9,200-a-year cop, anxious to put the bite on Joseph Cotten, a contemptibly corrupt Beverly Hills physician with money and heroin in his bedroom safe. . . . Ford's partner on the force, Ricardo Montalban, is also crooked, which is especially contemptible because he is a detective of poetically Mexican extraction whose eyes dream of little yellow birds while has hands reach for gold. Everyone dies in the end but Miss Sommer, who will know enough in the future to put her money more wisely into tax-free municipal bonds."

Time magazine said:

"Overburdened with social significance and sloppy syntax, *Trap* is chiefly notable for the appearance in a secondary role of a onetime glamour girl, Rita Hayworth. Rita, frequently cast opposite Ford since they co-starred in *Gilda* in 1946, plays a frowzy, pathetic old flame who knows the rackets but preserves all her secrets in booze. Puffy, plain-spoken, her veneer meticulously scraped away, Rita at forty-seven has never looked less like a beauty, or more like an actress."

Kevin Thomas, in the *Los Angeles Times,* said:

"*The Money Trap* has been sprung before—and far better. Once again a cop goes crooked when baited by a chance at the big loot, but rarely has one gone about it in such a dumb, implausible way. Consequently, such polished pros as Glenn Ford, Rita Hayworth, Joseph Cotten and Ricardo Montalban have been sagotaged by a mishmash of a script that is equal parts 30s gangster picture and 40s murder mystery . . .

"But it is Rita Hayworth who is best of all. Playing a worn-out waitress, she and Ford meet once again, and make love and realize what might have been. Miss Hayworth and Ford who have starred in several films, most memorably *Gilda,* are so sadly touching that for a moment you can see what *The Money Trap* might have been, too."

James Powers, in the *Hollywood Reporter,* said:

"There are indications that *The Money Trap* was intended to be more than just a crime story, perhaps a parable on a materialistic age. If so, this got lost. The script is sometimes confusing. . . . One flaw is that it is very, very hard to make a crooked cop sympathetic. Ford's problem, that the income of his rich wife, Elke Sommer, is temporarily interrupted, doesn't seem motivation enough. Montalban is given less reason for his fall from grace. . . .

"Ford contributes a thoughtful and appealing characterization, although he cannot extend his conviction beyond the limits of the script. Montalban is also attractive, but he is equally handicapped in capturing sympathy. Miss Sommer is pretty and personable, but she is not strong on drama. Miss Hayworth is good, and so is Cotten. . . . *The Money Trap* is an offbeat drama with some exceptionally good performers starred in it, but one that does not quite come off."

The Poppy Is Also a Flower

A Telsun-United Nations Production,
Released by Comet Films   1966

Produced by Evan Lloyd. Executive Producer, Edgar Rosenberg. Directed by Terence Young. Second Unit Director, George Lampin. Screenplay by Jo Eisinger, based on a story idea by Ian Fleming. Photographed in Eastman Color by Henri Alekan. Second Unit Photography, Tony Brown. Special Effects by Paul Pollard. Musical Score by Georges Auric. U. N. Delegate Producer, Simon Schiffin. Production Supervisor, Michael Delamar. Production Managers, Dennis Hall, Clo D'Alban and H. Shafti. Art Direction by Maurice Colasson and Tony Roman. Set Decoration by Freda Pearson. Released by Comet Films in association with Morin M. Scott. Edited by Monique Bonnot, Peter Thornton and Henry Richardson. 100 minutes.

CAST:

Nightclub Entertainer, SENTA BERGER; *Benson,* STEPHEN BOYD; *Colonel Salem,* YUL BRYNNER; *Himself,* BOB CUNNINGHAM; *Herself,* GILDA DAHLBERG; *Linda Benson,* ANGIE DICKINSON; *Superintendent Roche,* GEORGE GERET; *Tribal Chief,* HUGH GRIFFITH; *General Bohar,* JACK HAWKINS; *Monique,* RITA HAYWORTH; *Agent Lincoln,* TREVOR HOWARD; *Herself,* GRACE KELLY; *Herself,* MORTEZA KAZEROURI; *Society Photographer,* JOCELYN LANE; *Himself,* TRINI LOPEZ; *Herself,* VIOLETTE MARCEAU; *Agent Jones,* E. G. MARSHALL; *Inspector Mosca,* MARCELLO MASTROIANNI; *Capitano Dinonno,* AMEDEO NAZZARI; *Himself,* ALI OVEISI; *Leader of Tribesmen,* JEAN-CLAUDE PASCAL; *Captain,* ANTHONY QUAYLE; *Herself,* LAYA RAKI; *Herself,* LUISA RIVELLI; *Marco,* GILBERT ROLAND; *Martin,* HAR-OLD SAKATA; *Dr. Rad,* OMAR SHARIF; *Herself,* SILVIA SORRENTE; *Chasen,* BARRY SULLIVAN; *Dr. Bronowska,* NADJA TILLER; *Herself,* MARILU TOLO; *Himself,* HOWARD VERNON; *Locarno,* ELI WALLACH.

NOTES:

Ian Fleming, creator of James Bond, the intrepid agent 007, is credited with the original story idea of *The Poppy Is Also a Flower* but should really be credited with the idea of making an *uncredited* remake of the excellent 1947 Columbia film, *To the Ends of the Earth,* which *Poppy,* filmed on a grander scale with an all-star cast, resembles too closely to be just mere coincidence.

Originally conceived as a noble endeavor, made possible through the auspices of UNESCO, the film was to serve a double purpose: to unite the nations of the world in an international effort to curtail the illegal narcotics market, and to donate whatever profits there would be to aid the needy children of all countries.

The Poppy Is Also a Flower was originally planned as the fourth of a quartet of television specials dedicated to the work of the United Nations and all participating members of the entertainment involved donated their services and received a dollar each as token payment. Sponsored by the Xerox Corporation, it was first presented on U.S. television, without commercial interruption, as a ninety-minute special on the ABC-TV network on April 22, 1966.

Because of its dazzling all-star cast, the subject matter and its lofty purposes, it was one of the year's highest-rated entertainments and attracted a wide audi-

Narcotics agent Trevor Howard suspects that the husband of drug addict Rita may be the mastermind behind an international drug smuggling ring.

ence. Reaction to it was so intense, Comet Films took it over for theatrical distribution, adding ten minutes of footage that was considered "too strong" for tube viewers and gave it an immediate release.

Director Terence Young spent fourteen weeks on location in Naples, Monte Carlo, Iran, and the surrounding desert country, filming the exteriors. Said Young:

"It was a marvelous experience for me even though I didn't make a dollar. I've never seen anyone like those actors. Yul Brynner had to make five flights back to the United States during his work with us, and he paid all his own expenses. Rita Hayworth, then scheduled to make *The Rover* with me, spent a great deal of her own money to remain available and donate her services. Omar Sharif, who was in Spain making *Dr. Zhivago,* flew to wherever we were on weekends to do his role. It was all quite marvelous since many of the performers, in order to donate their talents, had to spend a great deal of money just to be available.

"Our story was from an idea of Ian Fleming's, who died before he was able to write the screenplay, and he was very knowledgeable about such things as opium traffic. Even the idea of impregnating some raw opium with radioactive material, then tracing it with a Geiger counter, is something which is actually possible. A Russian and a Spanish scientist working together in the U.N. laboratories at Geneva invented the idea."

Because *The Poppy Is Also a Flower* is quite explicit in saying that the international drug traffic is one of the business operations of the Mafia, there was, on various occasions, in various countries, opposition and a lack of cooperation in areas where part of the filming was done and the people there actually feared reprisals if they participated.

Said Terence Young:

"The Mafia has many heads, and when one is chopped off, there always are several others to take its place. I did not want to pinch toes of other countries, but it is a fact that no other country except Iran has put its poppy cultivating under U.N. supervision. And it costs Iran $50 million a year in illicit opium traffic, too, so you can see why the other poppy countries aren't particularly anxious to submit to U.N. control."

As a publicized theatrical attraction, after a television debut, *The Poppy Is Also a Flower,* did better commercially than it did critically.

Allen Eyles, in *Films and Filming* magazine, said:

"Films loaded with guest stars tend to veer all over the place in a way ruinous to story and pace in order to show off the special players. There's one example of it here, with Trini Lopez hogging the screen and trading on a magnetic appeal that is more presumed than established; but otherwise the stars, respecting the special crusading intent of the picture and taking only a token fee (the film's profits are said to go to UNESCO), all accept their place in the scheme of things, which in one case includes being very unexpectedly extinguished by the villains. They certainly help to keep one absorbed in the film which deals with the U.N.'s fight against opium smuggling. . . . The aim is apparently to make governments pool their efforts at the U.N. but a fictional format can hardly be as persuasive as statistics and undramatized documentation. Otherwise the old message about the dangers of drugs has become a cliché that no longer means anything in vague terms like this."

Motion Picture Herald said:

"A powerful lineup of marquee names makes the success of this film, which deals with the war against opium trafficking, practically assured. The subject matter also is likely to prove interesting in the light of present controversy over drugs of various kinds. The possibilities for exploitation of both the cast and the subject matter are nearly limitless, and provide alert exhibitors with all they should need to do well at the box office. It should be noted, however, that the film was shown on television in the United States earlier this year. . . . It is too bad, then, that the dialogue, from a script by Jo Eisinger, frequently falls far below what it ought to be. But the slick production, coupled with the other plus values, tilts the scales back again."

Film Daily said:

"A sizzling adventure thriller, *The Poppy Is Also a Flower* deals with the global efforts of the police of several nations to crack down on international traffic in drugs. The all-star cast, drawn from around the world, is the type to bring a beckoning glow to any showman's marquee. An added touch of appeal is the exotic sites in Europe and the Near East where the picture was filmed in Eastman Color. The picture is one of lively box-office appeal.

"The shrewd direction of Terence Young from the script of Jo Eisinger keeps things moving at a bristling pace as melodramatic surprise follows melodramatic surprise. . . . Star appearances sparkle throughout. Hugh Griffith puts shrewdness into his role of an Iranian chieftain; Jack Hawkins and Yul Brynner are brisk and neat as police officers; Omar Sharif is effective as a U.N. scientist; Marcello Mastroianni is dashing as the Italian inspector; Senta Berger writhes through the role of a drug-using nightclub entertainer; Trini Lopez plays himself, a nightclub singer; Eli Wallach is a reformed American gangster, now an Italian businessman; Anthony Quayle, a ship captain; and Rita Hayworth, the drug-addicted wife of Roland; and Barry Sullivan, a U.N. official."

Time magazine said:

"*The Poppy Is Also a Flower* is another James Bond movie made without James Bond, and many will wish it had been filmed without film.

"As it is, the picture offers one interesting scene: the screen credits. They reveal that *Poppy* was developed from an idea proposed by author Ian Fleming, who mercifully died before he could see what happened to it; that the man principally responsible for what happened is director Terence Young, who in *Dr. No* struck the first big Bondanza; and that what happened is performed by an awful lot of people who ought to know better. . . .

"*Poppy's* plot is poppycock. Two U.N. narcotics agents (Howard and Marshall), assigned to trace a shipment of radioactivated opium from the poppy fields of Persia to the junk shops of Harlem, whip out their trusty Geiger counters and go lickety-click from Teheran to Geneva to Naples to Nice. Enroute they run a grim gantlet of all-too-familiar thriller scenes (bang-bang on the Blue Train, hugger-mugger on the bad guy's yacht, hack the stripper in a nudie nightspot) and unpleasantly overripe chestnuts ("How'll we get there—take the midnight camel?"). By the time the heroes get the heroin the customers may find themselves in something of a narcoma. The very best that can be said about this picture is that it's junk, but hardly habit-forming."

And *Weekly Variety* said:

"From the opening shot, it is instantly apparent that director Terence Young never intended that this adventure-laden look at the international dope traffic should be limited to the small screen of a TV set. . . . Using a story outline by the late Ian Fleming, reportedly the last one written by the James Bond creator, screenwriter Jo Eisinger has fashioned an action-packed story that may not reform the world's dope addicts overnight, but provides a fascinating insight into the international traffic in the poppy's deadly by-product and the types of characters who move in this morbid milieu. If an occasional lapse in logic occurs, or a particular character doesn't quite come off, these moments are rare and there's almost no letup in the suspenseful scenario. . . .

"Fortunately, the big-name cast is uniformly able to restrain individual personalities sufficiently to make their brief roles believable . . . bits that linger in the memory are Hugh Griffith's hammy Iranian sheik, Rita Hayworth as Roland's dope-laden wife, Amedeo Nazzarri's Italian police captain and a brief but brilliant scene between Yul Brynner and Jean-Claude Pascal (as a rascally tribe leader). And always the excellent color photography. This one is much too good to let linger on the shelf of a TV film library and should have an excellent chance as a theatrical release once the word gets around."

With Anthony Quinn.

The Rover (L'Avventuriero)

An Arco-Selmur Production, Distributed by Cinerama Releasing Corporation   1967*

Produced by Alfred Bini. Directed by Terence Young. Associate Director, Giancarlo Zagni. Screenplay by Luciano Vincenzoni and Jo Eisinger, based on Joseph Conrad's novel. Photographed in Eastman Color by Leonida Barboni. Camera Operator, Idelmo Simonelli; Assistant, Sergio Rubini. Musical Score by Ennio Morricone. Conducted by Bruno Nicolai. Soloists, Angelo Stefanato and Dino Asciolla. Production Manager, Fernando Franchi. Unit Manager, Gilberto Scarpellini. Art Direction, Gianni Polidori; Assistant, Andrea Crisnati. Additional Art Direction by Alberto Cardone. Set Dressers, Dario Micheli and Luciano Spadoni. Costume Designer, Veniero Colasanti. Costumes by Casa D'Arte "Firenze" Di P. Peruzzi. Hair Stylist, Roccheti. Chief Hairdresser, Renata Magnanti. Chief of Makeup, Otello Fava. Fight Director, Franco Fantasia. Naval Advisor, Marc' Antonio Bragadin. Continuity by Joan Davis. Sound Recording by Franco Groppioni. Executive Producer, Selig J. Seligman. Associate Producer, Mike Stern. Filmed at Rome's Cinecitta Studios (in 1966). Edited by Peter Thornton. 103 minutes.

CAST:

Peyrol, ANTHONY QUINN; *Arlette,* ROSANNA

*Released in the U.S. in 1971.

SCHIAFFINO; *Caterina,* RITA HAYWORTH; *Real,* RICHARD JOHNSON; *Scevola,* IVO GARRANTI; *Dussard,* MINO DORO; *Michel,* LUCIANO ROSSI; *Jacot,* Mirko Valentin; *Lieutenant Bolt,* Gianni Di Benedetto; *Captain Vincent,* Anthony Dawson; *Summons,* Franco Giornelli; *Admiral,* Franco Fantasia; *Archives Officer,* Fabrizio Jovine; *Port Captain,* John Lane; *French Officer,* Vittorio Venturoli; *Sans-Culotte,* Gustavo Gionni; *Fisherman,* Lucio De Santis; *Arlette (as a child),* Raffaela Miceli; *1st Girl,* Paola Bossalino; *2nd Girl,* Rita Klein; *3rd Girl,* Cathy Alexander; *Hoodlum,* Ruggero Salvadori.

NOTES:

Completed in 1966, *The Rover* was first shown for one performance in the United States as the opening night attraction of the 11th Annual San Francisco Film Festival, in October 1967. In July 1967, under the title *The Adventurer,* it was shown at the Taormina Film Festival in Italy. Three of the film stars, Anthony Quinn, Rita Hayworth and Richard Johnson, were present for the screening which, like the one in San Francisco, met with a very unreceptive audience.

The screenplay is based on the posthumously published (1925) Joseph Conrad novel, which is usually regarded as one of his lesser works. *The Rover* did not

With Anthony Quinn.

With Rosanna Schiaffino.

play a theatrical engagement in the Los Angeles area until 1971 which then made it eligible to appear on the annual "Reminder List," published by the Academy of Motion Picture Arts and Sciences so members can know which films are eligible for consideration of Academy nominations. And because its local showing was at a Santa Monica theater, no Los Angeles newspaper thought enough of the occasion to cover it and review the film.

In *Films in Review,* William Thomaier, the astute historian of films made from the books of Joseph Conrad, said:

"*The Rover* appeared on the lower half of a mid-Manhattan theater's double bill and the reason for its delayed release was all too apparent. After a fairly promising beginning in which Anthony Quinn and crew run a naval blockade and elude a British warship during the Napoleonic wars, the plot goes to land and audience interest grinds to a halt. The story-line is never lucid, and the tempo is tedious as Quinn seeks refuge in a seacoast village with Rita Hayworth and her ward (Rosanna Schiaffino). The film is rather faithful to Conrad, perhaps too much so, for the book's weakness, the subplot about the young lovers, is chiefly responsible for the picture's turgidity. The film's ending, incidentally, in which Quinn, realizing the self-deception in his romantic feelings for Schiaffino, sets sail in a small boat toward his death from the guns of the British warship, is well done."

Because the Conrad novel is obscure and the film made from it even more unavailable, here's a brief synopsis of the film's story-line:

Peyrol, an aging, freewheeling pirate who has joined the counter revolutionaries fighting in the bloody Napoleonic War, crashes through a British naval blockade in Toulon harbor aboard a hijacked English ship in order to deliver a message to the port captain, another activist in the cause. Barely escaping arrest, Peyrol flees up the coast where he helps Arlette, a beautiful but deranged girl, escape from a mob of tormentors.

The grateful Arlette takes Peyrol to her home, where she lives with her aunt, Caterina, and a roomer, Real, a French naval officer in love with the mentally anguished girl. Jealous of Real's attentions to Arlette, Peyrol attacks him but stops when the helpless girl pleads with him. Before Real, who has learned Peyrol is a fugitive, can turn him in, a fire breaks out in the house which causes Arlette to recall a traumatic childhood experience—witnessing the brutal murders of her parents. The shock clears her mind and relieves the trepidations of Catherina, who has lived in dread of the girl's finding out about her parents' tragic fate.

Realizing that Arlette and Real truly love each other, Peyrol resumes his counterrevolutionary mission and is killed. Later Arlette, Real and Caterina watch a ceremony from shore in which Peyrol's body, in the true tradition of a sailor's funeral, is put to sea in a burning boat.

Sons of Satan (I Bastardi)

A Warner Bros.-7 Arts Picture   1969

Produced by Turi Vasile. Directed by Duccio Tessari. Screenplay by Ennio De Concini, Mario Di Nardo and Duccio Tessardi, based on an original story by Mario Di Nardo. Photographed in Technicolor by Carlo Carlini. Optical Effects Directed by E. Catalucci. Musical Score by Carlo Rustichelli. Conducted by Michel Magne. Production Supervisor, Danilo Marciani. Production Managers, Michele Marsala and Philippe Modave. Production Assistant, Franz Huttl. Art Direction by Luigi Scaccianoce. Assistant Art Director, Dante Ferzetti. Set Decorations by Bruno Cesari. Costumes by Danda Ortona. Makeup by Nilo Iacoponi. Hair Stylist, Amalia Paoletti. Sound Recording Engineer, Claudio Maielli. An Italo-French-German co-production of the Ultra Film-PECF-Rhein Main Enterprises. Edited by Mario Morra. 102 minutes.

CAST:

Martha, RITA HAYWORTH; *Jason,* GIULIANO GEMMA; *Adam,* KLAUS KINSKI; *Karen,* MARGARET LEE; *Jimmy,* SERGE MARQUAND; *Barbara,* CLAUDINE AUGER; *Doctor,* Umberto Raho; *Policemen,* Hans Thorner, Karl Cik; *Dancer,* Paola Natalie; *2nd Dancer,* Mireilla Pompili; *Television Announcer,* Detlef Uhle.

NOTES:

Rita Hayworth has said that her role of Martha, a former Ziegfeld Follies beauty who has become an alcoholic and unable to contend with her two grown sons, who plan, execute a jewel store robbery in Arizona and then die after doublecrossing each other, is one of the best roles that she had been offered in years and that her performance in *Sons of Satan* is her most dramatically demanding one. She is also perplexed that the film never had an official release in the United States or even trade-shown to exhibitors.

Originally titled *The Cats* and filmed on locations in Madrid, Rome, Arizona, New Mexico and Nevada, *Sons of Satan* was completed in mid-1968. It was released in Italy in 1969, under the title *I Bastardi,* and the following year a 92-minute version played in Great Britain.

Early in 1972, CBS-TV purchased it for network showings and announced that a reedited version would

Rita graciously accepts a birthday gift.

be available for late-night viewing *only,* sometime in 1973.

Miss Hayworth did all her own dialogue for the three versions made—in Italian, French and English—and is the only cast member whose own voice is on the sound track of these three versions.

Soon after its purchase, a CBS executive saw the English-language version and said in a TV column:

"It's an unbelievably bad film. The color doesn't always match and the story-line is just a ludicrous bloodbath. The performances are either stilted or over-acted and the poor dubbing just makes them seem that much worst.

"It's impossible to imagine how anyone as talented, beautiful and beloved as Rita Hayworth, could involve herself in such a farrago. Fortunately for her, but un-fortunately for the film, she doesn't have a very long part. But she's a real pro—and, with the exception of Claudine Auger, who is equally wasted in a thankless part, Miss Hayworth is the only thing professional about the film.

"I suppose it may have some curiosity value for Hayworth fans but they will be very disappointed with it. . . . Personally, I don't think it's worth the effort or the expense involved to reedit it and try and make it palatable."

Needless to say, the CBS executive who offered columnist Cecil Smith his candid opinion on *Sons of Satan* insisted that he not be credited for his comments.

Arriving unexpectedly at her son's garage, Rita is presented with a birthday cake.

When Robert Walker, Jr. tells Rita he is not her missing son, she ignores him.

Road to Salina (Sur la route de Salina)

A Corona Films–Transinter Films–Fono Roma Films Co-Production, Released by Avco Embassy   1971

Presented by Joseph E. Levine. Produced by Robert Dorfmann and Yvon Guezel. Directed by Georges Lautner. Assistant Directors, Claude Vital and Robin Davis Israel. Screenplay by Georges Lautner, Pascal Jardin and Jack Miller, based on Maurice Cury's novel. Photographed in Panavision and DeLuxe Color by Maurice Fellous. Second Unit Photography by Alain Boisnard. Photographic Lenses by Panavision. Musical Score and Songs: "Clinic" and "Bouree," by Bernard Gerard, Christophe and Ian Anderson. Music Conducted by Bernard Gerard. Production Supervisor, Louis Wipf. Second Unit Direction by Paul Nuyttens. Art Direction, Jean D'Eaubonne. Sound Recording by René Longuet and Louis Hochet. Filmed on location at Lanzarote (Canary Islands). Edited by Michelle David and Elizabeth Guido. 96 minutes.

CAST:

Billie, MIMSY FARMER; *Jonas*, ROBERT WALKER; *Mara*, RITA HAYWORTH; *Warren*, ED BEGLEY; *Charlie*, Bruce Pecheur; *The Sheriff*, David Sachs; *Linda*, Sophie Hardy; *Rocky*, Marc Porel; *Locals*, Ivano Staccioli, Albane Navizet.

NOTES:

After three obscure films of dubious quality, which have gained a certain notoriety solely by virtue of their frustrating unavailability to the cult of film students and buffs who see most films, especially those directed by or featuring a former film great, *Road to Salina* was something of an event: a Rita Hayworth film which actually had a release schedule and playdates in U.S. theaters! Unfortunately, its release schedule was modest and of short duration and its playdate was usually on

In an attempt to keep Robert Walker, Jr. from discovering why her brother mysteriously disappeared, Mimsy Farmer tries to get his mind on other things.

With vagabond Robert Walker, Jr.

the lower half of a double feature. But those who took the time and trouble to seek out *Road to Salina* found the effort more than worthwhile. Sloughed off by distributors and exhibitors and most critics (at least the few who did get to see it), *Road to Salina* is about 80 percent better than the average big film which rates prime play dates and high admission prices!

In fact, it has a sort of cinematic grandeur about it simply because of its superlative color photography and a semi-mystery-incest plot which manages to maintain audience interest throughout its entire running time and contains a brilliant performance by Mimsy Farmer, better than good performances by Robert Walker and Ed Begley and an excellently acted and thought-out performance by Rita Hayworth, as a woman who would rather be thought of as mentally deranged than face the fact that her daughter murdered her brother when he tried to break off their incestuous relationship.

Vaguely resembling *The Postman Always Rings Twice* in setting and irony and having some of the poetic

With old friend Ed Begley.

qualities of *The Petrified Forest,* it also captures an insight of human nature which very few films achieve.

Kevin Thomas, in the *Los Angeles Times,* said:

"The irony of Rita Hayworth's career is that she is making fewer (and increasingly obscure) pictures but is giving better and better performances. The greater irony, however, may be that perhaps it only seems that way: Anyone who is dubbed a 'love goddess,' as she was in the 40s, is going to find it hard even to be taken seriously as an actress. Nevertheless, in Miss Hayworth's recent pictures, notably *The Money Trap* and now in *Road to Salina,* she gives what are arguably the best performances of her career.

"But *Road to Salina,* an admirably ambitious film of strictly sophisticated appeal, has been dumped into a flock of drive-ins and neighborhood theaters where both it and its star are least likely to be appreciated.

"Instead of applauding Miss Hayworth's courage and honesty in acting her age, many of those who haven't seen her on the screen in a while will merely be dismayed that she no longer looks like the pinup girl she once was. By the same token a lot of people will probably write off her picture as arty and pretentious and therefore miss the impressive psychological validity of its characters and their tangled relationships. . . .

"Essentially, *Road to Salina* is a fable showing how tragedy can occur when reality intrudes upon the lonely lives of those who live in a world of fantasy. . . . Miss Hayworth evokes much sympathy for the anguished woman she portrays so well. Lean and intense as ever, Miss Farmer once again makes an invitation to certain disaster seem irresistible. Walker is likably naive and perplexed amidst decadence, and the late Ed Begley lends an appropriate sinister note. Subtle, delicate even, *Road to Salina* is a credit to Lautner and his impeccably

Said *Newsday:*

"The best things about the film are George Lautner's direction and the neurotic, almost carnivorous, energetic intensity of the many-toothed, broad-shouldered, predatory Mimsy Farmer and the introverted passion of Rita Hayworth, who presents the look of sorrow turned to madness and then to sleepwalking acceptance of any lie that will help her survive another day. In a small role, Ed Begley is impressive with his frightening vigor and insincere smile that seems to barely mask a desire to kill Robert Walker. . . . A very strange film! . . . More perversely compelling than it has a right to be."

In the *Village Voice,* Robert Colaciello said:

"What can one say about a film which features Rita Hayworth pumping gas? Rita Hayworth frying eggs! Rita Hayworth at a pot party! Rita Hayworth frugging with Ed Begley! Rita Hayworth *in competition* with that latter-day Doris Day on dope, Mimsy Farmer! . . . About a film which is innocent of any intent beyond its own making? Not much. Except that if your taste runs to 70s actors having 60s sex in a 50s film so that a 40s star can suffer, then *Road to Salina* is for you."

With down-on-his-luck writer
Stephen Oliver.

The Naked Zoo

Film Artists International   1971

Produced and Directed by William Grefe. Screenplay by Ray Preston and William Grefe, based on Preston's original screen story. Filmed in Eastman Color at Film World Studios in Fort Lauderdale and surrounding Florida locations in 1969. 78 minutes.

CAST:

RITA HAYWORTH; FAY SPAIN; STEPHEN OLIVER; FORD RAINEY; FLEURETTE CARTER.

NOTES:

Originally titled *The Grove,* this most obscure of all Rita Hayworth films, under the title *The Naked Zoo,* was released by Haven Films, Inc., in New York City where, for four days at one theater, and seven days at another, it played the lower half of a double bill. No metropolitan newspaper or trade paper reviewed it. In January 1972, under the title *The Hallucinators,* it was listed in *Boxoffice Booking Guide* as being available for rental from R&S Enterprises, a Florida film distributor. Under that title, it played a week in Chicago in early 1973 at a theater which specializes in nudie films. Since then, as far as I have been able to determine, it has gone into limbo.

In *Cue* magazine, critic Donald J. Mayerson, one of the chosen few people in the world to have seen the film, said:

"Perverse curiosity-seekers who want to see how former screen goddesses age may find this Rita Hayworth film of some minimal interest. Miss Hayworth—older, wrinkled and edematous—is seen to such disadvantage that it would be a kindness to her to avoid the film. She plays a wealthy wife and then widow (after her husband, strapped in a wheelchair, gets himself killed fighting over her boyfriend). Stephen Oliver plays the boyfriend, a writer who lives off women and on LSD. The entire affair is abysmal."

The Wrath of God

A Rainbow Productions Inc.—
  Cineman Films, Ltd. Production,
  Released by Metro-Goldwyn-Mayer   1972

Executive Producer, Peter Katz. Associate Producer, William S. Gilmore, Jr. Directed by Ralph Nelson. Assistant Directors, Mario Cisneros and Jerry Ziesmer. Screenplay by Ralph Nelson, based on James Graham's novel and excerpts from Ariel Ramirez's "Miss Criolla." Photographed in Panavision and MetroColor by Alex Phillips, Jr. Photographic Lenses by Panavision. Original Musical Score by Lalo Schiffrin. Music Editor, William Saracino. Special Effects by Frederico Farfan. Production Design by John S. Poplin, Jr. Unit Production Manager, Robert Watts. Construction Coordinator, Ralph DeLong. Acting Coordinator, Everett Creach. Set Decoration by William Kiernan. Property Master, Ray Mercer. Wardrobe Supervisor, Ted Parvin. Makeup Supervisor, Del Armstrong. Hair Stylist, Lynn Del Kail. Sound Recording by Peter Sutton and Harry W. Tetrick. Script Supervisor, Bob Forrest. Casting by Lynn Stalmaster. Edited by J. Terry Williams and Richard Bracken. 111 minutes.

CAST:

Van Horne, ROBERT MITCHUM; *De La Plata,* FRANK LANGELLA; *Señora De La Plata,* RITA HAYWORTH; *Colonel Dantilla,* JOHN COLICOS; *Jennings,* VICTOR BUONO; *Emmet,* KEN HUTCHINSON; *Chela,* PAULA PRITCHETT; *Jurado,* Gregory Sierra; *Moreno,* Frank Ramirez; *Nacho,* Enrique Lucero; *Cordona,* Jorge Russel; *Antonio,* Chano Uru-eta; *Pablito,* José Luis Parades; *Señora Moreno,* Aurora Clavel; *Delgado,* Vicor Eberg; *Tacho,* Pancho Cordova; *Diaz,* Guillermo Hernandez.

NOTES:

It's always an occasion of amazement when usually astute film critics suddenly suffer a mental block, en masse, revealing a denseness and lack of perception which, as a display of human frailty, would merely doubly endear them to their devoted readers were not the occasion when they chose to turn off their cerebral networks otherwise of such cinematic importance.

Less amazing, but more amusing, although equally frustrating, are some of the astounding and astonishing appraisals of films by the *Cahiers du Cinéma* types who can expound at length on the nonexistent symbolism of, say, a Samuel Fuller B film, when that which they are canonizing may be merely an awkward circumstance which a low budget, sloppy editing, inadequate script elucidation, or hazy direction, or a combination of them all, has wrought but which nevertheless sends these frenzied French film fanatics into fits of such ecstasy, erroneous but erudite, that they lose their cinematic cool.

But just let a filmmaker deliberately set out to spoof the medium, film genres in general, and all the famous stars who have appeared in famous roles in these genres —and the astute critics, including those of *Cahiers du*

Revolutionary Frank Langella shows his disapproval of his mother, Rita, worshipping in church.

Cinéma, suddenly go deaf, dumb and blind. Of course, I am alluding to only the successful, planned, well-intended spoofs, not to such a film as is only later called a spoof because it was so dreadful and amateur that the dedicated partisans of its director excused his ineptitude by saying he was only kidding the medium, everyone having been too stupid to realize it. The best way I know of to deflate that kind of logic is to cite an artistically successful spoof, such as John Huston's *Beat the Devil* (1954), which was never intended as anything else but a spoof, but which was a financial disaster in its initial release after a thorough critical panning. (It wasn't until a long time after Huston's little classic disappeared from release that the film started winning admirers among the critics and attracting a potential audience. A decade later, when it was reissued with great financial rewards, the publicity for it was simple and direct: "It's time . . . for the film that was ahead of it.")

The Wrath of God, 1972's most intriguing film, appears well on the way to facing the same early reception that *Beat the Devil* faced. Except in one, perhaps two, isolated instances, it has been reviewed only in terms of its values—as nothing more than a handsomely mounted and moderately well-budgeted adventure yarn. This, however, is hardly the case.

In actuality, *The Wrath of God* is a movie spoof of *movies* that has been so brilliantly executed that its seams do not show—which may, after all, be the *only* fault of an otherwise flawless piece of filmmaking.

Director Ralph Nelson, with tongue firmly in cheek, sets out to show us just how easy it is to equal, and better, the ridiculous bloodbaths created by Sam Peckinpah, by taking us for a slay-ride through a Central American republic, the likes of which even a *Mission Impossible* segment wouldn't possibly attempt. To this locale he adds three anti-heroes who, collectively, are a composite of every cinema standby from Sam Spade to *Hud*. Executing exploits of derring-do unequaled since the youthful days of Errol Flynn and Burt Lancaster, exploits plentiful enough to supply chapter climaxes for at least one whole serial, his unholy trio romp through an all-encompassing cavalcade of movie clichés, and a dozen variations of them, while delivering, usually with deadpan seriousness, the most deathless dialogue it has even been a film buff's pleasure to listen to.

Apparently, director Nelson, the scripter, did not overlook any movie, or even movie-movie, which has ever been lauded, applauded, admired, or listed among the box-office bonanzas, or has been an integral part of every filmgoer's happiest movie memories, for there isn't a single one of them which isn't, in some way, subtly, gently, outrageously, emphatically, and often hilariously lampooned—and for all that, with sly ingenuity and an equally fey innocence. There's a fistfight which betters those in all five versions of *The Spoilers* and *The Quiet Man* by several punches and more sight gags. And our motley trio of antiheroes are more idiotic, improbable, indispensible and so coolly cowardly, especially in moments of crisis, that no one who watches *The Wrath of God* can ever again watch *The Magnificent Seven, The Good, the Bad and the Ugly, The Professionals, The Dirty Dozen, The Wild Bunch, Straw Dogs,* or even the James Bond works with quite the same fascination, or repulsion, of yore.

Robert Mitchum, more laconic than ever, lampoons his own screen image, adding judicious bits of Bogart's Rick, Gable's Rhett, Tracy's Flanagan and a composite of all of Cagney's killers to his almost endless list of heroes and antiheroes to be delightfully deflated. Like Bogart, in *Casablanca,* who stands amusedly by without lifting a finger while the police haul Peter Lorre off to his doom, Mitchum, eyes twinkling, cigar firmly clenched between his teeth, stands beside a group of hostages facing a firing squad and goes through the business of offering them the last rites, in a deadpan delivery, which continues until all of them have been slaughtered, upon which he gingerly steps over the body of one of them, closes his Bible, flicks the ashes from his cigar, and goes on his way. Not since the village priest stopped praying and started machine-gunning down a company of German soldiers in *Edge of Darkness* (1943) has any screen clergyman been able to handle a machine gun as casually and adeptly as Mitchum, in a later scene, as he calmly mows down a cantina full of raping revolutionaries, afterwards lovingly wiping off his weapon with even more aplomb than Sean Connery managed after mowing down one of *Dr. No's* henchwomen.

Ken Hutchinson, second of the trio, in addition to spoofing his own role in *Straw Dogs,* also performs an Irish-flavored bottled-in-Bond burlesque, late 1920s style, while the third member of the trio, Victor Buono, takes at least one famous line of dialogue from each of a dozen Sydney Greenstreet films, rolls it around on his tongue, relishing the prospect of delivery, and then speaks the purloined line in a tone of mellifluent menace. Virtually his very first line in the film is "By gad, sir, you are a character," which he delivers so innocently and flawlessly you'd never even suspect he ever even heard of a Kaspar Gutman.

The ostensible heroine, Paula Pritchett, who, at first, appears to be the latest student of Maria Montez's old acting coach, quietly and successfully spoofs *Ramona,* a half dozen other Indian maidens of filmlore, and a few of Dorothy Lamour's *aloha* dollies. And by *quietly,* I mean just that. Because, until a climactic moment to approximate Dorothy McGuire's climactic moment in *The Spiral Staircase,* she too is a mute.

Frank Langella, using the same lesson in the acting handbook Jay Robinson used before undertaking his assignment as Caligula in *The Robe,* manages to convey some swishy and smirking menace before his own death scene when he's shot down and, in quick session, in

about three seconds flat, manages death-throe expressions that burlesque similar situations wherein Bruce Cabot, David Newell, and Paul Hurst, respectively, all faced demise at the hands of the trigger-happy heroines impersonated by, respectively Rochelle Hudson *(Show Them No Mercy),* Bette Davis *(The Letter),* and Vivien Leigh *(Gone With the Wind).*

In *The Wrath of God,* the pistol-packin' mama with the deadly aim turns out to be none but Rita Hayworth. And her appearance in it is by far the biggest and the best movie-within-a-movie- within-a-movie-within-a-movie joke of them all! Her name was bandied about in the dialogue of such recent films as *The Godfather, Made for Each Other* (1971), and *Sometimes a Great Notion,* but it was really way back in 1954 with *Beat the Devil* that the act of bandying her name about consumed a good minute's screen time (during a scene in which Humphrey Bogart finds the only way to get out of being liquidated by an Arab admirer of Miss Hayworth is by professing to know her personally and promising to send him her autographed portrait).

That Rita Hayworth has had her name put to other uses is, as Sam Spade woud say, "Just one more thing in your favor." In a World War II serviceman's publication, one of the most hilarious pieces of fiction ever published concerned a GI's account of a weekend in a blitzed building with a bevy of B-girls. It was called "The Night Rita Hayworth Fell Off My Locker Door." And recently, Argentine novelist Manuel Puig called his

With Robert Mitchum, a gun-slinging priest.

At the entrance to her silver mine, Rita receives the consolation of priest Robert Mitchum, a man not as saintly as she believes him to be.

new book *Betrayed by Rita Hayworth,* even though it otherwise had nothing whatever to do with the Love Goddess of the 1940s.

By seemingly being aware of all these references to herself while gunning down her screen son, Langella, and by simply maintaining a straight face while speaking some of the most trite and mundane dialogue ever awarded an actress, Miss Hayworth merely confirms my strong belief that she is, after all, an expert comedienne and that she personally possesses a very outré sense of humor.

But to return to *The Wrath of God* itself—

At the moment, it appears to be just a matter of conjecture as to how long it will take the U.S. critics, *Cahiers du Cinéma,* and the general public itself, which has been led astray, to discover *The Wrath of God* and begin paying it the homage it deserves. Second and third viewings of it confirm virtues which, like those of a well-constructed violin or a vintage wine, improve with age, and merely pique one's interest in still another viewing, this time taking along someone who hasn't seen it. In Los Angeles, it was a feat in itself to catch *The Wrath of God* at all, because within about a week of its arrival it had disappeared into limbo.

A total delight, *The Wrath of God* succeeds as the best spoof of *movies* in years. (Not *of a movie*—there's a difference!) And, like the movies it spoofs, it, too, is ageless.

But, as in the case of *Beat the Devil,* as I've said, the critics had little regard for it. For example, in the Los Angeles *Herald-Examiner,* Bridget Byrne said:

"The sort of old-fashioned nonsense which might make you believe once again in the magic of the movies and the power of a real star to turn dross to gilt. This MGM movie, starring Robert Mitchum, doesn't bear close scrutiny or cold analysis. It should be accepted with full-blooded relish, a sense of humor and all your dormant romantic instincts."

Kevin Thomas, in the *Los Angeles Times,* was equally dense in missing the whole point. Said he:

"A hypocritical, brutalizing cartoon of a film. *The Wrath of God* makes fun of much of the violence it ostensibly deplores. It assaults rather than compels and becomes a brutalizing, demoralizing experience. . . . Thankfully, Rita Hayworth, elegant and beautiful, fares pretty well. It is unfortunate she is not on-screen more often because she lends *The Wrath of God* a note of dignity it so desperately needs."

Arthur Knight, in the *Hollywood Reporter,* said:

"Much as I was engrossed by *The Wrath of God,* I found myself obsessed by a curious notion. Shouldn't it have been directed by Sam Peckinpah? And shouldn't Ralph Nelson have directed Peckinpah's serene *Junior Bonner?*"

Only in *Cue* magazine was there a hint of the pleasures to behold in *The Wrath of God.* William Wolf certainly hinted at them:

"Adventure? Philosophy? Comedy? Satire? These were questions for director Ralph Nelson, but no decision seems to have been made. . . . The result is an unsatisfactory mess of many elements. Appealing Robert Mitchum, giving one of his customary sincere performances, plays a profane hero in priest's clothing. . . . In Nelson's involved, corny script, he comes up against an evil tyrant played by Frank Langella, and Mitchum is determined to hold mass for the people. Rita Hayworth has the clichéd role as the unhappy mother of the tyrant. An assortment of character types find themselves aligned with Mitchum, including the very attractive Paula Pritchett as a mute Indian girl. The amusing presence of obese, waddling Victor Buono as kind of reincarnated Sydney Greenstreet hints at the sort of *Beat the Devil* atmosphere that might have developed."

A larger symposium of critical evaluations would be even more frustrating. Steal one bit of business, one line of dialogue, one unique camera angle from a film—and every reviewer in the world seems aware of it. But commit mass mayhem in one film with *all* movie clichés—and you leave the critics in complete puzzlement. Not so, however, with the audiences with which I viewed *The Wrath of God* three times. Sparse at one showing, middling at another, jam-packed at still another, they were with it all the way.

A RITA HAYWORTH
Miscellany

The following listing includes Miss Hayworth's television appearances, compilation films and unrealized stage and screen projects which, at one time or another, she had planned or been scheduled to do.

Television:

1: THE ODYSSEY OF RITA HAYWORTH (NBC; 1964)

One of David Wolper's half-hour series, "Hollywood and the Stars," produced by Jack Haley, Jr. and narrated by Joseph Cotten. Contained newsreel footage, candid photographs and footage from many of the films in which she appeared.

2: THE 1964 OSCARCAST (ABC; 1964)

In the course of telecasting the annual Academy of Motion Picture Arts and Sciences Awards, Miss Hayworth appeared as one of the presenters, for the "Best Director" Award, won by Tony Richardson for *Tom Jones* and accepted on his behalf by Dame Edith Evans. Broadcast live, from Santa Monica Civic Auditorium, Miss Hayworth appeared nervous while reading off the list of director nominees and misread director Richardson's name by calling him "Tony Richards."

3: FIRST TUESDAY (NBC; 1969)

A two-hour newscast roundup, presented in magazine format, which aired on the first Tuesday of each month. On the premiere program, Rita Hayworth was interviewed by Sandy Vanocur for a unique segment titled "Rita Hayworth at Fifty."

4: LAUGH-IN (NBC; 1971)

Miss Hayworth joined the dancing chorus for one musical number and then participated with Rowan and Martin in several blackout skits.

5: THE CAROL BURNETT SHOW (CBS; 1971)

As a guest star, Miss Hayworth exchanged banter with hostess Carol Burnett, did a pantomime sketch in which she and Miss Burnett appeared as the charwoman character. Miss Hayworth's appearance on this program came about after she telephoned Miss Burnett to tell her how much she had enjoyed the comedienne's lampoon of Miss Hayworth and her film, *Gilda,* on a previous telecast.

6: THE MERV GRIFFIN SHOW (CBS; 1971)

A special broadcast of the nightly series called "An Evening with Rita Hayworth" had host Merv Griffin join Miss Hayworth in a song-and-dance duet, discuss her film career and then be joked by another guest star, Anthony Franciosa, who had co-starred with her in *The Story on Page One*. Film clips from many of her movies were shown and commented on and Miss Hayworth discussed her film work and her private life.

Motion Picture Compilation:

THE LOVE GODDESSES (Columbia; 1965). A feature film consisting of film clips of screen vamps, sirens and sex symbols, written and directed by Saul Turrell and Graeme Ferguson, with an original musical score by Percy Faith. The footage included several film clips of Rita Hayworth in her various films.

NOTE: In such films as *Beat the Devil* (1954), *Made For Each Other* (1971), *Sometimes A Great Notion* (1971) and *The Godfather* (1972), Miss Hayworth has been alluded to in the dialogue. And the famous Bob Landry pinup picture of her, which was originally printed on page 33 of the August 11, 1941 issue of *Life* magazine, has been used as a prop in countless films in which the action takes place during World War II.

Unrealized Film Projects:

1: A brief role, as Barbara Stanwyck's sister in *A Message to Garcia* (1936), was actually filmed, but deleted from the final print of the film before it went into general release.

2: The title role in a Technicolor remake of *Ramona* (1936) for which she had made color screen tests with Gilbert Roland and Don Ameche. The role was ultimately played by Loretta Young when Darryl F. Zanuck canceled Miss Hayworth's contractual option.

3: The failure of Darryl Zanuck to renew her option at Fox also canceled another film Miss Hayworth was scheduled to make at that studio: the second feminine lead in *Señora Casada Necesita Marido,* a Spanish language version of *The Lady Escapes,* directed by Eugene Forde, starring Antonio Moreno (1937).

4: The lead in a Columbia B film, *Convicted Woman,* which, had she made, would have been her first film with Glenn Ford, who was the male lead. But because she was loaned to MGM *(Susan and God),* Rochelle Hudson replaced her.

5: While at MGM in 1940, she did a screen test for the role of the mantrap in *Boom Town,* ultimately played by Hedy Lamarr.

6: Previous to directing her in *Susan and God* (1940), George Cukor had considered and tested her for the role of Katharine Hepburn's sister in his 1938 remake of *Holiday.* The role eventually went to Doris Nolan.

7: The feminine lead in a Columbia wartime musical, *Tars and Spars,* a salute to the U.S. Coast Guard which had originated as a stage show with Victor Mature. Miss Hayworth's pregnancy forced her to withdraw. She was replaced by Janet Blair.

8: When she requested a complete rewrite of *Dead Reckoning* (1947), in which she was scheduled to co-star opposite Humphrey Bogart, Miss Hayworth was dropped from the film and replaced by Lizabeth Scott.

9: An untitled musical biography of the Duncan Sisters to be produced by George Jessel and made at 20th Century-Fox, with Miss Hayworth co-starring with Betty Grable was cancelled when Jessel was unable to obtain legal clearance. The property, still owned by 20th, has never been filmed.

10: The title role in *Lona Hanson,* a large-scale Technicolor western prepared for filming in 1947, postponed until 1949, and eventually canceled. It was to have been directed by Norman Foster and Miss Hayworth's co-stars were to have been William Holden and Randolph Scott.

11: The lead in a Columbia comedy, *Miss Grant Takes Richmond,* in which William Holden again would have been her co-star, was given to Lucille Ball when Miss Hayworth, insisting on script revisions, went on suspension to avoid making it.

12: The role of Billie Dawn in Garson Kanin's comedy *Born Yesterday,* which Harry Cohn especially purchased for Miss Hayworth but was ultimately played by Judy Holliday, who had originated the part on Broadway and in recreating her role in the film, won the 1950 "Best Actress" Academy Award.

13: *Human Desire,* a remake of the Emile Zola novel, directed by Fritz Lang, in which Miss Hayworth, scheduled to co-star with Glenn Ford and Broderick Crawford, failed to appear for the first scenes, to be filmed on location. She was put on suspension and replaced by Gloria Grahame.

14: The feminine lead in *Joseph and His Brethren,* a biblical spectacle scripted by Clifford Odets that was to be independently produced by Louis B. Mayer and released by Columbia was canceled when Harry Cohn refused to co-finance the film when Miss Hayworth requested Orson Welles (her second husband) and Dick Haymes (her fourth husband) as co-stars. (The 1962 film of the same title that was produced in Europe has

no relationship to this project, which never realized by Miss Hayworth.)

15: Because she felt that the lead in Joseph L. Mankiewicz's *The Barefoot Contessa* (1954) had too many similarities to her own life, Miss Hayworth rejected an offer to play the lead and the role was awarded to Ava Gardner.

16: Miss Hayworth rejected the role of Karen in *From Here to Eternity* unless Columbia would postpone filming it to allow her a vacation after completing *Miss Sadie Thompson* (1953), then being filmed on location in Hawaii. Joan Crawford, next offered the role, also rejected it and then it was offered to and accepted by Deborah Kerr.

17: The leading role in *I Want My Mother!* which was prepared for filming in late 1962 by Miss Hayworth's fifth husband, James Hill, but inexplicitly canceled just twenty-four hours before principal photography was to commence. Miss Hayworth was scheduled to play the mother of a psychopathic killer awaiting execution in San Quentin's gas chamber.

18: The role of a fading film star involved in a suicide scandal in a cinematization of James Kirkwood's novel, *There Must Be a Pony,* canceled after a stage production of it, starring Myrna Loy, failed to generate audience interest.

19: The feminine lead in *Welcome to Hard Times,* a Max E. Youngstein production, filmed at MGM, to be made immediately after *The Money Trap.* But when Glenn Ford bowed out of the male lead and was replaced by Henry Fonda, Miss Hayworth also withdrew, and was replaced by Janice Rule.

20: In late 1972 Miss Hayworth signed a contract to appear in *Tales That Witness Madness,* a World Film Services production, filmed at the Shepperton Studios, for Paramount release, and directed by Freddie Francis, and worked four days on it in England before quitting, without explanation, and returning to Hollywood. Her unusual behavior resulted in Kim Novak taking over her role.

Unrealized Stage Appearances:

1: Miss Hayworth bowed out of the leading role in *Step on a Crack,* after three weeks of rehearsal, before its scheduled Broadway opening in the fall of 1962. When it ultimately did reach Broadway, it closed after a single performance.

2: A Feuer and Martin melodrama, *Journey into Limbo,* scheduled for the 1965 New York theater season with Miss Hayworth but canceled when script difficulties could not be resolved.

3: Replacing Lauren Bacall in a musical version of *All About Eve* called *Applause,* which Miss Hayworth first agreed to do but then changed her mind when she felt she would have insufficient rehearsal time before opening. Anne Baxter later accepted the assignment.

NOTE:

Miss Hayworth claims that during her entire film career she never particularly sought to play any special role after attaining stardom but adds:

"I would have liked to played Federico Garcia Lorca's *Yerma,* the story of a barren woman who has no children and whose husband rejects her. It's a tremendous part and the few times I mentioned an interest in it, while I was still the right age, the people with whom I discussed it said they had never heard of it."